Military Strategy for Writers

Stephen Kenneth Stein

Published by Jeweled Sea Press, 2023.

While every precaution has been taken in the preparation of this book, the publisher assumes no responsibility for errors or omissions, or for damages resulting from the use of the information contained herein.

MILITARY STRATEGY FOR WRITERS

First edition. September 26, 2023.

Copyright © 2023 Stephen Kenneth Stein.

ISBN: 978-1737018742

Written by Stephen Kenneth Stein.

Table of Contents

Introduction 1
Chapter One: Building Your Strategic Vocabulary 17
Chapter Two: Classic Strategic Thought 45
Chapter Three: Strategies of Sea Power 75
Chapter Four: Strategies of Air Power 97
Chapter Five: Nuclear Strategy and Game Theory 121
Chapter Six: The People in Arms, Strategies of Insurgency ... 145
Chapter Seven: Fighting Insurgents, Counterinsurgency 167
Chapter Eight: Strategies of Terror 187
Chapter Nine: War in the Far Future and Strategy in Space .. 209
Questions to Ask as You Write 241
A Guide to Quick Military History Research 245
Ten Indispensable Books 253
Acknowledgments 257
A Word about the Cover 259
Bibliography 261
Additional Books by Stephen Kenneth Stein 267

To Carolyn

Introduction

Rambo does not win wars.
A thousand Rambos do not win wars.

Wars are won by the application of sound strategy to achieve rational political goals. Battlefield prowess—no matter how impressive—cannot win wars alone. Military forces correct poor tactics as their officers learn from experience. Poor strategy, though, endures and dooms one to defeat. Simply put, you cannot fight your way out of bad strategic decisions. The German army, despite its tactical proficiency, lost both world wars trying to do that. The great alliances that fought Germany in the first half of the twentieth century—and Revolutionary and Napoleonic France a century earlier—succeeded despite repeated battlefield failures. Similarly, the armed forces of the United States have won an impressive number of battles since World War II, but hardly any wars. This, again, resulted from poor strategy. Tactical proficiency cannot compensate for strategic ineptitude.

Yet, in fictional accounts, it often does. Whether heroic fantasy or space opera or more "realistic" technothrillers, heroes win wars by winning a succession of individual battles culminating in a climactic showdown. Their protagonists and antagonists may quote great strategists, but strategy itself is often absent.

This is unfortunate, because outlining the strategic situation and asking the hard questions posed by great strategic thinkers will clarify a story's context and stakes. Why are soldiers at a particular place? What strategic purpose does their mission serve? How will it help win the war? Why is Robert Heinlein's starship trooper Juan Rico battling "Bugs" on an alien world? Why is George MacDonald Fraser's cowardly Harry Flashman in Afghanistan? How will Mary Robinette Kowal's Ghost Talkers solve the communications problems of First World War battlefields? What's the importance of the Death Star? Will destroying it win the war for the Rebel Alliance? (Apparently not, since the Empire keeps "striking back.")

The emphasis on climactic battle also helps authors avoid discussing the complex aftermath of wars. J. R. R. Tolkien's *Lord of the Rings* is among the few exceptions. Following the destruction of the One Ring and annihilation of Sauron's army, Frodo and his victorious companions return home only to discover they have a mess to clean up. Sauron's henchman Saruman has wrought no end of violence and destruction on their beloved Shire. The victorious heroes must both end Saruman's evil reign and rehabilitate war-ravaged lands, as the Belgians and French had to after the First World War. Since the object of war is a better peace, it's worth saying more about that peace and how wartime decisions led to it.

While some novelists demonstrate an intuitive understanding of strategic issues, they often miss the practical details and subtle nuances of executing effective strategy. This is hardly surprising. Many military officers have trouble grappling with matters of policy and strategy. They spend most of their careers studying tactics and operations, turning to strategy only at higher rank. Military academies and similar undergraduate institutions focus on small unit leadership and tactics.

Postgraduate military institutions, such as the various U.S. war colleges, focus their attention on operations, strategy, and policy. Yet students at these higher institutions of learning, and senior officers in general, often remain more comfortable thinking about tactics than considering issues of strategy and policy.

Tactics involve how troops maneuver and fight in battle. The operational level of war describes the movement of military forces over larger spaces and periods of time. It describes how military forces position themselves advantageously for battle or to seize or threaten important places.

Strategy is the process that connects your goals to the actions you take to achieve them. What do you want? What resources do you have? How will you use these resources to achieve your goal? What are your military capabilities? In other words, what means will you apply to achieve what ends? What are the most effective ways to use your military, industrial, and other resources to achieve your political goals?

Strategy encompasses a host of high-level decisions, including resource allocation, operational targets, and, most important, how one expects to win a war. It is not about storming a hill or sinking a battleship. Strategy is not about winning battles, but rather about winning wars.

Anyone with goals, whether saving for retirement, getting into a good college, or finishing a novel, develops strategies to achieve them: invest in a balanced portfolio of mutual funds, couple good grades with extracurricular activities, write every day, and so on.

Whether it's time to write, money to invest, or the troops, industry, and allies needed to wage war, one's resources are always finite. Goals, though, can approach the infinite. Even Alexander the Great, perhaps history's most able general, faced this reality. He could not conquer the entire world. Successful strategists reconcile means and ends.

The Persian Empire fielded far more troops and warships than Alexander and generated more money than its ruler, Darius III, could effectively spend. Yet, Alexander consistently out-thought and outmaneuvered his Persian opponents. While impressive in themselves, Alexander's battlefield victories at Granicus, Miletus, Issus,

Tyre, and Gaugamela were part of a coherent strategy in which Alexander systematically dismantled and conquered the Persian Empire. Alexander approached battle carefully and fought only when necessary. A master strategist, he ensured every battle served his strategic purposes and advanced him toward his final goal.

Military Strategy

THIS BOOK DESCRIBES and explains military strategy, often defined as the use of military force—or the threat of military force—to achieve one's political goals. It is neither a primer on military culture nor an explanation of weapons and weapons systems. Rather, it is about how people—scholars, senior military officers, and political leaders—analyze, plan for, and win wars, and how understanding the strategic issues involved can inform fiction writing. It offers an introduction to military strategy aimed particularly at novelists and other writers. It aims to help them think more deeply about strategic issues and avoid common mistakes, such as confusing tactics and strategy.

Throughout this book, discussions of strategy are illustrated by historical, film, and literary examples, the latter from historical fiction, science fiction, and fantasy, the genres in which military strategy most appears. These necessarily involve spoilers. You have been warned.

While this book focuses on military strategy—and the robust literature on it—one can apply strategic principles to a host of nonmilitary situations, from orchestrating the perfect heist to advancing the cause of true of love. One can develop strategies for career advancement, retirement planning, and even writing novels. Almost any endeavor benefits from strategic analysis. Since the publication of H. Igor Ansoff's *Corporate Strategy* in 1965, people have applied strategic concepts to a host of topics, particularly business and marketing, hence such titles as *Business Secrets of Attila the Hun*.

Developing and executing military strategy, though, is more complex than beating a corporate rival to the next hot trend, planning your retirement, or writing a novel. Military forces operate in a dynamic environment in which enemies actively work against them—often in unanticipated ways. How much progress would you make on your novel if rival authors bombarded your office with discordant music, deployed malicious viruses against your computer, or arranged mysterious accidents to sap your time and energy?

Military strategy necessarily pits two or more antagonists against one another. Each seeks to outwit and outmaneuver the other. As a result, the most obvious strategy may not be the best. Like the duel of wits between Wesley and Vizzini in William Goldman's *The Princess Bride* (1973), trying to out-think and out-strategize your opponent can result in dizzying, paradoxical chains of reasoning.

A further complication, as the great Prussian strategist Carl von Clausewitz noted, is that wars take place in a realm of uncertainty and chance. The future is difficult to predict, particularly in military matters. In war, one must deal with the normal uncertainties that accompany any endeavor, such as poor weather or inaccurate maps, in addition to uncertainties one's enemies create. Military forces conceal their intentions and work to deceive their opponents. They use camouflage, false signals, night marches, and other tricks, as well as elaborate deceptions, such as Wesley's ruse to outwit Vizzini in the *Princess Bride*.

During World War II, for example, British agents created a false biography for a recently deceased man. They planted fake invasion plans on the body of this "man who never was," and tossed him into the sea to wash ashore and fall into Nazi hands. The Germans fell for the trick, as they often did, and concentrated their forces in Sardinia instead of the actual sites on Sicily where American and British troops landed in July 1943. Dubbed "Operation Mincemeat" this ruse saved thousands of Allied lives. As the ancient Chinese strategist Sun Tzu noted, "all warfare is based on deception."

Friction, Uncertainty, and Change

TO EASE HIS ANALYSIS, Isaac Newton envisioned physics in an environment free of gravity, atmospheric friction, and other external forces. Clausewitz similarly first examined war as an ideal type, borrowing the term friction to encompass war's many unpredictable factors. Armed forces operate in uncertain environments and suffer from supply, logistic, and other difficulties. These can make even simple tasks, such as moving a large column of troops from one place to another, difficult. Critical supplies fail to arrive. Storms wash out a road or block a mountain pass. An officer misreads a map and leads his unit in the wrong direction.

Equally important is war's inherent uncertainty, which Clausewitz compared to fog on a battlefield, hence the term "fog of war." Uncertainty is so central to Clausewitz's conception of war that he suggests games of cards like poker better reflect war's reality than games like chess in which opposing forces are clearly visible.

Luck, good or bad, also plays a role, so much so that Napoleon reputedly quipped, "don't tell me if an officer is skillful, tell me if he's lucky."

War is a dynamic and reciprocal process that takes place within this uncertainty. As events unfold, adversaries' initial assumptions are tested and often found false. Enemies learn about and adapt to one another. Strategy necessarily changes in a prolonged war—at least for the victorious side. This year's winning strategy may lead to disaster in the next.

Policy goals often change as well. During the Korean War, U.S. policy changed from preserving South Korea to liberating North Korea and then back to preserving South Korea after China's intervention made the costs of continued war unacceptable.

Military Strategy in Fiction

SOME NOVELISTS ADEPTLY interweave strategic considerations into their works. Too often, though, strategic considerations receive short shrift, even in military fiction. In place of strategic wisdom, naive farm boys and over-muscled barbarians carve their way through escalating numbers of enemies with little planning or forethought. Winning battle after battle leads to their inevitable victory. Among the best of these is Orson Scott Card's *Enders Game* (1985). Believing they are simulations, child prodigy Andrew "Ender" Wiggin defeats the alien Buggers in a succession of battles, eventually annihilating the species entirely by destroying their home planet.

Few wars unfold that way. American forces never lost a significant battle in Vietnam and yet lost the war. Napoleon similarly fought his way to Moscow, defeated the Russian army outside that city, and yet was forced into a disastrous retreat from which his army never recovered. Russia's generals lacked Napoleon's tactical virtuosity but proved superior strategists. Strategy trumped tactics.

In Robert Heinlein's *Starship Troopers* (1959), perhaps the best-known and most widely imitated military science fiction novel, we learn little about the causes of the war or the strategies involved. A series of unspecified incidents leads the "Bugs" to open war with humanity with a nuclear strike on Buenos Aires.

This is the proximate cause of the war, much like the attack on Pearl Harbor instigated war between the United States and Japan. We know the underlying causes of that historic war, but Heinlein never explains the underlying causes for war between humanity and the Bugs. Similarly, he never explains the Bugs' strategy. Why nuke

Buenos Aires? Why later nuke San Francisco? What is the strategic purpose of these nuclear attacks? What made Buenos Aires or San Francisco worth nuking? If the Bugs could nuke one city, why didn't they nuke others?

The human counteroffensive against the Bugs involves invading a series of planets in battles reminiscent of the Pacific Theater of World War II. Apart from one battle, which specifically aimed to capture an enemy leader, a "Bug Brain," these campaigns lack strategic context or explanation. Why, after capturing a Bug Brain, invade planets at all? Why not bombard them from orbit? Were any of them worth capturing? What were the strategic alternatives?

The same could be said of J. R. R. Tolkien's *The Hobbit* (1937). Following the death of the dragon Smaug, armies of dwarves, elves, and humans maneuver against one another to get a share of the spoils in Lonely Mountain. Before fighting breaks out, an army of goblins arrives and instigates what becomes the Battle of Five Armies. If the goblins have a plan, it's never explained. Lacking any objective other than fighting and looting, the goblins apparently exist solely to unite the good guys against them, prefiguring the alliance against Sauron and his orcs in Tolkien's *Lord of the Rings* trilogy.

Similarly, in the movie *Greyhound* (2020), why is Tom Hanks in the middle of the Atlantic? The movie glosses over the strategic importance of winning the Battle of the Atlantic. Yet, C. S. Forester's masterful novel *The Good Shepherd* (1955), on which the movie is based, explains this in detail. German strategy in World War II relied on cutting off American supplies to Great Britain. Tom Hanks, the captain of the *Greyhound,* commands warships escorting a vital convoy. If enough convoys get through, Allied victory is assured. If not, Nazi domination of Europe will endure.

Historian Eric Larrabee underlines this point. Strategy, he says, explains "the reason why." Why are "a given number of individuals with a given mission to accomplish" at a specific place at a specific time? "If the strategy is well conceived, they will be concentrated in greater strength than the enemy and will have caught him off balance. Contriving such circumstances is the strategist's never-ending preoccupation" (*Commander in Chief*, 8).

Why did an army of goblins march on the Lonely Mountain? What is its mission? How does this mission serve the goblins' larger strategy? We don't know. The goblins lack policy goal, strategic purpose, and operational plan. They're just looking for a fight. Nations that do the same don't last. Perhaps that's why Tolkien renamed the goblins to orcs in *Lord of the Rings*.

In *Lord of the Rings*, Frodo and his companions discuss how to defeat Sauron. Gandalf underlines the importance of destroying the One Ring, which is central to Sauron's plan for Middle Earth domination. While more strategically informed than *The Hobbit*, the good guys' strategy boils down to stalling Sauron's armies and destroying the ring. It is simplistic.

Sauron's plan, like those of too many villains, suffers from a single point of failure easily identified and exploited by heroes. Competent strategists avoid that problem and many others discussed in this book.

Published seven years after *Starship Troopers*, Heinlein's *The Moon is a Harsh Mistress* (1966) is more strategically nuanced. Drawing on the American Revolution, Heinlein considers strategies for a rebellion by lunar settlers to seize control of the Moon and pressure Earth's government to accept their independence. In doing so, he grapples with one of strategy's enduring questions. How can a weaker entity employ strategy to defeat a seemingly superior foe?

Outlining this strategic situation establishes the stakes for Heinlein's lunar insurgents, which is important for any historical or fictional work. What's at stake? What do the protagonists and their antagonists want? What resources will they commit and what actions will they take to get it?

The story of the 300 Spartans (and their oft-forgotten Thespian allies) offers a historical example. What were they doing at Thermopylae? Why did their commander, Leonidas, insist they stand and fight the Persians despite overwhelming odds?

Contrary to depictions in several movies, a large Greek army, supported by an equally large fleet, occupied the pass at Thermopylae to block the invading Persian army. The Persian army depended on supplies from its accompanying fleet and its own foraging as it advanced across Greece. The narrow passes at Thermopylae, and similarly constrained waterways off its coast, offered the perfect places to halt the enormous Persian fleet and army. If the Greeks could hold the Persians in place long enough, the Persians would eat up their supplies and be forced to retreat to avoid starvation.

Unfortunately for the Greeks, the Persians discovered a way to outflank their army at Thermopylae. Leonidas and his Spartan and Thespian hoplites held the pass while the rest of the Greek army (and fleet) withdrew to the south. The prolonged stand of the 300 at Thermopylae was strategically essential. It saved the Greek army and bought time for Athens, Sparta, and their allies to reassess their strategy, develop new plans, and eventually defeat Persia.

A good fictional example is Jack Campbell's *Lost Fleet* series. Inspired by Xenophon's *Anabasis*, Campbell opens the series with an outnumbered military force trapped deep within a foreign empire. How will its leaders guide it home? What are their strategic options?

Campbell establishes the political situation, which involves a protracted, attritional war between the Alliance and the Syndics. Strategically, the trapped Alliance fleet will avoid combat, seek indirect routes home to confuse pursuers, and raid enemy bases to gather supplies and keep the enemy off balance.

Unfortunately, other authors mimic Michael Douglas's character in the movie *Wall Street* (1987). They pepper their works with the names and common sayings of important strategists, but without explaining them—or in some cases even understanding them. What, for example, does Sun Tzu mean by "know your enemy; know yourself" or Napoleon by "the moral is to the physical as three is to one?"

In Greg Bear's *The Forge of God* (1987), a character suddenly suggests Earth's alien visitors have taken a page from British strategist B. H. Liddell Hart and are employing an "indirect approach" by misdirecting Earth's leaders as to their intentions. "Never do what your enemy expects," he tells colleagues.

The aliens, though, are involved in complex misdirections far beyond what Liddell Hart described as "the indirect approach," in his popular book, *Strategy* (1954). Misdirection features in every military thinker's arsenal and is as important to tactics as it is to strategy. As Sun Tzu said, "all war is based on deception." That ancient Chinese strategist is a much better choice to illustrate Bear's point. Sun Tzu describes elaborate ruses, including arranging for couriers with false orders to fall into enemy hands.

Liddell Hart's primary concern was avoiding the First World War's bloody trench warfare. He advocated attacking enemy forces from unexpected directions by taking indirect approaches as Hannibal did against Rome when he crossed the Alps.

In Bear's sequel, *Anvil of Stars* (1993), a character rattles off a list of strategic thinkers ranging from Clausewitz to Lawrence of Arabia with no explanation as to their ideas or how these applied to the situation at hand, an upcoming space battle against technologically superior (and deceitful) aliens. The implication is that characters who can name strategists understand strategy. Unfortunately, their actions often show otherwise.

Thinking Through Strategy in Fiction

IN LOIS MCMASTER BUJOLD'S *The Vor Game*, protagonist Miles Vorkosigan faces off against Commander Cavilo, a mercenary who condescendingly explains "the key to strategy... is not to choose *a* path to victory, but to choose so that *all* paths lead to victory" (613).

While seemingly clever, Cavilo's increasingly complex schemes and tangled alliances prove a vulnerability rather than a strength. Her efforts to plan for every possible contingency, alliance, and employer lead to strategic incoherence, which her "total self-interest" exacerbates. Rather than making Cavilo strong, her constantly shifting goals and related strategies made her "a rag in the wind, anybody's to pick up" and exploit (Chapter 16).

Frank Herbert's *Dune* (1965) features similarly confused planning by Emperor Shaddam IV and Baron Vladimir Harkonnen. Apart from their antipathy toward Duke Leto Atreides they have no common interests or shared goals. Like Cavilo's confused planning and ever-changing goals and strategies, they bring us back to Clausewitz. "No one starts a war—or rather, no one in his sense ought to do so—without first being clear in his mind what he intends to achieve by the war and how he intends to conduct it" (*On War*, 577). In other words, know what you want before going to war.

This is the question posed by the unsavory Mr. Morden in the television series *Babylon 5*. Proceeding through the eponymous space station, he asks various ambassadors "what do you want?"

Surprisingly, it is Centauri Ambassador Londo Mollari, presented as a buffoon in the first season, who articulates clear political goals. He wants to rebuild the Centauri Empire to command the stars in "a rebirth of glory" and "renaissance of power."

In contrast, the Narn Empire's Ambassador G'Kar can't think beyond revenge for past Centauri depredations. Blinded by their justified hatred, the Narn lack coherent foreign policy goals. Their on-

MILITARY STRATEGY FOR WRITERS 13

again, off-gain friendships with other civilizations demonstrate this. Alliances matter to the Narn only to the extent the Narn can use them against the Centauri. Blinded by their passions, the Narn have no coherent long-term policy goals or strategy. Like Cavilo, they are anyone's to exploit. They wind up as cannon fodder, dying by the millions.

Babylon 5's commander, Captain John Sheridan, emerges as a clear strategic thinker who maintains consistent goals. He learns the strengths and weaknesses of his enemies while forming a growing alliance to fight the ancient Shadows whom he deftly maneuvers into several mistakes, allowing him to use his limited forces to best advantage.

NOT EVERY FICTIONAL character is a strategic genius, nor should they be. Neither do fictional characters need to run around citing Clausewitz or Sun Tzu. They do, though, need a strategy, even if it's superficial, ill-informed, or unrealistic. Japan's decision to attack on Pearl Harbor ranks among the greatest blunders in military history. Nonetheless, it resulted from serious planning and a clear, if flawed, strategic concept. Germany's Nazi leaders invaded the Soviet Union with an equally flawed strategy. Every nation goes to war with a strategy for winning it. Some work out. Others don't.

Understanding strategy and strategic principles allows authors to create more compelling situations, explain villains' schemes, and develop ways for their heroes to foil them. No plan is perfect. Both heroes and villains may be guilty of common—or less common—strategic mistakes. They may focus on immediate, tactical opportunities rather than long-term strategic goals. Perhaps they misidentify enemy weaknesses, violate various principles of war, end wars in ways that provoke new wars, underestimate enemy strength, or overestimate their own.

Strategic thought offers neither simple solutions nor a rote system guaranteed to produce victory. Strategy is not prescriptive. No strategy guarantees success. The goal of strategic theory, as Clausewitz explained, is to "provide a thinking man with a frame of reference for decision making." It should encourage the critical thinking and thoughtful planning essential to translating political purpose into military action, whether real or fictional (*On War*, 141).

The same is true of this book. It does not provide a strategic checklist for fictional villains and heroes to follow. Rather, the point is to help authors think through strategic issues using the same ideas, principles, and tools historical leaders have.

Characters who develop and implement detailed and plausible strategies engage readers and drive exciting stories. The ever-changing goals and strategies of Bujold's Commander Cavilo kept readers turning the page. Your villain's schemes should do the same, as should your hero's desperate efforts to out-strategize them, as Miles Vorkosigan does Cavilo.

I organized this book into nine chapters. The first, Building Your Strategic Vocabulary, describes and explains the terminology and important concepts essential for strategic thought and planning. Chapter 2 addresses classic strategic thought, focusing on four foundational strategic writers: Thucydides, Sun Tzu, Antoine-Henri Jomini, and Clausewitz. It explores their conceptions of war and strategy and expands on points raised in this introduction, including cost-benefit analysis, decisive battle, winning without fighting, war termination, civil-military relations, and war's inherent nature as a realm of uncertainty, chance, and friction.

The next five chapters, each of which closes with a short case study illustrating important points, discuss how strategists adapted these strategic ideas to different kinds of wars and military environments. Chapters 3 and 4 discuss sea power and air power. Chapter 5 addresses the largely speculative field of nuclear warfare, which has proven a ripe playground for game theorists. To get the most out of this chapter, be sure to read the preceding chapter on air power first. Chapters 6 and 7 address strategies of insurgency and counterinsurgency, which have a long history. So, too, does terrorism, the subject of Chapter 8. These three chapters are best read together since the concepts relate and build upon each other.

Finally, Chapter 9 builds on the previous chapters to explore strategies in science fiction and fantasy, genres that frequently feature warfare. At the end of the book, you'll find questions to ask yourself to guide your strategic thought as you write your book.

Chapter One: Building Your Strategic Vocabulary

As Clausewitz noted, war has its own grammar, but not its own logic. Learning that grammar, though, is essential to understanding war. Scholars and military officers use terms with specific meanings to them, but which outsiders may employ casually and inaccurately. Tactics and strategy, for example, refer to different things, and there is no such thing as tactical strategy—no matter how many movies use the term. This chapter aims to acquaint you with terminology central to discussing war and assessing strategy. Military theorists and scholars assess the conduct of war at four levels: policy (political goals), strategic, operational, and tactical. Political leaders need to clearly articulate their nation's (or organization's) goals. What is their national policy? What is their vision for the postwar world? What is the desired end state for which they fight?

Strategy is how you intend to achieve this end state. How will you use your available means to achieve your desired end state? Operations and tactics involve the sharp end of the sword: maneuvering and fighting one's armed forces before (operations) and during (tactics) battle.

An effective strategy balances ends, ways, and means and weighs the risks involved in its execution. A Naval War College colleague of mine likes to use coffee as an example. Why has a student brought an enormous mug of coffee to class? The student's goal (policy) is to stay sharp and not fall asleep in class. To do that, he will rely on caffeine (strategy). Purchasing his huge mug of coffee brings us to the operational level, while sipping coffee during class takes us down to tactics.

In Lois McMaster Bujold's novel *Barrayar* (1991), the usurper Vordarian seizes power and ignites a civil war. Loyalist forces, led by Aral and Cordelia Vorkosigan, need to defeat Vordarian and restore Gregor, still a child, as emperor. While Aral works to woo vacillating military commanders to his side, besiege Vordarian's forces in the capital, and limit the damage of civil war, Cordelia cuts right to the heart of the matter. Her strategy is to undermine Vordarian's legitimacy by rescuing Gregor's mother, whom Vordarian holds captive, and reunite her with her child. So, Cordelia and her team infiltrate the capital and palace (the operational level of war) by sneaking through secret passages and avoiding or overcoming guards and other obstacles (tactics).

Policy

AS SERGEANT ZIM EXPLAINS in Heinlein's *Starship Troopers*, "War is not violence and killing, pure and simple; war is *controlled* violence, for a purpose." The goal of war, Sergeant Zim says, is to make the enemy "do what you want him to do" (Chapter 4).

Heinlein, of course, is paraphrasing Clausewitz who described war as "politics by other means" and warned: "no one starts a war—or rather, no one in his senses ought to do so—without first being clear in his mind what he intends to achieve by the war and how he intends to conduct it" (*On War*, 577). Mao Zedong similarly emphasized that war is "politics with bloodshed." It should aim to destroy the enemy's ability to resist so one can implement political change (*Selected Military Writings*, 229). In the absence of clear political goals and sound strategy, wars devolve into mindless violence—exactly what Clausewitz, Mao, and Sergeant Zim warn against.

The Atlantic Charter, a joint statement by U.S. President Franklin D. Roosevelt and U.K. Prime Minister Winston Churchill in August 1941 exemplifies superior policy making. It spelled out their long-term goals, which included people's rights to self-determination, the restoration of conquered territory, and the disarmament of aggressor nations. While Britain was then fighting for its existence against Nazi Germany and Fascist Italy, the United States was nominally at peace. It did not formally enter World War II until Japan attacked Pearl Harbor four months later. Yet, Roosevelt and his advisors were already considering how to shape the post-war world. They also recognized the strategic importance of supporting Britain and Russia.

Strategy

WRITING 1,000 WORDS a day will not give you a novel. A novel requires a clear goal combined with intellectual and creative effort: character development, world building, and a coherent plot with beginning, middle, and end. Similarly, killing enemy troops by the thousands does not, by itself, win wars. American forces killed far more enemy combatants than the 58,000 Americans who died in Vietnam, and yet lost the war. More Union than Confederates troops died in the American Civil War, yet the Confederates lost. In World War II, more Allied troops died than Germans, yet Nazi Germany lost the war. The reason, of course, is strategy. The Americans in Vietnam, the Confederates in the American Civil War, and the Germans in both World Wars were strategically inept.

In these cases, racism compounded poor strategic planning. Hitler and his senior generals believed the "mongrel" Soviet state would collapse in a matter of weeks. Confederate leaders believed northerners lacked martial values and that African Americans would prove poor soldiers. American politicians and generals believed Vietnamese peasants incapable of fighting and winning a modern, high-tech war.

In the distant past, when wars involved simply marching to and attacking an enemy village, there was little need to distinguish between tactics and strategy. A single engagement lasting a few hours could decide a war. This was the norm among Greek city states before the Persian invasions of the fifth century BCE. As wars became larger and more complex, distinguishing between tactics and strategy became essential.

Sixth century Byzantine manuals differentiate between tactics, which involve winning battles, and strategy, which considered the more complex issues of winning wars. Earlier Roman treatises probably did the same, but they have not survived. As European wars increased in scale and complexity, a new generation of scholars re-emphasized these distinctions. Writing in the late 18th century, French writer Jacques Antoine Hippolyte Guibert, differentiated between tactics and "grand tactics," the latter involving war aims. Dietrich Heinrich von Bülow, a Prussian army officer, revived the use of the word strategy for these matters and offered its first modern definition. Strategy involved the movement of opposing armies beyond sight of one another, while tactics was their movement within sight of each other.

A generation later, Clausewitz criticized Bülow's definitions for failing to explain the purpose of strategy and tactics. The point of tactics was to win battles, while strategy was the use of engagements (of whatever size) to win wars.

Clausewitz offered a more nuanced understanding of strategy, which included winning wars through means other than decisive battle, that is a battle so large or important it "decides" a war by so weakening an enemy that victory is inevitable. As he noted, "strategy is harder than tactics because you have more time to act and thus more time to doubt." Enemies, in turn, have more time to react and spring their own traps. In tactics, "you can see what is going on, in strategy you have to guess" (178-179). This observation remains as true in the age of spy satellites as when Clausewitz wrote almost 200 years ago.

Grand Strategy

CLAUSEWITZ ENCOURAGED commanders to seek decisive battle against an enemy but recognized this was not always possible or desirable. Wearing down an enemy over time was another option, which brings us to grand strategy. One rarely seeks victory solely through military means. Nations form alliances, pressure enemies economically, and make their case through international media to win adherents and sow dissension among enemies. Grand strategy includes military strategy and all the other tools one may use against enemies: cultural, diplomatic, economic, psychological, and so on. Some scholars represent this as DIME (Diplomatic, Informational, Military, and Economic). As Chou En-Lai (Zhou Enlai) once quipped, reversing Clausewitz's famous dictum, diplomacy can be "war by other means."

During World War II, for example, the Allies not only attacked Axis military forces but also blockaded Axis ports to strangle their economies, bombed their factories, supported resistance movements in occupied countries, broadcast propaganda, dropped counterfeit currency into enemy lands, and encouraged civilian resistance.

Grand strategy is important in peace as well as war, and you don't need to be a nation-state to have a grand strategy. During the Cold War, Jewish and Christian religious organizations smuggled prayer books into the Soviet Union along with magazines, music, and other popular media. By doing so, they not only countered Soviet efforts to suppress religion, but also undermined its claim of creating a socialist utopia. They demonstrated most West Europeans and

Americans lived in greater comfort than all but the highest placed Soviet citizens. They waged an ideological struggle in which they weaponized *Beatles* music and *Good Housekeeping* magazine to subvert existing power structures.

When the alliance between the United States and Soviet Union broke down after World War II, American diplomat George Kennan proposed the United States employ a strategy of containment against the Soviet Union. If the United States used its diplomatic, economic, and military resources to block Soviet expansion, Kennan argued, internal social and economic problems, combined with the inherent contradictions of its communist ideology, would inevitably tear apart the Soviet nation. Roughly 40 years later, the Soviet Union collapsed, much as Kennan predicted.

Geopolitical success requires economic vitality. In *The Rise and Fall of Great Powers* (1987), Paul Kennedy highlights how overexpansion and excessive military spending led empires to collapse. As empires grow, more and more of their resources go to the frontier to hold longer borders against growing enemies. This reaches a point—due to external threats or internal problems—where these commitments overwhelm the state and the empire collapses like Han China, and the Roman, Spanish, and British Empires.

Successful grand strategy, Kennedy argues, requires nations to combine "all the elements of national power," including diplomacy; national will, morale, and political culture; and the full range of economic resources, including industry, finance, manpower, and wealth, to enhance their "long-term (that is, in wartime and peacetime) best interests" (*Rise and Fall,* 5).

One may threaten a potential enemy with military force, economic sanctions, or other forms of coercion. Deterrence aims to convince enemies to avoid going to war or adopting a policy injurious to one's interests. Compellence, a term popularized by Lawrence Freedman, aims to convince the target to take action that helps you, such as ceding a territory, abandoning an ally, or changing their foreign policy. In the last year of World War II, for example, Allied threats compelled Sweden to stop shipping iron ore to Nazi Germany. Compellence and deterrence require both military capability and its demonstrated use. The ready willingness of ancient Romans to employ overwhelming military force and revel in what we today label war crimes proved effective for several centuries. Routine displays of military force deterred Rome's enemies and won them allies, no matter how reluctant.

For Edward Luttwak, "grand strategy is simply the level at which knowledge and persuasion, or in modern terms intelligence and diplomacy, interact with military strength to determine outcomes in a world of other states, with their own grand strategies" (*Grand Strategy of the Byzantine Empire,* 409). So, strategy or military strategy is a component of grand strategy—a very important part if you are at war.

Nations pursue grand strategies over decades. Luttwak argues the Roman and Byzantine Empires pursued coherent grand strategies across centuries despite recurrent political upheaval and civil war. For the Roman Empire, this involved pacifying and assimilating people along its frontier, securing that long frontier with fortifications, and conducting punitive raids to deter enemies or bend them to Rome's will. Byzantine strategy focused on turning enemies against one another and expanding or contracting imperial frontiers based on enemy pressure.

In Eric Flint's *Ring of Fire* series of alternate history novels, the town of Grantville, West Virginia is mysteriously transported from late twentieth century America into Germany during the Thirty Years War (1618-1648). Grantville's people apply all their resources, military, technological, and cultural, to survive. They develop a grand strategy that involves fielding their own military forces, forming alliances, selected sharing of technology, and promoting the economic and political development of their immediate region.

Historically, battles proved indecisive in the Thirty Years War. The antagonists fought to mutual exhaustion. They failed to develop and apply coherent strategies beyond living off the enemy's land and devastating it. Flint adeptly injects strategic purpose into this war. His protagonists pursue an effective grand strategy to change its outcome.

Strategy

THE INCREASING FINANCIAL resources of modern states after the Thirty Years' War allowed them to replace feudal levies and mercenaries with recruits trained to use gunpowder weapons. Armies grew larger and troops more specialized, reflecting the political, social, and technological developments of the last few centuries. As science fiction author and Vietnam veteran Joe Haldeman notes in his novel *Forever War* (1974), "modern warfare has become very complex." Wars are no longer "won by a simple series of battles." Rather, victory results from a "complex interrelationship among military victory, economic pressures, logistic maneuvering, access to the enemy's information, political postures, and dozens" of other factors that underpin strategy.

Strategy is the intellectual link between your political goals and the use of force (or threats of force) to achieve them. It is, as B. H. Liddell Hart wrote, "the art of distributing and applying military means to fulfill the ends of policy" (*Strategy*, 335). At its heart, strategy involves a search for comparative advantage. How do you apply your strengths against an enemy's weaknesses? How do you prevent the enemy from doing the same to you?

Strategy also requires reconciling ends with means. Can you achieve your political goals with the resources in hand? If not, you either need to change your goal or devote more resources to the struggle. Imperial Japan's decision to attack the United States while still embroiled in war in China was foolish. If Japan lacked the economic and military resources to defeat China, how could it simultaneously fight the United States? Their goals far exceeded their military capabilities.

Yet, Alexander the Great conquered the Persian Empire despite its vast superiority in finances and military manpower. Strategic calculations involve more than totaling up troops and money. Alexander conquered the Persian Empire piece by piece. He exploited the empire's fragility and disaffected subject peoples and lived off the enemy's land. Loot from each captured city and province funded his army's next advance, which continued into Afghanistan, a campaign highlighted and fictionalized in Steven Pressfield's novel *The Afghan Campaign* (2006)

A century later, Hannibal Barca, Carthage's foremost general, similarly tried to dismantle the Roman Empire. Repeatedly defeated in battle, the Romans resorted to what has since been called a Fabian strategy, named for Quintus Fabius Maximus Verrucosus, a veteran general recalled to service to stop Hannibal. Fabius avoided major battles and instead sought to wear down Hannibal's army in small harassing attacks, particularly against foraging parties, hindering its ability to live off the land. This earned Fabius the nickname Cunctator, or Delayer, and gave us the term Fabian strategy for avoiding battle and wearing down an enemy through gradual military attrition.

While Fabius limited Hannibal's depredations, his strategy proved unpopular among Romans accustomed to decisive battle. When Fabius stepped down from command, the Romans assembled their largest army ever, sought battle with Hannibal, and suffered a disastrous defeat at Cannae. Afterward, Rome returned to a Fabian strategy while it rebuilt its army and then went on to win the war.

Many nations have employed Fabian strategies against tactically superior enemies. Following a succession of defeats around New York in the American Revolution, George Washington avoided major battle and instead attacked isolated British garrisons. As Alexander Hamilton explained, facing the British in a major battle was "a desperate game" in which one gambled the revolution's success on "a single cast of the die." Losing a single major battle could wreck the Continental Army, making it "folly to hazard it."

Washington's Fabian strategy proved successful and paved the way for battlefield victories at Saratoga (1777), which brought France into the war as an American ally, and Yorktown (1781), which broke the back of British power in the American South. In Frank Herbert's novel *Dune* (1965), the Fremen and their Atreides allies similarly wear down their Harkonnen oppressors with a Fabian strategy.

Operations

THE CONCEPT OF AN OPERATIONAL level of war was not clearly articulated in Clausewitz's day. Nonetheless, nineteenth century officers had an implicit understanding of a realm of conflict linking tactics and strategy. Clausewitz himself refers to campaigns, campaign plans, and zones of operation.

Operations involve the movement of large military forces against the enemy. The U.S. Army defines operations as "the pursuit of strategic objectives, in whole or in part, through the arrangement of tactical actions in time, space, and purpose" (*ADP 3-0: Unified Land Operations*, 2011). The goal of operations is to maneuver one's forces against the enemy as advantageously as possible to win any resulting battles. Operations should advance one's strategy, hinder the enemy's, or both.

Examples of operations include the American, British, and Canadian amphibious invasion of Normandy in World War II, along with all the prior and subsequent amphibious operations in the European and Pacific theaters, Nazi Germany's invasions of Poland, France, Russia, and all the other offensives and campaigns of that war, such as the back-and-forth fighting in North Africa.

All of these campaigns aimed to advance their respective organizers' strategic goals, though these goals sometimes rested on flawed assumptions. Napoleon assumed his 1812 invasion of Russia would inflict such heavy losses on Russian armies that Tsar Alexander I would agree to Napoleon's demands. Nazi Germany's leaders were even more grandiose. In 1941, they assumed they could inflict such losses on Soviet armies they would precipitate the collapse of the Soviet government. Both, of course, were wrong.

Military operations are guided by doctrine, general principles that inform how military forces act, particularly at the tactical and operational level. Today, many military forces and governments issue formal statements of doctrine, but doctrine is shaped as much by past practice and tradition as it is by the pronouncements of senior political and military leaders.

Doctrine varies by time, place, service, and nation. Roman generals preferred to seek out enemy armies and force them to battle, rather than allowing their enemies to come to them. Rome carved out its empire following this aggressive doctrine, but also suffered numerous disasters, such as the annihilation of seven Roman legions at the Battle of Carrhae by Parthian cavalry and the destruction of three others in Germany's Teutoburg Forest.

While both the U.S. Army and U.S. Marine Corps face similar combat situations, they are guided by different doctrine, which explains their different approach to fighting the Vietnam War, World War II, and more recent conflicts in the Persian Gulf. Doctrinal differences helped produce the Smith-Smith controversy of World War II between two similarly named Army and Marine generals. As part of their training, Heinlein's *Starship Troopers*, are inculcated with their service's traditions and doctrine, including independent, aggressive action, and not leaving any comrade behind.

Tactics

TACTICS REFERS TO THE deployment of troops and weapons systems to win battles, sieges, or other military engagements. It is the use of maneuver and firepower (or hand-to-hand combat in earlier eras) to destroy an enemy's armed forces or attack or defend important positions.

Apart from direct assault on enemy positions (and their fixed defense), common tactics include ambushing an enemy force, turning its flank, or enveloping it entirely as Hannibal did the Romans at Cannae. Outnumbered armies seek strong defensive positions, or refuse to engage entirely, detaching small units to harass the enemy, but avoiding pitched battle. Or they might feign retreat to draw an enemy army into a trap, as the Parthians did the Romans at Carrhae.

The various principles of war apply most to the tactical and operational levels of war. The list varies among military services, but generally includes some variation of those identified by the U.S. Army in *Unified Field Operations* (FM 3-0): Objective, Offensive, Mass, Economy of Force, Maneuver, Unity of Command, Security, Surprise, and Simplicity. Briefly, these are defined as follows:

1. Objective: define and direct military operations toward clearly defined goals.

2. Offensive: gain and maintain the initiative to force enemies to react to you. As Clausewitz notes, defense is the stronger form of war, but it is difficult to win a war on the defensive.
3. Mass: concentrate combat power at a decisive point to achieve relative superiority.
4. Economy of force: don't use a hammer to smash a gnat. Don't commit the bulk of your forces to secure trifling objectives.
5. Maneuver: use mobility to gain advantage before battle.
6. Unity of Command: create and maintain a clear and direct chain of command to avoid confusion and ensure a united effort. Rivalries among allies, different military services, and commanders complicate this.
7. Surprise: plan movement and attack to catch an opponent unaware as the Japanese did at Pearl Harbor, the Israelis in the 1967 Six Day War, and the Egyptians in the 1973 Arab-Israeli War.
8. Security: ensure your defense through effective reconnaissance, spying, and other measures. Avoid enemy surprises while maintaining the secrecy of your own plans.
9. Simplicity: don't unnecessarily complicate your plans. To paraphrase Clausewitz, everything in war is very simple, but even the simplest things prove difficult to execute. Convoluted schemes may confuse your own commanders as much as your enemies.

Napoleon and other master tacticians rely on these. Story protagonists and villains ignore them at their peril.

Yet, no principle of war is valid for every situation, and they are often contradictory. Concentrating troops against an enemy's decisive point is important, but the larger an army becomes, the more difficult it is to maneuver and the harder it becomes to surprise an enemy.

Clausewitz encourages generals to seize and maintain the initiative by pressing their offensive operations, the principle of continuity. Yet, he also warns about the "culminating point of victory" (Book 7, chapter 22), the point after which a successful invading army necessarily grows weaker from casualties, garrisoning captured territory, and maintaining lengthening supply lines. Clever enemies draw successful armies past their culminating point of victory and then counterattack as the Russians did against Napoleon.

These contradictions create opportunities for both real and fictional commanders. Authors can use these to advance their plots and lure their heroes into traps from which they must extricate themselves and perhaps their armies. In Frank Herbert's *Dune*, for example, the Harkonnen launch a devastating attack against Atreides forces on Arrakis. Yet, Paul Atreides survives and develops a strategy to defeat the Harkonnens and regain control of Arrakis.

Tactics may change during wars, particularly prolonged wars in the modern era. At the outset of World War II, tanks often smashed their way through enemy positions. Within a few years, though, tanks found it difficult to advance, particularly if unsupported by infantry and artillery or air power. Infantrymen employed new tactics against tanks and benefitted from improved anti-tank guns and rocket launchers, like the American bazooka.

In 1944, the U.S. Air Force sought to apply the same tactics it used to bomb German cities against Japanese cities: high-altitude daylight precision bombing by airplanes flying in close formation. The jet stream, though, made accurate bombing difficult. Dispersed Japanese manufacturing compounded the problem. So, the Air Force changed to low-altitude night bombing with incendiaries. By the end of the war, its raids destroyed the built-up area of most Japanese cities, killed hundreds of thousands of people and left millions more homeless. The strategy remained the same—destroying enemy industry to cripple its war effort. The tactics to implement it changed.

Most movies focus on tactics. Intrepid teams battle their enemy opposite numbers, attack critical installations, and execute other acts of derring-do. Among the exceptions are *A Bridge too Far* (1977), which covers the entirety of Operation Market Garden, involving multiple paratroop drop and simultaneous combat at widely separated places, and *The Battle of Britain* (1969), which, in between numerous scenes of air combat, shows how superior British strategy foiled Germany's air offensive.

The Tacticization of Strategy

NAVAL WAR COLLEGE PROFESSOR Michael Handel coined the term "tacticization of strategy" to describe generals who assume superior tactics and successive battlefield victories win wars. Many generals are guilty of this. Handel highlights German General Erich Ludendorff. Abrasive, overconfident, and dictatorial, Ludendorff brushed aside critics and committed Germany to massive offensives along the Western Front in 1918. Using new tactics, German forces broke through British and French lines in several places, inflicted heavy losses, and drove forward dozens of miles. The offensive marked the first significant progress on the Western Front in almost four years.

Yet, these attacks lacked strategic purpose. They relied on elite units to break through enemy lines and move forward rapidly on narrow fronts. Successive attacks by fresh troops widened these breaches, sustained the offensives, and allowed the German army to move artillery forward to support the next assault.

Against Russia, whose military and civilian morale had reached its nadir, these tactics produced battlefield victories that precipitated the Tsarist government's collapse.

In the West, Allied morale, bolstered by fresh American troops, remained strong. German troops suffered heavy losses without capturing anything of strategic value. When the Allies counterattacked that summer, the German army, bled white from Ludendorff's offensives, cracked. Thousands of German soldiers surrendered, and tens of thousands more retreated in disarray. Ludendorff declared it a "black day" for the Germany army—one from which it never recovered.

Prioritizing tactics over strategy led Germany to defeat in both world wars. Focused on immediate tactical and operational problems, German generals failed to assess the strategic situation and develop sound, long-term plans. Gordon R. Dickson describes something similar in his science fiction novel *Tactics of Mistake* (1971). The protagonist entices the villain with a series of tactical opportunities that lure the villain into strategic mistakes. Substituting tactical acumen for strategic thinking leads to disaster.

Many of history's great generals were better tacticians than strategists, including Hannibal, Gustavus Adolphus, Napoleon, and Robert E. Lee, whose nemesis, Ulysses S. Grant, was a master strategist.

A surprising number of alternate history stories posit Confederate victory at Gettysburg would have won the American Civil War for the Confederates. These writers offer a tactical solution (winning a single battle) for a strategic problem.

By the time of Gettysburg, the Confederacy was in a dangerous strategic position. The Union strategy was working. The Confederacy lacked the troops to defend its long frontier. Mustering enough troops to defend Virginia left the Confederacy's western states vulnerable. The Union navy liberated New Orleans, the Confederacy's most important port and captured or blockade the rest. Union armies advanced steadily through Tennessee, Mississippi, and Louisiana. They captured Vicksburg, the Confederacy's last position on the Mississippi River, the day after Gettysburg.

These victories were far more consequential to winning the war. Lee's invasion of Pennsylvania, which ended at Gettysburg, was an act of desperation by a general who lacked good strategic options. Victory at Gettysburg would not have changed the Confederacy's desperate strategic situation any more than its earlier victories at Fredericksburg or Chancellorsville. Similarly, George Washington's grasp of strategy more than made up for his army's tactical failings.

Total, Unlimited, and Limited Wars

THE VALUE OF A BELLIGERENT'S political goals should reflect what they're willing to pay to achieve it. How many lives and resources will they risk for it?

The United States mobilized its citizens, resources, and troops to a greater extent in World War II, a total war, than any later war. Defeating Nazi Germany, which, along with its Italian and Japanese allies, posed an existential threat to the democratic world order, was far more important than winning the United States' later wars in Korea, Vietnam, and the Middle East. World War II was a total war, while the latter were all limited wars.

Historians and strategists confusingly use the terms total and limited to refer to both means and ends. Means involves the mobilization of population and resources for war. Ends refers to one's political objective, as in "the ends justify the means."

In terms of ends, one might fight for the elimination of an enemy government, as the Allies did in World War II. In the most extreme cases, one might fight to eliminate an enemy entirely. Rome's third war with Carthage ended in mass murder, enslavement, and razing

Carthage to the ground. Most people call these total wars, though some scholars prefer to call them "unlimited wars," reserving "total" for discussing mobilization.

Unlimited wars usually aim to overthrow an enemy government, regime change in today's parlance. The victor generally imposes terms on the loser after it is no longer willing—or perhaps even capable—of offering military resistance.

Limited wars seek something less, such as capturing a province or forcing the enemy to change its foreign policy. So, limited wars usually end in negotiated settlements. Borders may shift and territories change hands. Sometimes, the loser pays an indemnity to the winner, as China did to Japan following the 1895 Sino-Japanese War.

Ancient states were perfectly capable of fighting unlimited wars, as Rome repeatedly did. The mobilizations achieved by the major powers in the twentieth century, though, were impossible for ancient or medieval states. They lacked the administrative, financial, and industrial apparatus for these. Despite constant wars, Rome rarely had more than 1% of its population under arms. The United States put 16 million men and women into uniform in World War II, about 10% of its population. Great Britain, Japan, Nazi Germany, and the Soviet Union mobilized even greater shares of their population for that war.

Equally important for mass mobilization is a sense of patriotism and national identity, which most ancient and medieval states lacked. The nationalism sparked by the French Revolution allowed France to mobilize the state for war on an unprecedented scale. French armies dwarfed those of their immediate neighbors. Napoleon then led them on vast wars of conquest that transformed Europe despite his ultimate failure. Napoleon did not fight limited wars. He played for all the marbles.

The distinctions between total and limited wars are best seen as a continuum. As Clausewitz explained, all belligerents face limitations, both internal (resources, population, armaments, etc.) and external (distance from the war zone, international law, allies, pressure from neutral powers, etc.). In World War II, our exemplar of total war, only about half the American population served in the military or worked in war industries.

Historian H.P. Wilmott offers one of the simplest definitions of limited war. A limited war is one you're willing to lose. If you're not willing to lose, you commit more resources to winning, moving up the gradient from limited to total war and perhaps even to nuclear war, a prospect unimaginable to Clausewitz.

Chuck Jones lampooned this prospect in his 1953 cartoon *Duck Dodgers in the 24 1/2th Century*. Dodgers and his nemesis, Marvin the Martian, fight over an obscure planet, escalating their military efforts until they simultaneously deploy their most deadly and secret weapons. Their combined release destroys the planet, a totality of war one hopes to never see.

In the Chaco War (1932-35), Bolivia and Paraguay fought to mutual exhaustion. The war ended when Paraguay literally ran out of people to send into battle. In the American Civil War, the Confederacy similarly neared its mobilization limits. Roughly 80% of white men aged 15-40 living within the Confederacy served in uniform during the war. Their absence from home facilitated the escape of tens of thousands of slaves and undermined the southern economy.

In William Tenn's story, "Down Among the Dead Men" (1954), Earth fights a total war against an insectoid species with a nearly inexhaustible supply of soldiers. Earth devotes all its resources to war. Normal civil life disappears. As humanity runs short of soldiers, scientists patch together body parts of the slain, reanimate them, and send these zombies back into battle, a mobilization so total it includes the dead.

It's important to remember that a war may be total or unlimited for one belligerent but limited for its opponent. During World War II, Japan fought an unlimited war against China, but a limited war against the United States with whom it sought a negotiated peace recognizing its conquests in China. In contrast, the United States fought to replace the authoritarian regimes of Japan and Nazi Germany with democratic governments.

In Vietnam, the United States fought a limited war, in terms of both ends and means. Its North Vietnamese enemy, though, devoted all its resources to unify Vietnam under its rule. Nonetheless, it confined its war effort to Southeast Asia. North Vietnam did not send saboteurs or terrorists to attack the U.S. homeland, or even U.S. bases near Vietnam, such as the Philippines or Guam.

The Vietnam War was a small part of the Cold War between the U.S. and the Soviet Union. Some scholars describe wars like Vietnam as nested wars, small wars that take place within the context of larger struggles. Nested wars are usually limited wars since the belligerent must maintain its focus on its primary antagonist. During the Korean and Vietnam Wars, for example, the U.S. deployed more troops in Europe to deter a Soviet invasion than it sent into combat in Korea or Vietnam.

Net Assessment and Reassessment

NET ASSESSMENT REFERS to the analysis of one's own and an enemy's strengths and weaknesses. It is the application of Sun Tzu's dictum to "know the enemy, know yourself." Nations anticipate, evaluate, and plan for potential threats before war. Before World War II, for example, American officers successfully anticipated most of the problems they encountered fighting Japan. A generation earlier, failed net assessments by all the major powers produced the disasters of World War I.

Changing military and political situations force constant reassessment. Allies come and go, enemies change tactics and strategy, and new weapons appear, such as Japan's kamikazes or Germany's ballistic missiles. China's entry into the Korean War transformed the military situation and sent American and United Nations forces into precipitous retreat. Fifty years earlier, Emilio Aguinaldo's Filipino army, repeatedly defeated in conventional battles by American troops, transitioned to guerrilla warfare, forcing the Americans to change their strategy.

Strategic Errors and Simplifications

GLORIFICATIONS OF VIOLENT problem solving, and oversimplifications of complex strategic matters are so common in science fiction they've spawned an entire subgenre lampooning them. Among the first was Harry Harrison's *Bill the Galactic Hero* (1965), which satirizes overused tropes ranging from naive farm boy turned hero to genocidal wars against alien hordes. Like Harrison's Bill, the characters in Howard Tayler's *Schlock Mercenary* webcomic series (2000 - 2020) fight in wars and execute strategic plans that often make little sense, despite their reference to "seventy maxims for maximum effectiveness," a few of which echo past strategic wisdom.

Misquoting important strategic thinkers is common, as is quoting them out of context or paraphrasing them in ways that change an author's original meaning or elide nuances. The most common of the latter is probably "no plan survives contact with the enemy." Even boxer Mike Tyson had a go at this one, warning "everyone has a plan until they get punched in the mouth."

What Chief of the Prussian General Staff General Helmuth von Moltke, a sometime novelist, actually said (in *On Strategy*) is: "No plan of operations extends with certainty beyond the first encounter with the enemy's main strength." Only laymen, he continues, envision a complex military campaign executed consistently according to plan from beginning to end.

Moltke, having led Prussia to victory in wars against Denmark, Austria, and France (1864, 1866, and 1870-71), was the foremost military leader of his era. Military operations, he explained, unfold in a fluid, ever-changing environment. "Certainly, the commander-in-chief keeps his great objective in mind, undisturbed by the vicissitudes of events." But the path to reaching it "can never be firmly established in advance." Commanders must be flexible and adaptable. Successive operations are "spontaneous acts guided by military measures." Their success "depends on penetrating the uncertainty of veiled situations to evaluate facts, to clarify the unknown, to make decisions rapidly, and then carry them out with strength and consistency."

People who shorten Moltke's explanation miss his point. A few pebbles, or the famous lost horseshoe, are unlikely to halt an army's progress. Competent, prepared commanders anticipate these types of friction. They expect enemy resistance, just as boxers expect to be punched in the mouth (and other places). They are flexible and plan for likely contingencies and enemy countermoves, as Muhammad Ali did in his famous boxing match against George Foreman. It requires something significant or unexpected to derail well-made plans.

As such, military planning is far from pointless. Despite his later claims to the contrary, Napoleon spent long nights crafting plans with his chief-of-staff, Louis-Alexandre Berthier. The point of planning is not to produce a perfect, unchanging plan. Rather, it serves to focus commanders and their subordinates on the objective and acquaint them with the military situation. As American General Dwight D. Eisenhower noted: "Plans are worthless, but planning is everything" (*Papers of the Presidents of the United States, Dwight D.*

Eisenhower, 1957, p. 818). The movie *Dungeons and Dragons: Honor Among Thieves* (2023) picked up on this theme, emphasizing the mutability of plans and importance of planning.

In Poul Anderson's Dominic Flandry series, the Terran Empire's enemies, the Mercians, think deeply about strategy. They recognize Earth's weaknesses and seek to exploit them. Yet, time and again their complex plans, which require near simultaneous successes in a host of diplomatic, espionage, and military endeavors, are undone when Flandry throws a wrench in the works.

Successful strategies are focused, simple, and flexible. Rather than hard and fast rules, Moltke warned, strategy is a "system of expedients." Successful commanders adapt to ever-changing tactical, operational, and strategic situations, uncertainty, and friction.

In contrast, poor commanders may panic when their plans go awry, or simply freeze as German General Friedrich Paulus did at Stalingrad during World War II. Others are too cautious. As Moltke warned, great results require taking great risks.

Some commanders, like Anderson's Mercians and Japan's Second World War admirals, develop excessively complicated plans. Others get lost planning for contingencies, a process that can cascade infinitely as one plans for contingencies for contingencies for contingencies. Excessively complex planning is among the common errors critiqued in war colleges around the world.

Other common strategic errors to which both historical and fictional commanders fall prey include:

1. Expecting more from your military than it can deliver. During World War II, Italian dictator Benito Mussolini planned to conquer a new Roman empire. His poorly trained and led army could not even conquer Greece. Iraqi dictator Saddam Hussein overestimated his military capabilities in every war he fought.

2. Assuming you and your enemy share the same vulnerabilities; that what would defeat you would also defeat your enemy. This is often called mirror imaging—looking at the enemy but seeing yourself. During the Vietnam War, casualty-averse American leaders assumed inflicting high casualties on the North Vietnamese would force them to the peace table. Instead, the Americans, who lost far fewer soldiers than North Vietnam, made peace because of the war's high costs.
3. Script writing: expecting the enemy to behave as predicted, participating in one's military plans like choreographed performers. This is Maxim 47 in the *Schlock Mercenary* series: "Don't expect the enemy to cooperate in the creation of your dream engagement." An enemy is unlikely to follow your script. Japanese Admiral Yamamoto Isoroku made that mistake at the Battle of Midway. He expected the American fleet to sail into his elaborately crafted trap. Instead, he sailed into an ambush. Much like comic book villains who lure superheroes to their doom, Yamamoto's plan was undone by unpredictable American admirals.
4. Other military plans rely on shallow and simplistic assessments of the military situation. They dumb things down, oversimplifying complex situations. The Iraqi people will welcome Americans as liberators. The 7th Cavalry can defeat many Sioux warriors.
5. Misidentifying what Clausewitz called the center of gravity, the nexus of enemy strength, which might be its capital city, primary army, economy, popular will, or something else. Focusing on the wrong strategic target practically guarantees failure in war.
6. Sticking to a strategy despite changing military situations. Allies come and go. New weapons appear. Economies

falter. Popular support waxes and wanes. Following China's intervention in the Korean War, the U.S. leaders wisely changed both their policy goal and strategy. They accepted a limited war to preserve South Korean independence rather than liberating the entire Korean peninsula or invading China. Prolonged wars require constant reassessments of changing military and political situations.

7. Learning the wrong lessons from previous wars. At the Second World War's outset, French leaders assumed the new war would resemble the First World War. Troops would need massive firepower to breech enemy defenses. Offensives would unfold in short hops within range of friendly artillery. Instead, the motorization of armies and development of radio facilitated the rapid concentration of firepower and exploitation of battlefield success. Spearheaded by tanks and motorized infantry, the German army overran France in a matter of weeks.

8. Mistaking military victory for political success. Translating military success into political success is difficult, and many victorious powers have failed at this. Instead of a lasting peace, one gets mired in so-called "forever wars," or cycles of conflict in which antagonists fight, make peace, and fight again. Britain and France did that for centuries. Throughout a war, keep in mind the better state of peace for which you fight. If you focus solely on military victory, the resulting peace, Liddell-Hart argues, is likely to be "a bad one, containing the germs of another war." This has proved the case for the United States since World War II. Americans have repeatedly failed to translate military success into an advantageous and lasting peace.

Both villains and heroes may fall prey to one or more of these errors. Villains may expect heroes to mirror their own aspirations and vulnerabilities or to fall easily into their traps. They may misidentify an enemy's center of gravity and attack the wrong target or assume military victory will automatically lead to political victory, as the Empire does repeatedly in the *Star Wars* movies.

WHILE NO TWO WARS ARE the same, there is a universal grammar and shared conception of war and strategy that guides discussion and analysis of war. Understanding that grammar, along with important concepts like friction, fog of war, and center of gravity, will help you help you think strategically. It will also help you write characters who think, talk, and act like competent strategists, or perhaps wholly incompetent ones, if that better serves your story. Historically, numerous commanders diligently followed received strategic wisdom to their doom.

Important questions to consider include:

- What is the antagonist's goal?
- What is their strategy to achieve it?
- What enemy weaknesses will they target?
- What value do they place on their goal?
- What will they risk or sacrifice to get it?
- How can your hero exploit the villain's weaknesses or strategic errors to turn the tables on them?
- Will the hero's victory emerge from a climactic battle, or will they win some other way?
- Can they win without fighting?
- What will the post-war world look like?
- What is the nature of the peace for which your heroes and

villains contest?

These concepts and questions should guide every strategist, real or fictional.

Chapter Two: Classic Strategic Thought

From 1793 to 1815, Napoleon Bonaparte led French armies on dazzling military campaigns across Europe. Coalitions of major powers formed and fought to contain France only to see Napoleon unravel their plans. His military genius seemed unmatchable. Napoleon redefined what war could achieve. Decisive victories and vast conquests again seemed possible. His campaigns sparked a resurgence of military analysis by Clausewitz, Jomini, and other generals and scholars. Their debates reinvigorated strategic thinking.

Along with Sun Tzu and Thucydides, whose works date to the sixth and fifth centuries BCE, Clausewitz and Jomini remain the touchstones for modern strategic analysis. These four writers, two ancient and two modern, laid the foundation on which later strategists built. All four addressed when and why to go to war, how to win wars, civil-military relations, espionage and intelligence, net assessment, appropriate strategic objectives, and related issues. Nonetheless, there are important differences in their works.

This chapter presents brief biographies of these four strategists, surveys their contributions, and discusses their main ideas. It explores their points of agreement and disagreement on issues ranging from cost-benefit analysis and civil-military relations to battlefield intelligence and the inherent friction and uncertainty of war. Can one win wars without fighting or seek decisive battle? Are sequential strategies that rely on winning battles more effective than cumulative strategies that seek favorable rates of attrition? How does one successfully terminate a war?

These concepts lay at the heart of strategic analysis and are important for military commanders—real and fictional—to consider. Fiction writers can use these strategists, their concepts and disputes, to add verisimilitude and strategic competence to their characters.

Thucydides

A FIFTH CENTURY BCE Athenian general, Thucydides fought in the Peloponnesian War. His history of that 27-year war between landlocked Sparta and maritime Athens explores how one develops and executes effective military strategy. He analyzes a host of military, political, and strategic issues. He also critiques democratic government, exploring how it functions, for both good and ill.

Unfortunately, Thucydides is best known in recent years for the "Thucydides Trap," a fiercely disputed idea popularized by political scientist Graham Allison. Allison suggests that emerging powers, by challenging the existing status quo and threatening to displace established powers, almost always provoke war.

Yet, as many historians point out, they often don't. The United States displaced Great Britain as the world's preeminent economic and military power without the two going to war. In fact, they were allies in both world wars when the U.S. achieved its dominant position. History is not a predictive science.

For Thucydides, war is an innately human experience. He offers a master class in how passion and other human factors influence the decision for war, shape war's conduct, and hinder efforts to negotiate peace. As S.L.A. Marshall notes, "the basic study in all warfare" requires understanding "the mind and nature of the probable enemy." Compared to this, "a technical competence in the handling of weapons and engines of destruction is of minor importance. Failing in the first, one will most likely fail in everything" (*Sinai Victory*, p. 6).

Nations go to war, Thucydides argues, for three reasons: fear, honor, and interest. They may covet an economically important territory or fear a rival's ambitions. They may be bound by honor to support an ally or driven by honor to expand their empires, like the Persians who invaded Greece. These reasons ignite people's passions. Those passions make the outbreak of wars unpredictable and impede war's rational management.

Once at war, nations need to integrate their diplomatic, economic, and military efforts and maintain their focus on the primary objective. Athens, the world's first democracy and center of Greek culture, failed to do this. As Pericles, their foremost general and politician warned, "I am more afraid of our own blunders than of the enemy's schemes" (Thucydides 1.144).

Following Pericles' death, Athens lost its way. It overreached militarily, committed large forces to secondary theaters like Sicily, and bungled opportunities to secure a favorable peace. Pressured by prolonged war, Athenians turned against one another and their allies. They massacred defeated foes and executed several of their own victorious generals. To paraphrase Sophocles, an Athenian playwright, "evil appears as good to those the gods lead to destruction."

The Athenians lost the characteristics that made them successful leaders of Greece's anti-Persian alliance. They descended into madness and lost sight of the reasons they went to war, the political goals for which they fought, and the strategic wisdom that guided them.

Thucydides' insights remain as apt today as they were 2,400 years ago. As he boasted, his work remains "a possession for all time" (1.22).

Sun Tzu

THUCYDIDES' LIFE IN classical Athens is well documented. In contrast, Sun Tzu may not be a real person. Rather, Sun Tzu's *Art of War* is probably a composite from several Chinese authors and generals who wrote and fought during China's Warring States Era when dozens of local rulers fought to reunite China under their rule. This makes Sun Tzu the first literary pseudonym.

While Thucydides embeds his strategic analysis in his narrative of the Peloponnesian War, Sun Tzu gets right to the point in short, specific strategic guidelines. Next to Clausewitz, Sun Tzu's *Art of War* is the most influential text on strategy—and far more quoted thanks to aphorisms like "appear weak when you are strong, and strong when you are weak," and "know your enemy, know yourself."

Sun Tzu's fortune cookie-like aphorisms conceal deep thought and complex ideas. You win wars, Sun Tzu argues, by outwitting the enemy. Ideally, one so misdirects and confuses the enemy, that battles—and even wars—are won with a minimum of bloodshed and destruction, perhaps without fighting at all.

During one of Rome's many civil wars, Gaius Marius repeatedly outmaneuvered enemy armies, defeated them, and then retreated to strong defensive positions. Frustrated, enemy commander Quintus Poppaedius Silo demanded: "If you are a great general, come down and fight." Marius replied: "If you are a great general, make me" (Plutarch, *Lives,* p. 572). This epitomizes Sun Tzu's teachings. Great commanders make the enemy dance to their tune. They fight on their own terms or not at all. They shape their enemy's movements and "bring the enemy to the field of battle and are not brought there by him" (Sun Tzu, VI.2).

Sun Tzu often uses water metaphors to express his ideas. "As water has no constant shape so war has no constant form." Water takes the most efficient route along paths of least resistance. So, too, should armies, as long as we understand this to mean the most militarily efficient route, not the shortest or most obvious route where enemies likely await. Water can eat away at obstacles, eventually carving the Grand Canyon, crash down from a great height in a raging torrent wreaking sudden, tremendous damage, or simply flow around obstacles and encircle them. Hence, actor and martial arts savant Bruce Lee's advice to "be like water." Be flexible and adaptable. Strike when and where you're least expected.

Jomini

ANTOINE-HENRI JOMINI, a Swiss general who fought both for and against Napoleon, became the nineteenth century's most popular and prolific strategy writer. Military academies taught his works. Officers studied them assiduously, including most of the generals who fought in the American Civil War. Of the four foundational strategists, Jomini focuses most on geography, logistics, maneuvering troops, and fighting battles. Despite his protestations that war is an art, not a science, he is also the most didactic.

Unlike his contemporary Clausewitz, Jomini articulated fixed principles to guide the conduct of war. While adhering to them does not guarantee victory, Jomini argued they should guide strategic and operational planning. Understanding them helps officers manage the chaos of battle. The principles of war taught by today's military academies derive from Jomini.

Jomini argues wars are won by concentrating one's forces, taking the offensive, and seeking decisive battle. Strategy determines where to focus one's forces and effective logistics allow them to reach that point. After that, one must maneuver advantageously to mass your army against the enemy at a decisive point to win a climactic, war-ending battle. Jomini focused particular attention on the advantages of interior lines, that is occupying a central position between more numerous, but dispersed, enemy armies. Napoleon frequently did this, taking advantage of interior lines to isolate and overwhelm each opposing army in turn. Interior lines, though, are not a panacea. Napoleon failed to isolate the British army at Waterloo. The Confederacy lost the American Civil War despite benefiting from interior lines.

Clausewitz

PRUSSIAN GENERAL CARL von Clausewitz is history's most profound—and complex—strategic thinker. Clausewitz died before revising his magnum opus, *On War*, around two central ideas: the primacy of politics in shaping war, and war's inherent uncertainty. His wife Marie revised and published *On War* in 1832, but the scholarly consensus is that only the first and last of *On War*'s eight books fully express Clausewitz's intent. *On War* was not translated into English until 1873, and not translated particularly well until much later.

A 1976 English translation of Clausewitz by Michael Howard and Peter Paret renewed interest in Clausewitz. It appeared at just the right time. Stung by defeat in Vietnam, American military leaders reinvigorated institutions of professional military education that had languished since World War II. Within a decade, students at the Naval War College, the Army's Command and General Staff College, and other military graduate institutions read Clausewitz. In the last half century, no book has influenced military thought more than Clausewitz's *On War*.

While Clausewitz's insights are profound, his prose is ponderous. In places it's almost impenetrable. Clausewitz attacked ideas from every possible direction, producing difficult to follow circumlocutions of reasoning that confuse readers. Like religious texts, one can pull quotations from Clausewitz to justify any military decision. As General Gunther Blumentritt once remarked, having young officers read Clausewitz was "like letting a child play with a straight razor" (Handel, 25).

MILITARY STRATEGY FOR WRITERS

Clausewitz examined war as a totality, portraying it as a collection of forces trying to escape human control. His study revolves around three main ideas. First, you cannot separate strategy from its political and social context. Second, the ever-present uncertainty of war, combined with war's social and political context, make it impossible to reduce strategy to fixed rules and principles. Third, commanders require a combination of theoretical knowledge and practical experience to cope with war's complexity.

Clausewitz emphasized war's political nature. War is "an act of force to compel the enemy to do our will" (*On War*, 75). It is a violent clash of wills to achieve political aims. One goes to war to achieve specific, rational political goals. Anything else was madness. Yet, Clausewitz warns, the conduct of war itself is not necessarily rational.

Victory requires both understanding a war's nature and making correct strategic choices. "The first, the supreme, the most far-reaching act of judgment that the statesman and commander have to make," Clausewitz wrote, is to determine "the kind of war on which they are embarking, neither mistaking it for, nor trying to turn it into, something that is alien to its nature" (*On War*, 88). This requires, as Sun Tzu noted, knowing both oneself and one's enemy. When going to war, what are you getting yourself into?

American leaders failed this test in Vietnam. Instead of understanding the nature of the war (and the enemy), they played to their strengths. They devoted most of their military resources to conventional operations and intense bombing campaigns, rather than counterinsurgency. Defeat necessarily followed.

Military victory requires targeting an enemy's center of gravity. Clausewitz borrowed the term from physics, explaining it as the "hub of all power and movement, on which everything depends." It is a point that if successfully attacked collapses enemy resistance.

Determining that point, as Clausewitz's contemporary Antoine-Henri Jomini warned, can be difficult (Jomini, 70-71). It could be an enemy army, capital city, or perhaps the community of interest that binds together a multi-national alliance. In popular uprisings or insurgencies, it is likely the "hearts and minds" of the people, or the political will to continue fighting (*On War*, 595-6). Successful leaders apply maximum pressure against an enemy's center of gravity. They do not waste their strength on secondary objectives unless they "look exceptionally rewarding" (*On War*, 618).

Identifying an enemy's center of gravity is often difficult. During the American Revolution, the British worked their way through several possible American centers of gravity. At various times they hounded the Continental Army to near destruction, occupied Philadelphia and other major cities, and worked to win American "hearts and minds." Yet, Britain lost the war. Targeting an enemy's center of gravity does not guarantee victory. Directing one's strength at the wrong objective, though, guarantees defeat.

For all his genius, Clausewitz ignores several important factors in war, most noticeably technological innovation. This is understandable since weaponry hardly changed during his life. The British army, for example, employed the Brown Bess musket as its primary infantry firearm for over a century. Clausewitz is also very landlocked. He says little about naval power, despite recognizing its importance to defeating Napoleon.

Strategic Debates and Questions

CLAUSEWITZ, JOMINI, and other modern strategists wrote in dialogue with one another. Clausewitz critiqued Jomini, and Jomini critiqued earlier writers. Alfred Thayer Mahan, Julian Corbett, and other naval strategists built on this foundation and applied their ideas to sea power. Later theorists applied Clausewitzian and Mahanian ideas to air power and nuclear weapons. Debates among leading theorists enrich strategic thought and have produced a wide and varied body of knowledge and theory on which we can draw.

Clausewitz compared war to a chameleon. Its form always changes. Enemies react and adapt to one another. Allies come and go. Wars may begin in one form, such as the insurgency in Vietnam, but end in another with North Vietnamese tanks rolling through Saigon. Change and uncertainty make it impossible to develop fixed and enduring rules for war.

Nonetheless, one can extract general principles, ideas, and theories to help commanders ponder military situations and inform the authors who write about military matters, both real and fictional. Rather than offering a prescribed path, theory aids judgment. It establishes a baseline and helps, as naval strategist Julian Corbett wrote, determine an action's likely outcome. Theory warns us when we "leave the beaten track" and enables us "to decide with open eyes whether the divergence is necessary or justifiable" (Corbett, 9-10). Theory helps answer the question "is this a good idea?"

In the past, some writers differentiated between Asian and European approaches to strategy. Few would agree today. Michael Handel put this bugaboo to rest in his book *Masters of War*, underlining the many points of agreement among history's great strategic thinkers. Strategic concepts are universal, as are the important questions one asks before embarking on war and while conducting war. What is the war's nature? What are your and your enemy's strengths and weaknesses? What is the enemy's center of gravity? Has an offensive reached its culminating point of victory?

Cost-Benefit Analysis and Value of the Object

"WAR IS NOT AN ACT OF senseless passion," Clausewitz warned. One needs to reconcile means with ends. One fights for a specific political objective. The value of this objective "must determine the sacrifices to be made for it in magnitude and also in duration" (*On War*, 92).

War necessarily involves a cost-benefit analysis. What price in blood and treasure are you willing to pay to secure a particular objective? Is it achievable? Will a bloody war reduce that objective's value? Ideally, as Sun Tzu advised, one captures a state intact. Ruining a territory to capture it makes its acquisition pointless. To paraphrase the Roman historian Tacitus, no one benefits from laying waste a territory "and calling it peace." Once a war's cost exceeds the value of its objective, one should end it.

While logical, this advice is difficult to follow. How does one value a political objective? Clearly Vietnamese communists valued uniting Vietnam under their rule far more than several American presidents valued preserving a stable, non-communist South Vietnam. Yet despite placing a lower value on their objective, Americans fought that war longer than made rational sense.

The First World War offers an extreme case. Rather than encouraging leaders to seek peace, the hundreds of thousands of deaths at Verdun, the Somme, and other bloody battles strengthened their determination to fight. Politicians not only insisted on continuing the war but promised to extract territorial and monetary concessions from defeated enemies. The only way to justify the war's enormous bloodletting was to expand their political objectives.

This underlines another problem with valuing wartime objectives. As wars progress, objectives, and their perceived the value, may change. The American Revolution offers an example. At the war's outset, Britain fought to retain its thirteen rebellious colonies. After France and Spain declared war on Britain, British leaders reassessed their objectives. Preserving the British Empire's other overseas territories, particularly in the Caribbean and South Asia, proved more important than reestablishing British rule throughout North America. So, the thirteen colonies won their freedom. Britain, though, defeated the French navy and preserved the rest of its empire.

The longer a war lasts, the more likely it is to shape policy and strategy. Abraham Lincoln did not set out to free southern slaves. Only after 17 months of hard fighting did he announce the Emancipation Proclamation. Freeing African American slaves undermined the Confederacy's planation economy and offered the prospect of recruiting them into the Union Army. Similarly, Franklin D. Roosevelt did not announce the United States sought the "unconditional surrender" of Germany, Italy, and Japan, until a year after Japan's attack on Pearl Harbor. As soldiers fought, leaders reassessed their objectives and the strategies for achieving them.

Winning Without Fighting vs. Decisive Battle

SUN TZU URGES HIS READERS to win wars at the least possible cost, ideally without fighting at all. One could so out-strategize an enemy that victory becomes certain. Recognizing they'd been outmaneuvered, wise enemies would concede without fighting a major battle. The great Byzantine general Belisarius similarly opined "the most complete and happy victory is this: to compel one's enemy to give up his purpose, while suffering no harm to oneself."

In contrast, Clausewitz urged readers to seek battle as the primary means to win wars. "The decision by arms is for all major and minor operations in war what cash payment is in commerce." Destroying an enemy army "is always the superior, more effective means" to victory (*On War,* 97). A single, strong blow can bring a half-hearted enemy to the peace table or cripple a more determined adversary.

Clausewitz decried sentimentally and warned against aiming for bloodless victories. "Kind-hearted people" wish "there was some ingenious way to disarm or defeat an enemy without too much bloodshed," but this "is a fallacy that must be exposed." War, he argues, "is such a dangerous business that the mistakes which come from kindness are the very worst" (*On War*, 75). "Sooner or later," a general like Napoleon who welcomes battle "will come along with a sharp sword and hack off our arms" (*On War*, 260).

Napoleon's fixation on decisive battle transformed how people thought about war. Nineteenth century commentators pilloried the previous century's cautious commanders and venerated daring generals. They even wrote admiringly of Charles XII, the "Swedish Meteor," who fought his way across Russia, winning victory after victory until larger Russian armies finally overwhelmed his dwindling force at the Battle of Poltava. As always, superior strategy trumped tactical acumen.

Leaders should prosecute wars ruthlessly, but also efficiently. Even Clausewitz agreed that sometimes a show of force and willingness to seek battle was sufficient to achieve one's goals. Leaders should seek battle as part of a coherent strategy. Pointless battles squander lives and waste resources.

In Sun Tzu's era, dozens of rival states fought to unite China. Sun Tzu warned against paying such a high cost to defeat a single rival state that it left the military too weak to fight the others. In the third century BCE, Pyrrhus of Epirus sought to conquer Italy, but his costly victories over Rome's legions bled his mercenary army white and forced him to abandon his campaign, hence the term "Pyrrhic victory."

Instead of rushing to battle, Sun Tzu encouraged commanders to "attack the enemy's strategy" and disrupt their alliances. Isolated and confused the enemy might seek peace. If not, "the next best [strategy] is to attack his army" (III:4-7).

Sun Tzu warned against finding oneself on, or forcing an enemy army on to, "death ground" (or desperate ground, in some translations). As Samuel Johnson quipped, "when a man knows he is to be hanged in a fortnight, it concentrates his mind wonderfully." While some trapped armies collapse in disorder, others fight ferociously. Sometimes, it's best to leave enemies a way out. Saladin may have done this at the Battle of Hattin, allowing some Crusaders to escape while completing his encirclement and destruction of the rest of Guy of Lusignan's army. The alternative may be a Pyrrhic victory.

If the primary enemy is too strong to confront directly, Clausewitz also encourages attacking its allies. The British and Americans did this in World War II and knocked Italy out of the war. In Heinlein's *Starship Troopers*, Earth similarly first defeats the Bugs' allies, the "Skinnies."

The worst thing to do, Sun Tzu suggests, is attacking cities. "Attack cities only when there is no alternative" (III:7). As Stalingrad and other bloody urban battles demonstrate, his warning remains valid today.

Winning without fighting is an ideal few have achieved. American victory in the Cold War remains one of the few examples of a major power defeating a rival without major war.

Usually, one fights one's primary enemy. So, Sun Tzu devotes most of his book to maneuvering armies and winning battles. The key is to seek major battle with advantage.

Ideally, commanders determine "the enemy's dispositions" while concealing their own. Their superior situational awareness allows them to keep the enemy off balance. They concentrate their forces against a divided, uncertain enemy, setting them up for a precisely timed attack (VI:13). "When the strike of a hawk breaks the body of its prey, it is because of timing" (V:14). One wins the decisive battle in a single stroke.

The Americans did this at the Battle of Midway. They concealed the size and location of their fleet, exploited their superior intelligence and reconnaissance capabilities, and struck the Japanese fleet by surprise, sinking all four of its aircraft carriers while losing only one of their own.

William the Conqueror defeated Harold Godwinson at the Battle of Hastings to win England's crown. Seven hundred years later, defeat at Culloden ended Bonnie Prince Charlie's bid for the same. Waterloo similarly ended Napoleon's military career. Historically, such decisive battles are rare, and they became rarer as wars became more complex. Waterloo was a fluke. Napoleon's army retreated from Russia without fighting a decisive battle. Neither world war ended with a decisive battle, nor did the Seven Years War, the American Civil War, or even the Greco-Persian Wars 2,500 years earlier.

Trafalgar, the 1805 naval battle at which British Admiral Horatio Nelson crushed a combined French-Spanish fleet, is often called decisive. Yet, Britain's war with Napoleon continued into 1815. While important for securing command of the seas and preventing a French invasion of Britain, Trafalgar was clearly not decisive. The French navy recovered and remained a threat until 1812 when Napoleon stripped the fleet of cannon to rebuild his army following the disastrous retreat from Moscow.

Wars open with the grand schemes and hopeful expectations for quick, decisive victory. No nation goes to war hoping for a long, bloody conflict.

Yet, decisive battles and short victorious wars are rare. They're usually the product of a serious mismatch in strength, such as the 1898 Spanish-American War, or the rare instance in which one enemy dramatically outstrategizes its enemy, as Israel did in its 1967 war with Egypt, Jordan, and Syria. The Israel army also proved superior at the tactical and operational level, defeating numerically superior Arab antagonists in six days, a feat it failed to repeat in later wars.

Even Clausewitz, who advocated massing one's army for a decisive thrust at the enemy's center of gravity, cautions his readers about expecting too much from a single battle. "A government must never assume that its country's fate, its whole existence, hangs on the outcome of a single battle, no matter how decisive." There's always a chance to turn things around "by developing new sources of internal strength," securing allies, or exploiting enemy mistakes and the natural decline in strength of advancing armies (*On War,* 483).

In modern fiction, though, decisive battles are practically the norm. This is particularly true of future war stories, science fiction, and technothrillers. Practically every future war story written between the Franco-Prussian War and the First World War ends in decisive battle.

These stories invariably involve surprise attacks by better prepared and often technologically superior enemies. In George Chesney's "Battle of Dorking" (1871), which launched the genre, Germany uses new super weapons to destroy the Royal Navy and then invades Britain and crushes its feeble, ineffectively led army. Meant as warnings and encouragements to military preparedness, these pedantic stories reflected the rapid technological progress of the late nineteenth and early twentieth century, which fueled arms races among Europe's major powers.

Similarly, Ender Wiggin annihilates the alien Formics in a final climactic battle in Card's *Ender's Game* (1985). Jerry Pournelle's stories of mercenary commander John Christian Falkenberg similarly build to decisive battlefield victory. So does E.E. "Doc" Smith's classic Lensman series about the long war between the Arisians and their human allies against the evil Eddorians. The Arisians execute a sequential strategy, pushing back the Eddorians in novel after novel. Each novel ends with a decisive battle, marking a turning point in the war and leading to the final climactic battle and eradication of the Eddorians in *Children of the Lens* (1954).

Authors should consider these issues in their fictive worlds.

- Why have the antagonists gone to war?
- How do they plan to win?
- Do they seek decisive battle or have they some other plan in mind?
- What happens if the grand battle they seek isn't decisive?
- How does one recover from a major battlefield defeat?

Asymmetries in War: Seeking Decisive Advantage

ONLY FOOLS PIT THEIR strength directly against an enemy's strength, as Saddam Hussein did against the American-led coalition in the First Gulf War. Overconfident, he chose to fight a conventional war of firepower and maneuver against a tactically and technologically superior force. Unlike the Vietnam War twenty years earlier, the United States military faced exactly the type of conflict for which it prepared. The result was one of the most lopsided victories in recent history. Coalition forces gained air supremacy, destroyed important strategic and tactical targets in a 40-day bombing campaign, and then smashed through Iraqi forces to liberate Kuwait in a 100-hour ground campaign.

Such wars are rare. Usually, belligerents apply their strengths against enemy weaknesses. They seek an asymmetric advantage. Confusingly, military analysts recently began using the term "asymmetric war" to describe wars between belligerents with significantly different capabilities, weaknesses, and goals. It appears almost as a synonym for insurgency, particularly in reference to recent American wars in the Middle East and Afghanistan.

Military asymmetries are not new. Good commanders have always sought to exploit them. In the Hundred Years' War between England and France, new English tactics incorporating dismounted

MILITARY STRATEGY FOR WRITERS   61

knights and archers wielding fearsome longbows shattered French armies at Poitiers and other battlefields. Afterward, French kings refused to face the English in pitched battle. Instead, they adopted a Fabian strategy, harassing the English in small engagements and attacking their supply lines. Neither army would fight when and where terrain and other circumstances favored its opponent.

Hoping to force the French into battle, the English responded with chevauchées, devastating raids that laid waste vast swaths of French countryside. These aimed to sustain English armies at French expense, loot the countryside, and pressure French kings to face them in battle. After all, a king who could not defend his lands was no king at all. A generation later, believing new tactics and heavier armor would neutralize the English longbow, the French faced the English at Agincourt. There, Henry V lured French knights into battle on ground of his choice and smashed the French army outnumbering his by four-to-one. England's asymmetric advantage endured.

In Lois McMaster Bujold's *Warrior's Apprentice* (1986), protagonist Miles Vorkosigan faces a more experienced and numerically superior mercenary space fleet. Unable to face it in battle, Vorkosigan focuses on its vulnerability. Mercenaries, he notes, will not fight for long if not paid (Chapter 16). Following the capture of several monthly pay shipments, the enemy admiral, unable to pay his disaffected troops, agrees to Vorkosigan's demands.

Exploiting asymmetric advantages is a hallmark of the Vorkosigan series. It's alluded to in the bitter insurgency waged by Miles's grandfather to liberate their world from Cetegandan invaders, and features in several of Miles's own adventures. Miles's father, Admiral Aral Vorkosigan, similarly exploited "every natural weak point in mercenary-employer relations" to drive a wedge between the planet Komarr and its mercenary defenders and capture the planet (Chapter 13).

Competent commanders apply their strengths against an opponent's weaknesses, hence Sun Tzu's famous dictum "know your enemy, know yourself." This applies not only to military capability, but psychology, culture, and other less quantifiable categories. Any advantage must be sought and exploited. Interestingly, "know yourself" was engraved on the wall outside the sanctuary of Delphi whose seers provided famously cryptic and oft-misinterpreted predictions. Successful foresight requires insight.

Cumulative and Sequential Strategies

DIFFERENT WARS REQUIRE different strategies. American Rear Admiral J.C. Wylie distinguished between what he called "sequential" and "cumulative" strategies. Sequential strategies involve a sequence of operations and battles that aim to destroy the enemy's primary military forces and threaten key objectives. Alexander's conquest of the Persian Empire and the American advance across the Pacific in World War II exemplify these, as do the fictional advances of human space armadas in Heinlein's *Starship Troopers* and Card's *Ender's Game*.

Hans Delbruck, a much-revered German historian (whose brain featured in the 1974 film *Young Frankenstein*), divided military strategy into two categories: annihilation and attrition. Generals who pursue strategies of annihilation seek battle with the enemy's main force, believing its destruction (annihilation) will end the war. They seek a decisive battle.

In that regard, the World War II victories of the Americans at Midway and the Soviets at Stalingrad are often labeled decisive. Even though the war against Nazi Germany and Imperial Japan continued into 1945, these battles marked clear turning points in the war. The Axis powers proved unable to recover from these defeats. The initiative shifted to the Allies whose sequential campaigns brought them to Berlin and Okinawa.

Enemies, though, may refuse battle or otherwise frustrate sequential strategies. Instead, they embrace what Wylie labeled a cumulative strategy and which Delbruck labeled attrition. Like Fabius Maximus, they aim to wear down an enemy in a prolonged war that saps its economic and military strength and erodes its political will. Americans won their independence this way.

Naval powers may employ a strategy of economic attrition, sinking an enemy's commercial shipping or blockading its ports to starve it into submission. Air power allows a combatant to attack an enemy's economy directly, bombing factories, transportation hubs, and other installations.

Achieving both the military destruction and the political dislocation of one's enemies proves elusive. Hannibal managed the former at Cannae, a masterpiece battle in which his army killed or captured as many as 70,000 of the 80,000 soldiers Rome sent against him. Yet, Rome refused to surrender.

When Nazi Germany invaded Soviet Russia in June 1941, its leaders implemented a sequential strategy. They aimed to destroy the Soviet army in a series of encirclement battles they thought would precipitate the unpopular Soviet government's collapse. Instead, Soviet armies recovered, learned from their mistakes, and continued the war. The Germans found themselves in a prolonged war of attrition they were ill-equipped to win. Their sequential strategy failed.

Britain and the United States also adopted a strategy of attrition against Nazi Germany, wearing down its military forces and bombing its cities in raids that killed several hundred thousand civilians, left millions more homeless, and wrecked factories, oil refineries, and transportation networks. These raids impeded Germany's war effort and forced its overstretched air force into daily combat that destroyed it.

Cumulative strategies like the Anglo-American bombing campaign are harder to implement and analyze, but often prove effective in the long run. They involve the minute accumulation of small events and successes until they reach a critical point. In both world wars, Germany unleashed submarines to sink British shipping, hoping to reduce Britain's economy below the level needed to sustain its war effort. It was, Winston Churchill noted, a "shapeless, measureless peril." Rather than clean lines on a map showing frontlines and advancing armies, victory or defeat in the U-boat war was "expressed in charts, curves, and statistics." Unlike the similar American campaign against Japanese commerce, Germany's submarine campaigns never reached a critical point. Britain fought on.

Ideally, sequential and cumulative strategies work together. British blockades weakened France's economy and forced Napoleon to garrison coastal positions, weakening his armies. American submarines, which by the end of 1944 had sunk roughly 90% of Japan's shipping tonnage, supported the advance of American fleets and armies across the Pacific. Similarly, American and British bombing aided their amphibious invasion of France by targeting Germany's air force, transportation network, and fuel supplies. These cumulative strategies supported the sequential advance of the Allied armies that liberated Western Europe from Nazi rule.

Victory and War Termination

ENDING A WAR MAY PROVE as complex and messy as fighting it. Some wars end in decisive battle, such as Scipio's victory over Hannibal at Zama, which ended the Second Punic War. Some enemies sue for peace while still capable of military resistance, as Austria did repeatedly in the Napoleonic Wars. Other enemies may disintegrate from the pressures of prolonged war, casualties, and lost territory, as the Confederacy did in the American Civil War. History texts note the dates wars end, but wars rarely end in a neat and tidy fashion. At their conclusion, there's still much work to be done, both by soldiers occupying enemy territory and the civilian agencies that assist them.

Regardless of how wars end, the winner's objective is to secure a lasting, beneficial peace. That requires imposing their will on the defeated enemy and cleaning up whatever problems the war created. Alexander campaigned for years to secure his conquests following his decisive victory at Gaugamela. Defeated Confederate officers formed the backbone of the KKK and other hate groups that terrorized post-war African American communities. Combating them required prolonged occupation by U.S. troops. It took many years for the newly created United Nations to repatriate the millions of people displaced by World War II. Rumors of Nazi holdouts persisted as the Allies implemented denazification measures in occupied Germany. Guerrilla resistance to Soviet rule simmered for years in the Ukraine and Eastern Europe. Anti-colonial resistance movements spread through Africa and Asia, igniting new wars.

Good strategists consider war termination. Yet, successfully ending a war and establishing a durable peace is difficult. Perhaps that's why novels like *Starship Troopers* and *Enders Game* conclude with the enemy's extermination. Genocide obviates the need to negotiate peace and simplifies post-war considerations, such as the treatment of civilians in occupied territories, the repatriation of military prisoners, and resettlement of displaced civilians.

In practice, genocide is both morally reprehensible and poor strategy. Enemies facing utter annihilation are on "death ground." They devote every resource to war. Their desperate plight might even win them allies. Regardless, defeating them will prove costly.

Rather than annihilation, wars generally end in one of two ways. First, one side's military power is so reduced that effective military resistance is no longer possible, as was the case of Carthage in the Second Punic War, the Confederacy in the American Civil War, and

Nazi Germany in World War II. Once military resistance becomes impossible, governments either surrender or, like the Confederacy, collapse.

Alternatively, one or both parties seek a negotiated peace. This proved the case for the United States in Vietnam, both Russia and Japan in the Russo-Japanese War, and Japan in World War II, though the latter is an extreme case. When a war is no longer worth the social or economic or military cost, wise leaders seek peace.

The goal of strategy is to produce one of these results and create a post-war situation more advantageous to you than your recent enemy. So, how do you convince an enemy to accept a disadvantageous peace?

More than two thousand years ago, Thucydides suggested "if great enmities are ever to be really settled," it will not be "by the system of revenge and military success, and by forcing an opponent to swear to a treaty to his disadvantage, but when the more fortunate combatant waives these privileges, to be guided by gentler feelings, conquers his rival in generosity, and accords peace on more moderate conditions than he expected. From that moment, instead of the debt of revenge which violence must entail, his adversary owes a debt of generosity to be paid in kind and is inclined by honor to stand to his agreement" (4:19).

Such, though, is rarely the case. Leaders usually choose coercion. They aim, as Clausewitz wrote, to put the enemy "in a situation that is even more unpleasant" than conceding to the victor's objective (*On War*, 77). Doing that requires destroying the enemy's means or will to resist, preferably both. A coercive peace, though, often lays the seeds for renewed conflict. As Clausewitz warned, "the result of a war is not always final" (*On War*, 80). Defeated foes rise again, particularly if subjected to harsh peace terms. Resentment burns, fueling calls for revenge, as in France after the Franco-Prussian War and Germany following the First World War.

In the absence of a just peace, philosopher Immanuel Kant observed, one can always find new pretenses for war. Naomi Nagata makes the same point in *Tiamat's Wrath,* the penultimate novel in James A. Corey's Expanse series. "Wars never ended because one side was defeated." They end when enemies are reconciled. Anything else just postpones "the next round of violence."

Clausewitz's Paradoxical Trinity and Civil-Military Relations

AMONG CLAUSEWITZ'S most profound discussions is what he labeled the "paradoxical trinity." War's three "dominant tendencies," he suggests, are "primordial violence, hatred, and enmity, which are to be regarded as a blind natural force; the play of chance and probability within which the creative spirit is free to roam;" and war's "element of subordination, as an instrument of policy, which makes it subject to reason alone" (*On War,* 89). One can reduce these to passion, chance, and reason.

"The first of these," Clausewitz explains, "mainly concerns the people; the second the commander and his army; the third the government." These three elements of war, passion, chance, and reason, mirror three elements of a state: the people, the armed forces, and their government. When going to war, governments should provide reason (rational policy goals and effective grand strategy). The people, in turn, support the war effort through passion and patriotism. The military develops strategy in concert with civilian leaders and executes that strategy at the operational and tactical level, the realm of chance and uncertainty.

Ideally, these elements are in balance. The people support the war. Senior civil and military leaders determine rational goals and produce an effective strategy to achieve them, which military forces implement in the field. The U.S. and Britain did this superbly in World War II.

Yet, Clausewitz warns, when nations fight for "minor objectives, the emotions of the masses will be little stirred." Support for these wars may dwindle, as it did among Americans during the Vietnam War.

On the other hand, emotions may become "so aroused" that politicians are "hard put to control them." During the First World War, Germany's senior generals overrode civilian leadership and committed the nation to an unwinnable war. In the Peloponnesian War, the passionate, increasingly optimistic citizens of Athens committed their military to risky campaigns, exiled or executed insufficiently successful generals, and insisted on continuing a war that bled them white, emptied their coffers, and alienated their allies.

Military coups or popular revolts have toppled a host of rulers who mismanaged and lost wars, including Argentina's ruling junta after the Falklands War, Egypt's King Farouk following the 1948-1949 Arab-Israeli War, and Tsar Nicholas II of Russia during the First World War.

Since wars are fought for political goals, successful strategy requires the primacy of political authority. As Sun Tzu wrote, rulers deliberate upon plans. Generals execute them. In Heinlein's *Starship Troopers*, Sergeant Zim similarly explains "it's never a soldier's business to decide when or where or how—or why—he fights; that belongs to the statesmen and the generals. The statesmen decide why and how much; the generals take it from there and tell us where and when and how" (Chapter 4).

Jomini and Sun Tzu present a clear divide between political rulers and military leaders. Politicians decide to go to war and specify the objective. After that it's the military's responsibility to develop and execute plans to win that war. As Sun Tzu wrote, "he whose generals are able and not interfered with by the sovereign will be victorious" (III:29). He even suggests there are "occasions when the commands of the sovereign need not be obeyed" (VIII:8).

This contrasts sharply with Thucydides and Clausewitz. They emphasize the interrelationship between war and politics, which continues throughout a war. Policy, wrote Clausewitz, permeates "all military operations" and necessarily influences the conduct of war. Political and military leaders must together assess changing military situations and alter political goals and strategy, as needed. Yet, political considerations do not determine "the posting of guards" nor should they extend their "influence to operational details" (*On War*, 87).

In practice, clearly demarcating where political authority ends and that of military commanders begins is difficult. Only rarely has one person successfully served as both head of state and army commander. Alexander the Great managed these joint tasks well. Napoleon failed. The growing size and complexity of modern wars make them impossible for even a genius to manage alone.

Strategy making involves compromises among rival politicians, branches of the military, allies, and other interested parties. Even in dictatorships, strategic debates are fierce. It's a myth that Hitler was solely responsible for Nazi Germany's many military blunders. Germany's senior military leaders participated fully in strategic decision-making in the war's first years and encouraged Hitler every step of the way. They, too, assumed air power would overwhelm Great Britain, their tanks would storm the gates of Moscow, and their submarines prevent effective American intervention.

In the generation preceding the First World War, political leaders largely abdicated their role in strategy-making to the military. As a result, all of Europe's major powers embraced war plans emphasizing aggressive offensive action with little thought to their allies or the prospects of prolonged war. Senior military leaders gambled on winning quick, decisive victories and led their nations to disaster. Almost too late, Premier Georges Clemenceau of France declared war "too important to be left to the generals," reasserted civilian authority, and purged the French army of incompetent generals.

In the Second World War, Winston Churchill and Franklin D. Roosevelt effectively oversaw their nation's war efforts, limited their intervention into purely military matters, and ensured Allied strategy supported Allied political goals. Even Josef Stalin learned to rely on his generals' military expertise and limit his intervention in operational matters. Adolf Hitler, of course, took the opposite approach, intervening more and more in military operations as the war turned against Germany.

Successfully managing civil-military relations is essential for crafting sound policy and strategy. Whether military leaders override civilian policymakers, as in Imperial Germany, or civilian authority stifles military input, as in the United States during the Vietnam War, the result is usually failure. Nonetheless, as Clausewitz explained, "when people talk ... about harmful political influence on the management of war, they are not really saying what they mean. Their quarrel should be with the policy itself, not with its influence. If the policy is right—that is, successful—any intentional effect it has on the conduct of the war can only be to the good. If it has the opposite effect the policy itself is wrong" (*On War*, 608). Strategy and military operations must align with political goals. If they don't, disaster will surely follow.

Uncertainty, Chance, and Friction

WAR IS "THE REALM OF uncertainty," Clausewitz writes. "No other human activity is so continuously or universally bound up with chance" (*On War,* 104). While Clausewitz repeats the old saw that time spent on reconnaissance is rarely wasted, he warns "many intelligence reports in war are contradictory." Others "are false, and most are uncertain" (*On War,* 117). This resonates with Schlock Mercenaries' Maxim 53: "the intel you've got is never the intel you want." So, gather all the information you can, but don't trust it too much.

Friction makes matters worse. "Everything in war is simple," Clausewitz explains, but achieving even the "simplest thing is difficult. The difficulties accumulate and end by producing a kind of friction that is inconceivable unless one has experienced war." War places combatants in mortal danger and makes intense physical demands on them, exacerbating friction and uncertainty. As "conditions become difficult, as they must when much is at stake, things no longer run like a well-oiled machine." As a result, "countless minor incidents—the kind you can never really foresee—combine to lower the general level of performance, so that one always falls short of the intended goal" (*On War,* 119).

Training and careful planning reduce friction but cannot eliminate it. So, a commander "continually finds that things are not as he expected" and must decide and act within "a fog of greater or lesser uncertainty" (*On War,* 101-2).

Sun Tzu similarly notes "that which depends on me I can do; that which depends on the enemy is uncertain" (IV:3). Yet, war is not an exercise in pure chance. As Louis Pasteur noted, "luck favors the prepared mind."

Jomini suggests commanders can master war's complex nature with almost mathematical precision. At times, Sun Tzu is equally confident. In the midst of battle's "tumult and uproar," everything appears chaotic, but the clear-minded commander sees through this and perceives "no disorder" (V:17). Skilled leaders, those who know the enemy and themselves, can pierce the fog of war to inflict uncertainty and friction on their enemies while avoiding it themselves.

This is what "Black Jack" Geary does in the first books of Jack Campbell's *Lost Fleet* series. Apart from a few disobedient subordinates, Geary's plans unfold as he intends, while his enemies are plagued with uncertainty and friction.

Sun Tzu relies on intelligence, deception, maneuver, and surprise. He argues prepared commanders can minimize—even master—war's uncertainty. Clausewitz, though, warns against this. He also cautions against elaborate deceptions. Preparing "a sham action with sufficient thoroughness to impress an enemy requires a considerable expenditure of time and effort." Its "costs increase with the scale of the deception." Further, tying down forces "to create an illusion" is dangerous when those troops may be needed at the decisive point (*On War*, 203). For Clausewitz, deception and surprise are useful, but should never be relied upon for victory. Instead, focus your efforts to apply concentrated force at a decisive point.

THIS CHAPTER OFFERED a host of sometimes contradictory ideas. How then does one apply them to develop an effective strategy?

Successful strategy begins with net assessment. Commanders must "know the enemy" and oneself and use that knowledge to determine the "nature of the war" on which he embarks. The war effort should pursue clear, rational, obtainable goals and aim to win as quickly as possible at the lowest cost.

Like Sun Tzu, the commander should seek to outsmart the enemy. Find opportunities to employ deception, psychological warfare, surprise and a "mix of orthodox and unorthodox strategies." Seek allies for yourself while isolating the enemy. Seek asymmetric advantages. Target the enemy's vulnerabilities while protecting your own.

Ultimately, though, war is a violent contest of wills. Identify and target the enemy's center of gravity. Apply maximum force against it. That may lead to a major battle that ends the war in a quick, decisive victory.

If, instead, the war is prolonged, one must continually reassess the military and political situation. Use those assessments to guide both the conduct of war and essential changes in policy and strategy. Abandon flawed strategies and objectives that prove unobtainable. Learn from the enemy and adapt to their preferred tactics and strategies. Has the nature of the war changed? Have its costs escalated to a point at which continued fighting no longer makes sense?

Throughout a war, keep its termination in mind. In a limited war, don't put your enemy on death ground. Leave them ways to seek an honorable peace. Conversely, don't fight in ways that encourage your enemy to seek a vindictive peace should you lose. Always keep in mind the post-war world you wish to create. Don't impose a peace that lays the seeds for future wars nor lay waste a territory and mislabel that desolation peace.

All this seems simple but remember Clausewitz's warning. In war, even the simplest things often prove difficult.

Chapter Three: Strategies of Sea Power

As the Roman politician Cicero wrote, "the master of the sea must inevitably be master of the empire." For most of history, strategic discussion focused on war on land. Clausewitz neglected sea power entirely. His contemporary Jomini noted its importance in Napoleon's eventual defeat, but still focused almost all his attention on analyzing Napoleon's campaigns on land, searching for strategic and tactical lessons. This reflected the reality that only recently had naval technology reached a point where sea power could have independent strategic effect.

This is the first of a set of chapters dealing with special strategic situations. Strategies of Sea Power will be most useful to those writers developing characters and settings at sea; however, they also provide a potential model for strategic principles in other environments. For example, many science fiction stories use sea power strategies as a basis for strategy in space. The *Babylon 5* space station is plagued by pirates and commerce raiders. The planetary invasions of *Starship Troopers* resemble the amphibious invasions of World War II. The battles between space fleets described by novelists ranging from Isaac Asimov to "Doc" Smith resemble historic fleet actions at sea, such as Trafalgar and Jutland.

Until the development of full-rigged sailing ships, which facilitated European overseas trade and expansion after the fifteenth century, navies functioned as adjuncts to armies. They operated within sight of land, carried supplies for nearby armies, and sometimes transported troops short distances, such as across the Hellespont in the wars between Greece and Persia. Decisive naval battles, such as Salamis or Actium, were rare and were important because of their effect on nearby armies. The Greek victory at Salamis forced Persian king Darius to withdraw two-thirds of his army from Greece due to lack of supplies. Antony and Cleopatra's defeat at Actium undermined their legitimacy and led their soldiers to defect.

In contrast to older warships, such as the oared galleys of ancient Greece and Rome, full-rigged sailing ships could stay at sea for months. This made prolonged blockades of enemy ports and attacks on their commerce possible, as well as the conquest and defense of overseas possessions. Various statesmen recognized how this changed the strategic environment, among them William Pitt, who led Britain to victory in the Seven Years War and dramatically expanded Britain's overseas empire.

Yet, sailing ships were limited by wind and weather. Ships might be trapped in port by contrary winds or becalmed at sea. Whole fleets were regularly scattered by storms. So, it is not surprising that the first detailed considerations of sea power and naval strategy appeared in the late nineteenth century as warships shed their sails and adopted steam power, which allowed them to travel great distances and maneuver at will.

Navies' growing capabilities fostered discussions of naval strategy by a host of naval officers. Alfred Thayer Mahan, an important voice for reform in the U.S. Navy, was preeminent among them. Mahan drew heavily on Jomini, while Julian Corbett, a British scholar, drew on Clausewitz to rebut several of Mahan's points.

Alfred Thayer Mahan

ALFRED THAYER MAHAN'S *The Influence of Sea Power Upon History* (1890) laid the foundation for modern naval strategy. A relatively obscure captain in the U.S. Navy—and a poor sailor who disliked life at sea—Mahan joined the faculty of the U.S. Naval War College in 1885, the year after it was founded as the world's first postgraduate military school. In 1886, he succeeded Admiral Stephen B. Luce as the college's president. Mahan lectured on tactics and strategy. Encouraged by Luce, he revised his lectures and published them as *The Influence of Sea Power Upon History*.

Mahan's book captured attention around the world. It was translated into foreign languages and influenced naval thought and strategy in Germany, Japan, and other countries. Mahan's ideas, which he developed in numerous books and articles over the next two-dozen years, centered on winning "command of the sea" and using that maritime dominance to enhance a nation's economic and military power. His essay "America Looking Outward" (1890), for example, encouraged the United States to expand its influence in the Caribbean and construct and secure a canal through the Isthmus of Panama.

Mahan wrote as much about the relationship between economic and naval power as he did about strategy. Maritime trade, he argued, offered the best route to national prosperity. Naval power and maritime trade operate synergistically. Each benefits the other and facilitates its growth. The role of navies was to secure a nation's sea lines of communication to both protect and expand this trade. In war, navies should seek out enemy fleets and destroy them in decisive battles to win command of the sea. With sea control assured, navies would then blockade the enemy's coast to starve it into submission and support army operations on land, as needed.

For Mahan, the point of sea command is to enable a nation's use of the sea for military, commercial, or other purposes, while preventing enemies from doing the same. Yet, developing effective sea power is far from easy.

Mahan suggested there are six foundations to sea power:

- Geographical position

- Physical conformation
- Extent of territory
- Size of population
- National character
- Government character and policy

Mahan offered Great Britain as the preeminent example of these. Its long coastline and geographic position facilitated maritime trade, as opposed to continental powers like Germany and Russia whose access to the sea was limited by geographic chokepoints. Similarly, Mahan thought some peoples and governments, particularly democracies, such as Great Britain and the United States, were more inclined to commerce, maritime trade, and life at sea than autocracies like Imperial Germany or Tsarist Russia.

Jomini deeply influenced Mahan and his work reflects this. Like Jomini, Mahan argued that fixed, enduring principles determine victory in war. For Mahan, these include never dividing one's battle fleet, maintaining the offensive, and seeking decisive battle with the enemy's primary fleet.

Mahan argued the best way to protect one's maritime commerce and choke off the enemy's was to seek out and destroy the enemy's main fleet and largest warships. Attacking lesser targets, such as enemy commerce, was pointless. So, Mahan emphasized the construction of capital ships, the largest warships, to fight a decisive naval encounter. In the Age of Sail, these were ships of the line, such as the 100-gun *HMS Victory,* Horatio Nelson's flagship at the Battle of Trafalgar. In Mahan's day, they were heavily armed and armored steam-powered battleships.

War at sea is different from war on land. Apart from a handful of critical maritime chokepoints, such as the Straits of Gibraltar, Hormuz, and Malacca (and the modern Panama and Suez Canals), the sea is a vast and relatively undifferentiated terrain. Unlike land, no particular advantage accrues to defenders at sea unless they are close enough to land that land-based defenses, such as gun emplacements—or aircraft in the modern era—can participate in battle. Therefore, Mahan argued, naval forces must take the offensive and force battle on the enemy. A fleet that surrendered the initiative to the enemy and merely defended its coast was doomed to defeat.

Mahan largely ignored amphibious warfare and treated navies as almost autonomous and independent military forces. Instead of projecting naval power onto land, Mahan emphasized sweeping an enemy navy from the seas and then imposing a crippling naval blockade to strangle its economy. The blockading nation would benefit from maritime trade and have access to all the world's resources, while the blockaded nation would be starved into submission. This made sea power a slow, but cost-effective, way to win wars.

Julian Corbett

JULIAN CORBETT WAS a contemporary of Mahan and sometime advisor to the Royal Navy. A civilian scholar, he thought deeply about maritime strategy and naval history and challenged many of Mahan's points, either explicitly or implicitly.

Corbett saw defense as the stronger form of war, even at sea. An inferior navy, he warned, would hardly cooperate in its destruction by a superior force. It had no reason to seek the decisive battle Mahan encouraged. It would explore strategic alternatives. In fact, Corbett argued, an inferior fleet in a strong defensive position, such as a well-protected port, could significantly hinder the operations of a larger, enemy fleet. The larger fleet would need to detach significant forces to watch this "fleet-in-being," and have other warships ready to sail to intercept it, if it sortied.

During the First World War, for example, the British and German fleets sailed against one another only a handful of times in the four years of war. Only once—at Jutland on 31 May 1916—did they engage one another in what could have been a decisive battle. Germany's battle fleet, only two-thirds the size of Britain's, adopted a fleet-in-being strategy. The possibility of it sailing forced Britain to maintain the bulk of its largest ships in home waters. Instead of the close blockade of the enemy coast Britain employed in previous wars, Germany's powerful fleet-in-being, along with the threat of mines and submarines, forced Britain to impose a more cautious, distant blockade. This made it easier for blockade runners to slip into German ports and for German submarines to attack British shipping.

Germany's fleet-in-being limited the Royal Navy's ability to project power elsewhere. Had Britain been able to deploy all of its largest and most modern ships in the Dardanelles to suppress Turkey's coastal fortifications and assist the amphibious landings at Gallipoli, things might have gone differently.

Germany's dilemma in the First World War showcases the traditional problems land powers have fighting naval powers, and vice versa. Victory in such a war requires the land power to successfully challenge the enemy at sea. Sparta eventually did this in the Peloponnesian War. After repeated failures and 27 years of war, Sparta destroyed the Athenian fleet at Aegospotami and then blockaded Athens into submission.

Historically, that victory was unusual. Usually, the sea power emerges victorious in a prolonged war. As Sarah Paine argues in *The Japanese Empire: Grand Strategy from the Meiji Restoration to the Pacific War* (2017), military power ultimately rests on economic power. Maritime states develop their economies through trade, while continental powers often expand their economies by conquest.

The inevitable destruction accompanying wars of conquest, such as Russia's 2022 invasion of Ukraine, reduces the value of conquered territory. It is far better, Paine argues, to engage in equitable trade.

MILITARY STRATEGY FOR WRITERS   81

While land powers are often tempted to expand their borders in bloody wars, maritime powers are more inclined to trade peacefully and grow wealthy as a result.

Sun Tzu emphasized the goal of war is to enrich the state. Mahan and Corbett agree, seeing this as the navy's primary role, whether in war or peace. Britain exemplifies this. Britain supported its European allies in a succession of wars, usually against France, but often devoted equal or greater resources to expanding its overseas empire and trading networks. Britain's allies raised large armies to fight great battles on land but emerged from even victorious wars economically and militarily exhausted. In contrast, Britain prospered.

Corbett often agreed with Mahan on general principles but cautioned against regarding the ideal situations described by Mahan as the norm. Similarly, one shouldn't take to heart simplistic strategic advice, such as Mahan's repeated warning against dividing one's fleet. "There is nothing so misleading," Corbett warned, as a strategic maxim.

Corbett agreed "the object of naval warfare must always be directly or indirectly either to secure the command of the sea or to prevent the enemy from securing it" (*Some Principles of Maritime Strategy*, 91). Yet, he questioned what "command of the sea" actually involved. As he notes, seas are normally uncontrolled. A fleet's ability to command a sea is limited by the speed of its warships and the range of their weapons. Since no fleet could be everywhere at once, most of the world's oceans will remain open to the enemy.

Throughout the Napoleonic Wars, for example, French warships and privateers preyed on British commerce despite overwhelming British naval superiority. The same proved true for American warships and privateers in the American Revolution and War of 1812. Outnumbered as much as five to one by British fleets, American warships and privateers nonetheless avoided the British blockade, attack British commerce, and inflict considerable damage to it.

Achieving complete control of the sea proved impossible for even the largest fleets. What mattered, Corbett concluded, was controlling the sea when and where it mattered to facilitate particular military missions. During World War II, for example, German submarines challenged Allied command of the seas. Yet, the Allies always achieved control of the sea when it most mattered, as during the evacuation from Dunkirk early in the war and the later Allied amphibious invasions of North Africa, Sicily, Italy, and France.

After World War II, two developments further undermined the notion of command of the sea. First, the deployment of nuclear weapons aboard warships and aircraft threatened even the largest and most heavily defended capital ships. Second, the development of nuclear-powered submarines whose long range and quiet engines made them far deadlier and much harder to detect than older diesel-electric submarines. Prompted by Admiral Stansfield Turner and other senior officers, the U.S. Navy accepted the more limited idea of sea control, that is control over vital passages and areas of strategic importance at particular times. Command of the sea in a Mahanian sense was no longer possible.

Commerce Raiding

WHILE MAHAN ARGUED commerce raiding could not win wars, Corbett emphasized the importance of protecting one's commerce. What was the point of seeking decisive battle to achieve "command of the sea," if doing so required so many warships that few remained to protect merchant shipping from enemy raiders? Contrary to Mahan, commerce raiding could, Corbett argues, have strategic importance, and even win wars. Much of the Anglo-Dutch Wars, for example, revolved around commerce. The advent of submarines in the twentieth century and the threat they posed to commercial shipping underlined Corbett's point.

Commerce raiding is also a fruitful enterprise for novelists and their protagonists, particularly at the peak of sailing ship era, from the Seven Years War through the Napoleonic Wars. The latter wars provide the setting for numerous fictional sea captains, including C. S. Forester's Horatio Hornblower who spent more of his fictional naval career protecting British commerce from French warships and privateers and attacking French commerce than he did sailing in line of battle against enemy fleets.

Forester's Hornblower inspired numerous other authors whose works also trace the careers of daring sea captains, including Alexander Kent's Captain Richard Bolitho, and Patrick O'Brian's immensely popular duo of Captain Jack Aubrey and ship's doctor Stephen Maturin. One can similarly point to the popularity of commerce raiding submarines, historical and fictional, in books and movies like *Run Silent, Run Deep* (1955).

Sometimes, particularly clever authors successfully insert their protagonists into major events, allowing them to play a minor role in Trafalgar or other great battles, sharing the spotlight with Nelson and other great admirals. More often, though, fictional ship captains miss major battles. Nonetheless, these battles provide essential background do their own deeds of derring-do.

Historically, pirates were as likely to attack isolated coastal towns as they were to hunt down heavily laden cargo ships. Vikings raided towns and besieged cities across Europe, including Paris. Caribbean pirates attacked and raided the rich ports of the region's sugar islands. From the thirteenth through the sixteenth centuries, large fleets of pirates, called wokou, raided China's long coastline and periodically attacked Korea and Japan. Piracy remained endemic in the region long afterward and inspired a host of novels and movies, as well as Milton Caniff's long-running comic series *Terry and the Pirates* (1943-1973).

Homer's epic poems, the *Iliad* and the *Odyssey*, present literature's most famous naval expedition, the Greek invasion and siege of Troy. On his voyage home, people repeatedly ask Odysseus whether he's a merchant or a pirate. For much of history, the line between the two was very thin. Piracy was so common that all maritime states maintained swift warships to hunt down pirates and deter their depredations.

Limited Wars

WHILE MAHAN FOCUSED on major wars, Corbett highlighted the utility of sea power in limited wars. Only island powers. Corbett concludes, have the ability to permanently keep a war limited. As Francis Bacon wrote: "he that commands the sea is at great liberty and may take as much or as little of the war as he will, whereas those that be strongest on land are many times nevertheless in great straits" (Essays 29). Continental powers always faced the possibility of escalation. Yet, island powers who commanded local waters were immune from invasion.

Island powers like Britain could engage with overseas enemies as much—or as little—as they chose. This allowed Britain to maintain a small army while building the world's most powerful navy, which it used to build an overseas empire so vast "the sun never set on the Union Jack." During the Napoleonic Wars, Britain's navy blockaded France, sustained Britain's Continental allies, and supported a British army in Portugal and Spain that proved impossible for the French to dislodge.

As Corbett noted, the goal of naval strategy is always to influence war on land. The overwhelming majority of people live on land and will continue to do so until advanced technology (or magic) offers alternative living spaces. Similarly, people acquire most of the resources to support their economies from the land. At best, the sea is a secondary source of resources, though a primary means of their transportation. How then can sea power affect war on land?

One thing a superior navy can do is to isolate a theater of war. The United States conquered the Philippines, in part, because its superior naval power allowed it to isolate the Philippines' major islands, trapping insurgent groups on individual islands. U.S. troops then overwhelmed insurgent forces one island at a time. Similarly, in the Russo-Japanese War, Japan effectively used its navy to isolate the Russian army in Manchuria, forcing it to rely on the inadequate Trans-Siberian Railway for supplies and reinforcements. The Russian navy's effort to break this blockade ended in disaster at the Battle of Tsushima. With its major warships sunk or captured, along with Port Arthur, its major eastern port, Russia's leaders agreed to negotiate peace.

Peacetime Navies and Gunboat Diplomacy

WHILE ONE GENERALLY thinks of strategy in terms of war, navies have substantial peacetime roles. In recent decades, U.S. warships were often the first to arrive and render assistance to communities struck by natural disasters. The same was true in ancient times. A Roman fleet helped evacuate Pompei as Vesuvius erupted. Similarly, both ancient and modern warships visit foreign ports to "show the flag," reassuring allies and reminding enemies of the threat they pose. When American President Theodore Roosevelt spoke of speaking softly and carrying "a big stick," the stick he had in mind was the U.S. Navy. During Roosevelt's presidency it became one of the world's largest.

In times of crisis, states can mass warships near an enemy state, engaging in what strategist Edward Luttwak terms "naval suasion." The threat of naval force can either deter an enemy from acting against one's interests or compel them to act in some favorable way. As a result, navies are often at the forefront of implementing grand strategy.

In the nineteenth century, imperial powers frequently engaged in gunboat diplomacy, threatening lesser states and securing concessions from them at gunpoint. American Commodore Matthew Perry famously forced open Japan to foreign trade in 1854. In 1882, the British fleet bombarded Alexandria, Egypt for 10 hours, inflicting considerable damage. Britain extracted growing concessions from Egypt and soon reduced Egypt to a British protectorate. A decade later, the cruiser *USS Boston* helped overthrow Hawaii's legitimate government and installed a group of U.S. settlers in its place.

After World War II, the United States frequently used its large navy to deter or compel potential enemies. Its utility was such, that beginning in the 1970s the Soviet Union enlarged its navy to challenge U.S. naval predominance. In the first decades of the twenty-first century, China is doing the same to facilitate "naval suasion" in the waters it claims. It has periodically threatened Indonesia, Vietnam, and other nations whose maritime claims conflict with China's whose government also maintains constant pressure on Taiwan, a "lost province" it hopes to reclaim.

Amphibious Warfare

WARSHIPS OFTEN RAID enemy coasts, sometimes landing troops, as in the "cutting out" expeditions featured in Forester's Hornblower stories. In these raids, Hornblower led sailors and marines who snuck into enemy ports in the dead of night to set fires to sink ships and destroy supplies. Gunboat diplomacy often required landing troops, as in the many U.S. interventions in the Caribbean and Central America.

However, these are small amphibious operations. The famous Allied invasion of Normandy in World War II required thousands of ships and planes to land and sustain hundreds of thousands of troops. Large amphibious operations are among the most difficult military operations. Many never get much past the planning stages, such as France's repeated efforts to invade Britain in the eighteenth century. Others fail before a single soldier is landed, as was the case for Spain's famous armada, which met fierce opposition from a smaller, but better prepared English fleet. Repulsed by the English in several battles, storms then scattered Spain's armada before it landed a single soldier.

Other landings fail on the beachhead, as the British landings at Gallipoli did in the First World War. A combination of factors including lack of experience and poor leadership slowed the British advance, allowing Ottoman troops, ably led by Kemal Ataturk, to seize the high ground overlooking the beaches. Repeated efforts to break out from the beaches failed. After suffering heavy casualties, particularly among Australian and other Commonwealth troops who accounted for the bulk of the landing force, the British withdrew. A fictional amphibious landing in the *House of the Dragon* television series similarly failed, despite aerial support provided by dragons.

Disposal Forces

BRITAIN WON THE FIRST World War, along with its allies. Its failure at Gallipoli and ultimate success in the war demonstrates another advantage of maritime powers and the importance to them of what Corbett labeled a "disposal force." These epitomize what Francis Bacon meant when he wrote that command of the sea allowed one to "take as much or as little" part in a war as one wishes. Britain's troops at Gallipoli were a disposal force, a force British leaders could expend in a risky operation. If they succeeded, it would hasten the war's end. If they failed, as the Gallipoli landings did, their failure would not materially change the strategic situation. Many of the troops were from Australia and New Zealand, and bitterness over Britain's mismanagement of that campaign lingers in those countries and is highlighted in the movie *Gallipoli* (1981).

Historically, Britain's most famous disposal force was the army it landed in Spain following Napoleon's invasion. Eventually commanded by Arthur Wellesley, who later defeated Napoleon at Waterloo and became the Duke of Wellington, this small army and its Portuguese ally contested French control of Spain. Between 1808 and 1812, Wellington outfought and outmaneuvered larger French forces and supported Spanish irregulars who nibbled away the French army. Sustained by the Royal Navy, Wellington's strength grew over time, allowing him to eventually seize the initiative and drive France out of Spain.

Wellington's Peninsular Campaign provides the setting for Bernard Cornwell's novels featuring Richard Sharpe who eventually rises to command a British rifle regiment. Inspired by C. S. Forester's Horatio Hornblower series, Cornwell developed Sharpe as Hornblower's roguish, army counterpart. In adventure after adventure, Sharpe bedevils larger French forces, supports Spanish partisans, and collects vital intelligence for Wellington. While only sometimes alluded to, Sharpe's adventures, like Wellington's campaign as a whole, relied upon Royal Navy support.

Disposal forces are fertile ground to set stories and torment protagonists. The personal stakes are high, the danger great, and the level of support from those they serve, inconsistent. At the same time, the opportunity and rewards for courage and success are also high. We use the term "disposal force" because no one, particularly not marines, likes be referred to as disposable.

Sea Power in Major Wars

IN THE AMERICAN CIVIL War, the U.S. Navy quickly captured New Orleans, the Confederacy's most important port, and supported the advance of Union armies along the nation's major rivers. The Navy raided and blockaded the Confederate coast but executed few successful large amphibious operations. Mahan served during the Civil War and wrote his first book, *The Gulf and Inland Waters: The U.S. Navy in the Civil War* (1883) about naval operations in that war. This may explain why he devoted relatively little attention to amphibious operations in his later works on sea power and naval strategy. Contested amphibious invasions appeared too risky, as a disastrous British amphibious invasion of Walcheren Island during the Napoleonic Wars demonstrated.

World War II shows the strategic benefits of sea power and utility of properly executed amphibious invasions. While Nazi Germany conquered a far larger resource base than Imperial Germany in the First World War, it still suffered serious shortages of war materials, particularly petroleum, rubber, and alloying metals, such as wolfram and tungsten.

American and British naval superiority gave them great flexibility, threatening the long coastlines of Nazi occupied Scandinavia and southern and western Europe. The Germans never knew where the Allies would land and were forced to garrison long coastlines with troops desperately needed on the Russian Front. The Germans also repeatedly fell for Allied deception operations. They massed troops in Norway, Sardinia, and France's Pas de Calais, while leaving the Allies' actual targets, Sicily, Normandy, and southern France, less well defended.

The Allies' first major amphibious operation of the war, the invasion and liberation of French North Africa, illustrates how one can use naval power to isolate a theater or war. While the Germans were able to rush in reinforcements by air for a few months, superior Allied and naval power soon halted the flow of German troops and then trapped this new German army, along with Erwin Rommel's retreating Afrika Korps, in Tunisia and forced their surrender, dealing a critical blow to German military strength.

Naval operations in major wars provide settings for many movies and novels, though writers generally focus their attention on the exploits of smaller warships. Torpedo boats, such the famous PT 109 commanded by future American president John F. Kennedy, feature in novelist Robb White's works. In C. S. Forester's *The African Queen* (1945), and the better-known movie (1951) of the same name, the civilian protagonists (Humphrey Bogart and Katharine Hepburn in the movie) arm their small steamboat and attack a superior German gunboat.

Risking the Fleet

WHETHER ANCIENT GREEK triremes, eighteenth century ships-of-the-line, twentieth century battleships, or today's nuclear-powered aircraft carriers and submarines, large warships represent a society's cutting-edge technology. These capital ships require considerable time, expertise, and resources to build. They are hard to replace and should not be risked lightly.

Napoleon invaded Russia because he lacked a fleet. After Britain imposed a blockade on France, Napoleon pressured Russia and other European states to ban trade with Britain. This embargo, called the Continental System, aimed to hurt Britain's economy, and bring its leaders to the peace table. Instead, the mutual blockade and embargo hurt Europe more than Britain. British merchants traded around the world and cemented their hold on lucrative markets and trade routes. When Russia broke with the Continental System in 1812, Napoleon invaded, hoping to force Russia back into the Continental System. Instead, Napoleon's invasion ended in disaster.

Each year, Napoleon could draft another batch of 19-year-olds into his army. Replacing all the ships he lost at the Battle of Trafalgar in 1805, though, required seven years. By then, Napoleon had invaded Russia and was on his way to losing the war and his empire.

The time and expense required to replace large warships makes the decision to risk one's fleet in battle one of the central questions of naval strategy. It is a particularly fraught question for nations who lack facilities to build large warships and instead purchase them from those that do. During the Russo-Japanese War, for example, Japan relied on British shipyards to construct its largest warships. This made Admiral Togo Heihachiro understandably cautious early in the war, particularly after he lost two of his six battleships to a Russian minefield.

Fictional characters, though, are often surprisingly willing to risk ships and fleets, regardless of the odds against them. Horatio Hornblower and Jack Aubrey win promotion by attacking and capturing enemy ships that substantially outgun their own. In both instances, they lure enemy ships into carefully planned traps.

In James S. A. Corey's *Expanse* series, the crew of the *Rocinante* do much the same. While they sometimes have battle forced on them, they try to plan in advance to lure superior enemy ships and fleets into situations where they have the advantage. The Greeks, of course, did the same at Salamis, luring a numerically superior Persian fleet into congested waters.

Historically, Horatio Nelson repeatedly led British fleets to victory against enemy fleets that outnumbered his own, were in a superior tactical position, or both. He risked his fleet in situations that daunted other commanders. He did so only after careful planning and thoroughly briefing his subordinates. Like their historical exemplars, fictional captains and admirals should only take these risks after careful consideration and planning.

So, when should a nation risk its fleet? When do the likely outcomes of battle outweigh the risks of losing major warships? Admiral Chester W. Nimitz, who commanded the U.S. Pacific Fleet in World War II, addressed this question succinctly in his orders to Admirals Frank Fletcher and Raymond Spruance on 28 May 1942 when they sailed to confront a much larger Japanese fleet near Midway Island. "You will be governed," he told them, "by the principle of calculated risk which you shall interpret to mean the avoidance of exposure of your force to attack by superior enemy forces without good prospect of inflicting, as a result of such exposure, greater damage to the enemy." Nimitz's order encouraged boldness, and it paid off. The U.S. fleet caught the Japanese by surprise and sank four Japanese aircraft carriers, while losing only one of its own. It was exactly the result for which Nimitz hoped and prepared.

Another admiral, though, might have issued different orders. As Fletcher and Spruance's three aircraft carriers sailed toward Midway, the United States had more than a dozen even larger aircraft carriers under construction. Funded by the Naval Act of 1940, the first of them, *USS Essex,* entered the war 11 months after the Battle of Midway. Even if the United States had suffered greater losses in at Midway, it had under construction the largest fleet in world history—a fleet far larger than Japan could ever hope to match.

Nimitz understood this. He could risk his three aircraft carriers in battle, because more were on their way, because a war of attrition favored the United States, and because Midway was close to American bases in Hawaii and far from Japan and its Pacific bases. While the U.S. fleet benefited from search and attack planes operating from Midway and Hawaii, the Japanese fleet lacked similar support. It sailed almost blindly into the American ambush. Every battle is something of a gamble, but at Midway the odds favored the Americans. An American victory would speed the path to victory, while an American defeat would not have significantly delayed it.

Case Study: Russo-Japanese War

THE RUSSO-JAPANESE War (1904-1905) offers an interesting example of a war between two second-tier naval powers. Japan opened the war with a surprise attack on the Russian Fleet at Port Arthur, its primary Pacific Ocean naval base. The attack failed to inflict significant damage on the Russian fleet but left it in such confusion that it failed to sortie. This allowed Admiral Togo to blockade the entrance to the harbor.

With the Russian fleet trapped in Port Arthur, Japanese troops conducted amphibious landings in Korea and Manchuria. The Japanese army quickly conquered Korea, left a large force to besiege Port Arthur, and marched up the South Manchuria Railway into Russian-held Manchuria with the rest of its troops.

When the Russian fleet finally sailed from Port Arthur months later, Togo's fleet intercepted it and outfought it in the Battle of Yellow Sea. Poorly led and inexperienced, the Russian fleet fell into confusion following the destruction of its flagship and retreated to Port Arthur. The Japanese army captured the city five months later following a prolonged and costly siege.

Russian cruisers based in Vladivostok had greater success. They sortied on six raids, harassed Japanese supply convoys, and sank ships carrying valuable cargo, including siege guns destined for Port Arthur. Because of the inaction of Russia's other warships, though, a superior Japanese fleet eventually caught and overwhelmed Russia's Vladivostok-based cruisers.

On land, Japanese troops won several costly battles and advanced steadily northward. In contrast to the Russians (and Japanese conduct a generation later in World War II), Japanese soldiers treated local Chinese well and benefitted from their reports on Russian troop movements. On the other hand, Russia's army retreated toward its supply lines. Steady infusions of fresh troops and supplies arrived along the Trans-Siberian Railroad. So, despite its defeats, the Russian army grew larger. Meanwhile, the pursuing Japanese were drawn farther and farther from their seaborne sources of supply.

The capture of Port Arthur allowed Japan to shift those troops north. These sustained Japan's advance and helped Japan win the Battle of Mukden. It was the largest battle fought thus far in history, with over 250,000 troops on each side. Both commanders had difficulty maneuvering such large forces, but Japanese troops proved more aggressive, maintained the initiative, and won the battle, forcing Russia's army to retreat yet again.

Two months later Admiral Togo's fleet engaged Russia's Baltic fleet, which had sailed from Europe, around Africa, and across the Indian Ocean. While an impressive feat of logistics, the long voyage left Russian crews exhausted and their ships fouled with marine growths that reduced their speed. Togo's ships repeatedly outmaneuvered Russia's warships and sank or captured most of them. Roughly a month later, Japanese amphibious forces invaded Russian-controlled Sakhalin Island, hoping its loss would force Russia to negotiate peace.

Both Mahan and Corbett wrote about the Russo-Japanese as it unfolded and used the war to illustrate their strategic ideas. Mahan, for example, praised Togo for keeping his fleet united and condemned Russia for dividing its Pacific fleet between Port Arthur and Vladivostok, and its slowness to dispatch the Baltic fleet to reinforce the Pacific. While Togo opened the war with a daring surprise attack, he otherwise handled his fleet cautiously and carefully. In contrast, Russia's Port Arthur fleet was cautious to the point of inaction; its Baltic fleet daring to the point of madness.

Corbett pointed to the early successes of Russia's cruisers, which cost Japan dearly. He focused most of his attention, though, on how Japan used its fleet to isolate Korea and Manchuria and choose when and where to fight. By the time Russia's Baltic Fleet arrived in East Asia, Japan had secured most of its objectives.

Yet, despite Japan's overwhelming superiority at sea after destroying the Russian Fleet at the Battle of Tsushima, Russia negotiated surprisingly moderate peace terms. Russia refused to pay Japan the cash indemnity it demanded. It even refused to admit it had lost the war. The problem, as Japan's leaders discovered, was that their overwhelming naval superiority in the Pacific could not influence the conduct of war deep in Manchuria.

The Russian army, fed by the Trans-Siberian Railroad, grew, while the Japanese army, which had exhausted its reserves, shrank due to heavy losses in battle and the prolonged siege of Port Arthur. On land, Russian losses exceeded Japan's by a factor of two to one. Russia's army, though, outnumbered Japan's by five-to-one. So, the loss rate actually favored Russia. Had the Russian Navy managed a similar exchange rate, the war would have ended differently.

Naval power allowed the Japanese to have "as much or as little" of the war as they chose, but it could not alone force Russia to concede the war. Losing naval superiority would have exposed Japan, an island nation dependent on trade for food and other critical resources, to blockade and starvation, as happened later during World War II.

Japan's leaders recognized the tide of war would soon turn against them. They had reached their culminating point of victory. So, they negotiated the best deal they could get, which was pretty good. Japan gained control of Korea and the southern half of Sakhalin Island, displaced Russia from Manchuria, and picked up some fishing rights and other minor concessions.

HISTORICALLY, NATIONS employed three primary naval strategies:

1. seek battle to attain command of the sea to facilitate a blockade of the enemy's coast and amphibious invasions;
2. raid enemy commerce to hurt its economy and hinder its ability to continue the war; and
3. maintain a "fleet in being" to deny a superior enemy command of the sea and limit its operations against one's coast.

In general, the larger navy seeks the first, while inferior navies do the second and—if possible—the third. And of course, inferior fleets seek opportunities to engage isolated parts of the enemy fleet in advantageous conditions, hoping to whittle down the enemy's numbers and eventually reverse their inferior position.

Debates on these options continue today. Seek battle or avoid it? How much of one's fleet should target enemy commerce? Can commerce raiding win a war? What about a blockade? Is a fleet-in-being a useful strategic asset or a waste of resources better devoted to the army and war on land?

Regardless of the chosen strategy, the advantages of sea power highlighted by Mahan and Corbett are immense. Despite the development of airplanes, a century ago and railroads a century before then, 90% of world trade still moves by sea. The ability to threaten or cut off this trade has great strategic value.

Equally important is the flexibility and strategic reach of navies. They can isolate a theater of war, conduct amphibious operations, sustain operations on land, and dispatch disposal forces to harass enemies at unexpected locations and force them to garrison long coastlines. That said, the vulnerability of enemies to sea power varies dramatically from island nations like Japan to continental powers like Russia.

Chapter Four: Strategies of Air Power

Humans have made boats since prehistoric times and developed specialized warships more than 3,000 years ago. Yet, strategists were slow to explore the possibilities of sea power. Debates on the utility of air power and strategies for its employment, though, developed as quickly as the aircraft themselves following the Wright Brothers' first public flights in 1908. In fact, discussions of the military applications of air power frequently outpaced the capabilities of existing aircraft. The possibilities airplanes offered, whether executing pinpoint attacks on critical targets or laying waste to entire cities, captured the imagination. According to their proponents, airplanes offered quick, decisive military victories at low cost. They would revolutionize warfare and military strategy.

Others recognized the importance of air power but insisted that aviation was best used to support troops on the ground and ships at sea. If the point of war is to seize and hold territory, "boots on the ground" are critical.

Thankfully, settling these debates is not essential to discuss the role of airplanes in war and strategies of air power.

Aviation before the Great War

PRACTICAL AVIATION began on 4 June 1783 when two brothers, Joseph-Michel and Jacques-Étienne Montgolfier, ascended aloft in their hot air balloon, the first humans to do so. Other demonstrations followed, including one for King Louis XVI of France and his wife, Marie Antoinette. A few years later, France's revolutionary army employed balloons and used them to observe enemy troop deployments in a few battles. Napoleon, though, shunned them. His armies moved too fast to make balloons practical. Balloons took hours to get into the air. Once in the air, they were stationary and could only communicate what they saw to their ground crews by dropping messages to them.

The U.S. Army found occasional uses for balloons during the American Civil War and later in the Spanish-American War. These newer balloons rose faster, thanks to hydrogen gas, but still required relatively static troop dispositions to be useful. They could, though, communicate with ground crews via telegraph (invented in 1837). This allowed balloon crews to report more quickly on enemy troop movements and direct artillery fire on distant enemy positions.

The British army also experimented with balloons in the nineteenth century. They proved useful in a few colonial conflicts, including the Boer War, when the military situation was static, such as the Siege of Ladysmith.

In 1900, Ferdinand von Zeppelin, who observed balloon operations during the American Civil War, demonstrated the first practical airship. Named after himself, the first zeppelin employed a cigar-shaped aluminum framework containing 17 individual cells filled with hydrogen gas. Gasoline engines powered the craft and fins and other control mechanisms allowed pilots to steer it. Zeppelin refined his design over the next decade, producing ever-larger airships with greater speed and lift. While airships like the zeppelin were more militarily useful than static balloons, they were expensive to build and troublesome to operate.

Orville and Wilbur Wright developed the first airplane, which they tested in 1903 at Kitty Hawk, North Carolina. They refined their design over the next few years and demonstrated a new Wright plane to the U.S. Army in 1908. Despite a crash that killed an army observer, Lieutenant Thomas Selfridge, the first airplane fatality, they signed a contract and began supplying the army with airplanes the following year.

Across the world, pioneering military officers realized the potential of airplanes. They could scout for enemy ships or troops, serve as the eyes of fleets and armies and direct long-range gunfire. As technology improved, these officers argued, airplanes would also be used to attack enemy bases, troops, and warships.

These discussions outpaced the capabilities of early airplanes. Long before airplanes could carry significant bomb loads, strategic theorists and future prognosticators, among them science fiction author H. G. Wells, predicted devastating aerial bombardments that destroyed entire cities. In the United States. Alarmists warned a surprise air attack could destroy the recently completed Panama Canal. Yet, no aircraft at the time carried bombs powerful enough to damage the canal's locks.

Senior political and military leaders refused to be rushed and funded aircraft purchases in dozens, rather than the mass aerial fleets of hundreds or thousands of planes aviation advocates demanded. The Italian army used a few scouting airplanes when it conquered Libya in 1911. The following year, the Ottoman Empire, Serbia, Greece, and Bulgaria all used airplanes to scout enemy positions in the Balkan Wars. It was the First World War, though, that showed the full potential of military aviation and the possibility they could have strategic, rather just tactical, utility.

The First World War and Developing Air Power Thought

BALLOONS FEATURED PROMINENTLY in the First World War. Hundreds were often deployed along the Western Front during major offensives. Zeppelins and other airships also flew in the war. Like balloons, though, they proved increasingly vulnerable to airplanes, whose capabilities improved dramatically. Between the outset of war in August 1914 and its conclusion in November 1918, military airplanes almost doubled in speed and dramatically increased their carrying capacity and weapon loads.

Even the most conservatively minded thinkers recognized the rapid advances of aviation technology during the First World War. Airplanes became increasingly specialized and executed all the military missions we associate with aircraft: reconnaissance (both visual and photographic), directing artillery fire, air defense, bombing enemy troops and cities, and even air transport, which included ferrying officers to important locations and landing and retrieving spies behind enemy lines.

Throughout the First World War, though, reconnaissance remained airplanes' primary mission, closely followed by air defense to prevent enemy reconnaissance of one's own positions. In the last months of the war, Allied armies massed their air power against German defenses. Bombing and strafing by Allied planes helped their soldiers break through German defenses. Yet, bombing targets in the enemy's homeland, such as factories, ports, and railroad yards, failed to produce results. Aircraft lacked the accuracy and bomb load to significantly damage urban targets.

Air power theorists predicted this would soon change. Drawing on the previous century's discussion of naval strategy, they adapted ideas of blockade and deterrence to air power. Much as Corbett and Mahan advocated command of the sea, air power advocates saw command of the air as the path to victory. Corbett argued a naval blockade could exert such "pressure on citizens and their collective life" that they demanded their governments make peace (Corbett, 97). Aerial bombing, aviation advocates argued, could do the same, only faster and more cheaply than expensive battleships. As French General Jean-Henri Jauneaud noted, mirroring Cicero's observations on sea power, "whoever is master of the air will be master of the world."

In the 1920s and 1930s, air power theorists debated the best use of air power. Many focused their attention on urban bombing. Did air power offer a more direct way to target civilians and civil society? Could air power circumvent enemy defenses and be employed in an "indirect approach" against a nation's vital areas? Could air power target enemy transportation nodes and production centers to produce results similar to naval blockade? If so, could air power win wars alone?

Alternatively, was air power best applied behind the fronts line, attacking enemy supply columns, bridges, road junctions, and other "soft" targets beyond the range of friendly artillery. These attacks would interdict the flow of enemy supplies and reinforcements to the front line, starving armies of the soldiers and material needed to sustain them. In contrast to attacking cities, these interdiction attacks would limit civilian casualties. Road-bound convoys and similar targets were also easier to spot, identify, and attack from the air than munitions factories scattered through dense urban conglomerations.

Other officers argued wars were won on the battlefield. Air power should concentrate there to aid troops on the ground and ships at sea. Airplanes should provide what came to be called close air support. It followed from this argument that air power should be subordinated to army and navy commanders, rather than operating independently.

Fictional characters will encounter these debates. They might debate the issue themselves, arguing over how best to use air power in the military situation they face. More likely, they will be the pilots or other air crew carrying out these missions—missions they may disagree with for moral reasons or practical military considerations.

Most air-minded officers opposed making close air support their primary mission. They objected for three reasons. First, because these missions were dangerous and produced high aircraft losses. Second, because tactical air support had not produced dramatic successes in the First World War. Third, because these officers wanted air forces to develop independently of armies and navies. They wanted to create independent air forces coequal to their nation's armies and navies, which Britain's Royal Air Force became in 1918.

Novelists joined these debates, among them H. G. Wells and Edgar Rice Burroughs whose works portrayed European cities devastated by war and aerial bombing. Few considered the issue settled. Debates continued throughout the 1920s, 1930s, and World War II. Even after the war, few regarded the issue as settled. Disputes over air power missions, and the aircraft to execute them, continue to the present day. They should be as important for fictional characters as for contemporary and historical political and military leaders. How can one best apply air power against an enemy's vulnerabilities? What are the ethical considerations of bombing particular targets?

Maturing Air Power Thought and World War II

THE MOST VOCIFEROUS post-war air power advocates, among them Italian Giulio Douhet, advocated direct attacks on enemy cities and factories. They soon labeled these *strategic bombing* to emphasize the airplane's strategic, as opposed to tactical, role. What better way to starve enemy armies of supplies than by destroying the factories supplying their munitions? This, they argued, was the surest, quickest, and most efficient way to end wars.

In *Command of the Air* (1921), Douhet argued the First World War demonstrated the futility of traditional ground warfare. Instead of bloody ground battles, he thought militaries should use airplanes to bomb centers of economic, military, political, and social importance. Airplanes' advantages of speed, elevation, and striking power made them both deadly instruments of war and impossible to defend against. By dropping poison gas, incendiaries, and conventional explosives in the "correct proportions," airplanes would destroy enemy industrial capacity.

Unlike ground officers, whose obsession with offensive warfare died in the trenches as machine guns and rapid-fire artillery ripped apart advancing troops, air power advocates remained committed to offensive warfare. Douhet, for example, advocated surprise attacks and preemptive wars without formal declarations of war. A handful of strikes, he believed, could cripple an enemy nation. So, it was vital to strike first in war, both to destroy the enemy's air force on the ground and deal the first blow against the enemy's industrial capacity. Douhet made no distinction between civilians and soldiers. In war, everyone was a legitimate target.

German zeppelins and airplanes bombed British cities during World War I, but inflicted little damage and achieved no strategic effect. Nonetheless, post-war air power advocates offered increasingly strident arguments for air power and strategic bombing.

About 250,000 Germans died of starvation in 1917 due to food shortages caused by Britain's naval blockade, exacerbated by German agricultural and economic mismanagement. Air power advocates used these deaths from starvation to undermine the moral argument against bombing cities. What difference did it make if a civilian died from war-induced malnutrition or an aerial bomb?

Airplanes steadily improved their speed, range, and carrying capacity after World War I. As bomb loads rose, air power advocates argued airplanes could inflict much greater losses on civilian society much faster than the slow starvation of naval blockade.

Hugh Trenchard, who commanded Britain's Royal Air Force in the First World War, developed ideas similar to Douhet's. While there's no indication they read each other's work, both denigrated air defense and encouraged all-out aerial offensives against enemy cities. Both believed defending against air attacks was impossible. As British politician Stanley Baldwin later proclaimed, "the bomber will always get through." So, the only way to stop an enemy air attack was to strike first against the enemy's factories and air bases.

Douhet, Trenchard, and others believed city bombing offered the additional advantage of eroding civilian morale. Much like Corbett, who believed civilians would demand their government make peace to end the deprivations of prolonged naval blockade, Douhet believed urban bombing would shatter the enemy's "physical and moral resistance." Terrified civilians would demand their governments make peace. If necessary, they would overthrow leaders who refused to do so, bringing wars to rapid conclusions.

Based on these assumptions that air power could win wars quickly—and unaided by ground or naval forces—air power advocates argued that air forces needed to be independent services. They should not be adjuncts of armies or navies, as they were for every nation before World War I and remained so for most nations, including the United States, long after that war.

During the 1920s, Britain's Royal Air Force, again led by Trenchard, helped police Britain's vast empire by visiting devastation on towns and villages whose people rebelled. For a time, this proved effective. Air attacks helped quell rebellions in Iraq and other colonies whose peoples were unaccustomed to air attack and lacked any means of retaliation or defense. Once World War II came, though, Britain faced a new, much larger Iraqi rebellion, which air power alone failed to stem.

In contrast to strategic bombing advocates, Ferdinand Otto Miksche warned against expecting too much from aircraft. Writing in the middle of World War II, he noted that fighting on land decided all the war's early campaigns. Even the invasion of Crete by German paratroops was decided on land in the fierce fighting for the island's handful of air bases. "While the aircraft has a place in the war machine," he wrote, "it can never of itself become the war machine." Air power's proper role was to support land power (Miksche, p. 9). In this regard, his ideas mirrored those of Corbett on sea power. As important as sea (or air) power might be to winning wars, people lived on land and that was where wars would be decided.

American Air Power Thought

YET, THE ALLURE OF strategic air power remained. Alexander de Seversky, a Russian emigre to the United States, captured this in his book *Victory Through Airpower* (1942). Walt Disney was among his fans, and he produced the animated film *Victory Through Airpower* (1943), which promoted Seversky's ideas. Disney's film brought these arguments into the mainstream and popularized strategic bombing as a cheap, efficient, and relatively bloodless (for one's own people) route to military victory.

Like Seversky, American air power advocates accepted Douhet's ideas. Many, though, including Billy Mitchell, who commanded the U.S. air service in the First World War, hoped to humanize them. Instead of mass air attacks on enemy cities, they advocated precision attacks on enemy "vital centers." Pinpoint attacks on a handful of vital production centers, they thought, would paralyze enemy industry while keeping civilian deaths to a minimum. Americans developed accurate bomb sights to facilitate these attacks, but they proved ineffective in Europe's cloudy skies. American assumptions that their heavily armed bombers could fight their way through German defenses with minimal losses also proved false. In 1943, they suffered significant losses without inflicting crippling damage on German ball bearing plants at Schweinfurt and Regensburg and other targets.

Post-War Air Power Debates

DESPITE THE DEVASTATING bombing of German and Japanese cities in World War II, which killed hundreds of thousands and left millions more homeless, the war failed to settle whether air power alone could win wars. Contrary to prewar predictions, the morale of British, German, and Japanese civilians did not crack despite heavy bombing.

Civilian morale proved equally resilient in later wars. H. G. Wells accurately predicted this in *War in the Air* (1908). Despite the horrific destruction he expected aerial armadas to inflict on heavily populated cities, Wells believed people would fight on in prolonged, bloody wars in which as many civilians as soldiers died.

There have been many devastating aerial surprise attacks, including Germany's opening air assault against the Soviet Union, Japan's attack on Pearl Harbor, and Israel's destruction of Egypt's air force in the 1967 Six Day War. Yet, these and similar surprise aerial attacks did not produce the enemy's physical and moral collapse. Both the Soviet Union and the United States went on to win World War II. Israel's 1967 victories enhanced its security by capturing the Golan Heights, Sinai Desert, and the West Bank, but failed to change its strategic situation. It remained surrounded by heavily armed, hostile nations that attacked again only six years later.

Air power debates continue today. Some insist, like Miksche, that air power's role is to facilitate the advance of ground and naval forces. Others argue air power can win wars alone, either through the devastation of massive bombing or by decapitating enemy leadership with precise strikes by guided weapons, an option unavailable in twentieth century wars. As Air Force historian Phillip Meilinger notes, the "history of air strategy is really a history of air targeting" (Meilinger, 170). What targets can planes hit with what strategic effect?

Strategies of air power exist at this intersection between capabilities and targets whose destruction will produce strategic results. The mass urban bombings of World War II proved the only effective way to use the heavy bombers of the era. Despite claims to precision bombing, American B-17 and B-24 bombers were lucky if their bombs fell within 1,000 feet of their targets. Early in the war, British planners discovered that most of the bombs they dropped fell more than a mile from their targets. The only way to achieve their strategic aim of destroying vital German industry and transportation nodes was to level whole cities to the ground, a strategy Britain's leaders adopted before their American allies. Bombing accuracy has improved with each succeeding generation, but its ability to produce strategic results is inconsistent.

Bombing Korea and Vietnam

AMERICAN AND ALLIED forces dominated the sky in the Korean and Vietnam Wars, yet suffered significant losses, particularly over North Vietnam, which came to boast the world's densest air defense network. In Korea, American bombers leveled Pyongyang and other North Korean cities and smashed dykes and irrigation systems. The latter caused widespread starvation and influenced Chinese leaders to seek peace, less because of civilian deaths than because Chinese troops relied on food grown in North Korea to feed themselves.

A generation later, American bombing in Vietnam proved much less effective. Its use remains fiercely debated. The United States steadily increased military aid to South Vietnam in the 1960s, including aircraft. In 1965, the United States deployed troops to protect the airbases from which these planes operated. The growing commitment of American troops to the war, who eventually numbered over 540,000, was matched by increasing U.S. air operations, both in tactical roles to support American and South Vietnamese troops, and in a strategic bombing campaign. Named Rolling Thunder, it aimed to pressure North Vietnam to end the war—or at least cease supporting communist insurgents in South Vietnam with supplies and reinforcements.

North Vietnamese troops and supplies traveled down the Ho Chi Minh Trail, a growing network of roads, trails, and supply depots in neighboring Laos and Cambodia. Despite massive American bombing, supplies kept flowing down the trail. Even worse, Communist insurgents became expert at defusing unexploded American bombs and reusing their components to kill American and South Vietnamese soldiers.

U.S. Air Force leaders also promised to shut down North Vietnam's economy by bombing key industrial nodes, but this effort also failed. North Vietnam was not Germany. The nation possessed few industrial targets worth bombing, and their destruction made little difference in North Vietnam's ability to wage war, since China and the Soviet Union supplied it with arms. For much of the war, tens of thousands of Chinese troops stationed in North Vietnam helped repair damage from American bombing raids.

In developing its bombing campaign, the Johnson administration relied on Robert Osgood, Thomas Schelling, and other political scientists who applied game theory to war. They applied mathematical models developed for games like prisoner's dilemma, in which accused criminals must decide whether to keep their mouths shut or rat out their friends. They compared strategic bombing to the pressure police and prosecutors apply to accused criminals in their custody.

Increased bombing of North Vietnam, they believed, would communicate U.S. intentions to North Vietnamese leaders and punish them for continuing the war and supporting the insurgency in the South. Bombing pauses, in turn, would convince them of American sincerity and encourage them to negotiate a peaceful end to the war. So, Americans would reward good North Vietnamese behavior with bombing pauses and punish North Vietnamese troop infiltration and other escalations with increased bombing or the bombing of more vital targets.

The effort failed. North Vietnamese society not only adjusted to American bombing, but North Vietnamese diplomats manipulated American leaders into a succession of bombing halts by promising negotiations that never materialized. As physicist Albert Einstein once noted, "in theory, theory and practice are the same. In practice, they are not."

Game Theory proved inapplicable to strategic decision making and the conduct of war. Osgood later admitted that "punitive bargaining" failed. Games rely on a shared understanding of the rules and players' willingness to operate within those rules. They don't flip over the board when they're losing. They don't escalate the conflict by pulling out knives or guns during a Monopoly game. In actual wars, they do.

As Clausewitz noted, there are no fixed rules in war. North Vietnam's leaders not only refused to play by the United States' rules, but also used those rules to manipulate American leaders. Following Sun Tzu's dictum, they knew their enemies and used that knowledge to confuse them.

Tiamat's Wrath (2019), the eighth book in James A. Corey's Expanse series, offers a similar example. The Laconian Empire attempts to apply prisoner's dilemma to a diplomatic problem with an alien species they do not understand and with whom they cannot communicate except through violence. The result, of course, is disastrous. Like the North Vietnamese, the aliens have no obligation to play the game by its rules—rules one cannot even communicate to them.

American bombing toward the end of the Vietnam War proved more effective. This resulted from the introduction of a new generation of guided bombs, which facilitated accurate strikes on difficult to reach targets. Equally important were American diplomatic overtures to China and the USSR. Their leaders assured Richard Nixon they would not intervene in the war if the U.S. escalated its bombing around North Vietnam's capital of Hanoi and its major port at Haiphong. In contrast to the Johnson administration, which avoided bombing Haiphong, fearing hitting Soviet freighters and triggering Soviet retaliation, the Nixon administration heavily bombed and mined Haiphong, closing North Vietnam's primary entry point for munitions critical to its war effort.

Many scholars credit these late war bombing campaigns (Linebacker 1 and Linebacker 2) with convincing North Vietnam's leaders to sign a peace treaty with the U.S. In exchange for the return of American prisoners of war, the United States withdrew its troops from South Vietnam and abandoned its ally. It was hardly the "peace with honor" Nixon promised, but it was peace.

John Warden, Five Rings, and the Gulf War

AMERICAN DEFEAT IN Vietnam encouraged dramatic reform at U.S. war colleges, particularly the Naval War College, Army War College, and Command and General Staff College. Senior military leaders, such as Admiral Stansfield Turner, recommitted the nation's war colleges to teaching classic strategic thought to mid-grade officers. Clausewitz became the centerpiece of war college curricula. Air power's failure in Vietnam similarly reinvigorated discussions of air strategy.

As military historian Hew Strachan notes, new technologies mostly "enable tactical and operational effects." Rather than changing the strategic situation, they act as force-multipliers, increasing one's lethality and effectiveness in battle. Only rarely, he argues, has air power proved "independently and strategically decisive." The First Gulf War, in which the United States led a coalition of allies to defeat Iraq and liberate Kuwait, offers a rare example in which air power dramatically influence a war's outcome (Strachan, *The Direction of War,* 191).

After building up forces in Saudi Arabia, the American-led coalition opened the war with a 38-day air campaign. Influenced by John Warden and other U.S. Air Force theorists, coalition air attacks struck targets throughout Iraq and occupied Kuwait. Nicknamed "Instant Thunder" (to contrast it with Vietnam's Rolling Thunder) Warden's plan aimed to knock out Iraqi political and military leadership and rapidly reduce Iraq's ability to wage war. Air power would directly target enemy centers of gravity to sever the connections between enemy leadership, its troops in the field, and civilian population.

Warden grouped his target priorities into five rings. He proposed coalition forces attack critical targets in each ring, aiming to paralyze Iraqi commanders and force their surrender.

First came national leadership, followed closely by what Warden termed "organic essentials." These second priority targets included military and political command, control, and communications systems, as well as energy production, such as oil refineries and electrical power plants, systems Warden labels as "essential for waging war." As part of these attacks, coalition forces would also attack Iraqi air bases, radar stations, and ground-based air defenses to eliminate Iraq's air force and win command of the air.

Critical infrastructure constituted the third ring. By this Warden meant the systems that bind together a modern economy. These include bridges and other transportation nodes, energy transmission lines, airfields, and factories.

Fourth came the enemy's civilian population. Like Douhet and Trenchard, Warden believed bombing could produce profound psychological effects among the civilian population. Unlike them, though, Warden declared direct attacks on civilians morally reprehensible. Instead, he advocated "indirect" attacks to encourage civilians to oppose the war and turn against their government. This is the fuzziest part of Warden's proposal. It's unclear what targets could be destroyed to influence a civilian population without killing civilians.

Fifth and final, Warden advocated attacks on enemy military forces, but only if attacks on rings one through four failed to produce results. This prioritization of civilian over military targets underlines the continuing influence of Douhet on air power theory.

In the Gulf War, coalition commander General Norman Schwarzkopf overruled Warden's acolytes and insisted on significant attacks on Iraqi armed forces, which critics derided as pointless, "tank plinking." Following weeks of air attacks, which Schwarzkopf and his staff thought had destroyed about half of Iraq's tanks and other military vehicles, the coalition ground forces began their offensive. In fact, these air attacks only destroyed about a tenth of Iraq's tanks. Nonetheless, coalition ground forces inflicted heavy losses on the Iraqi army and liberated Kuwait in about 100 hours.

Whether air power alone could have won the Gulf War, as Warden and his acolytes argue, is uncertain. The air campaign, though, paved the way for a stunningly rapid advance by American and allied ground forces.

The *Gulf War Air Power Survey,* a multi-volume analysis of the campaign produced by leading scholars, proclaimed: "for the first time in history, air power had reached the expectations of its proponents" (1993, II, 327). A decade later, in its second war with Iraq, the United States repeated its success in a combined air and ground campaign that aimed to "shock and awe" Iraqi troops and their leaders. Precision air attacks and "thunder runs" by rapidly advancing American tanks and other armored vehicles quickly overwhelmed a much weaker Iraqi army. This success, though, failed to prevent the emergence of a determined Iraqi insurgency. Even in such a military mismatch, air power alone could not win a war.

Case Study: Bombing Germany in WWII

AMERICAN, BRITISH, and German leaders entered World War II confident air power would have a significant, even decisive, effect on the war's outcome. All three devoted substantial funding to their air forces. The U.S. and Britain constructed large, four-engine bombers, the American B-17 and B-24 and the British Halifax, Lancaster, and Stirling. German efforts to do the same failed, in part because German civil aviation lagged that of Britain and U.S. and provided an insufficient foundation to develop large aircraft and the large engines needed to power them. So, Germany relied on two-engine medium bombers throughout World War II.

Early in the war, German bombers inflicted heavy damage on Rotterdam, Warsaw, and other cities. Yet, German efforts to bomb Britain into submission over the summer and fall of 1940 failed, despite killing 50,000 civilians and inflicting considerable damage. Germany failed to win air superiority. Despite some trying days, the Royal Air Force won the Battle of Britain.

German bombers suffered heavy losses from British defending aircraft in daylight raids, so the Germans switched to bombing at night. Britain, which continued to send bombers against Germany, faced similar problems and did the same. Since bombers could not distinguish factories, airfields, and other targets at night, both

British and German leaders transitioned to area bombing. Leveling whole cities in nighttime raids seemed the only way to destroy enemy industry.

Over time, British bombing accuracy improved thanks to better training, the creation of an elite "pathfinder" force to lead raids, and the adoption of radar and various electronic navigation devices.

In July 1943, British bombers struck Hamburg in force over two consecutive nights. American bombers hit the city during the day. Britain's pathfinders hit the Hamburg's lumber yard, the largest in Europe, which was packed with Baltic timber dried by the summer heat. Fires broke out across the city, overwhelming firefighters. Bomber after bomber dropped their bombs into these fires, igniting the war's first firestorm. Winds reached 300 miles per hour and temperatures soared over 1,500 degrees. Wooden structures burst into flame. Asphalt streets ignited.

Germany's most successful raid against England destroyed 100 acres of Coventry. Britain's raid on Hamburg destroyed over 6,000 acres (four square miles) and killed about 40,000 people, many of whom asphyxiated in bomb shelters. The raid knocked out about 75% of the city's electric works and other critical infrastructure, dropping industrial production by half. Albert Speer, who coordinated Nazi Germany's economy, suggested a half dozen similar strikes on major cities could end the war.

That didn't happen. Supreme Allied Commander Dwight Eisenhower redirected American and British bombers against Nazi defenses in France to prepare for the Allied landings in Normandy the following year.

Before then William Harris, who commanded Britain's Bomber Command, committed his planes to bomb Berlin. They struck Berlin night after night for most of five months. Bomber Command, which rarely had more than 1,000 bombers available, lost 1,128 planes in these raids. While they reduced large parts of Berlin to rubble, the sustained bombing did not force Germany's surrender as Harris expected. Instead, the heavy losses decimated his own command. Morale among air crews plummeted.

American bombers suffered similarly heavy losses against defending German aircraft in daylight raids in 1943. Contrary to prewar predictions, heavily armed American bombers could not fight through to their targets and bomb accurately with minimal losses. The bomber did not "always get through." Yet, American industrial production was such that its air forces grew despite its losses. Soon, the U.S. sent 500, 1,000, and eventually 2,000 bombers on missions.

By 1944, escorting fighters protected American bombers. American leaders changed from targeting ball bearing plants, which proved difficult to destroy, to aircraft factories, air bases, oil refineries, and synthetic oil plants. Their idea was to destroy the German air force by targeting the installations on which it depended.

The German air force, of course, fought back, and suffered heavy losses against numerically and qualitatively superior American aircraft. Between January and May 1944, Germany's air force suffered 91% losses in pilots. It never recovered.

Heavy raids against German cities resumed following the Allies' invasion and liberation of France in the summer and fall of 1944. Yet Allied bombers failed to replicate the success of Hamburg until the last months of the war. In February 1945, a raid on Dresden produced similar devastation. By then, though, Allied troops had entered Germany and were advancing at will. The Dresden raid did nothing to hasten the war's end. Germany surrendered three months later, on May 7, following Hitler's suicide and Berlin's capture by Soviet troops.

Heavy bombers were expensive to build, required large crews, and suffered heavy losses. At its peak, Bomber Command accounted for about a third of British military spending. Bomber Command lost 12,000 planes and 55,000 dead during the war, the highest attrition rate of any British service (44% of the 125,000 who flew died; another 10,000 were captured by the Germans). About 40,000 American bomber crewmembers died in the air war with Germany, along with thousands more in training accidents.

So, what did American and British bombing contribute to Allied victory?

All told, American and British bombers dropped about 1.6 million tons of bombs on Germany, which killed over 300,000 people and left millions more homeless. The 161,000 tons of conventional bombs Americans dropped on Japan, many of them incendiaries, killed even more people, a death toll increased by two atomic bombs. Yet, the strategic efficacy of bombing remains debated. Air power advocates like Harris argued bombing alone could have defeated Nazi Germany, if only his bombers had stayed focused on smashing German cities. Yet, the findings of the post-war *Strategy Bombing Survey* were inconclusive.

Certainly, the bombing campaigns gave Allied forces command of the air, which facilitated the advance of their armies across occupied Europe and into Nazi Germany. While Soviet leader Joseph Stalin complained Britain and America were slow to open a second front, by which he meant a full-scale amphibious invasion of Western Europe, Nazi leaders treated the air campaign as a second front. Roughly a third of German war production went to aircraft, two-thirds of which by 1944 were fighters to defend against Allied bombers. In 1944, a third of all large caliber guns produced in Germany were anti-aircraft guns, as was 20% of the ammunition (by tonnage). That year, half of Germany's large caliber guns were deployed in Germany to shoot down Allied bombers.

Yet, many argue the resources devoted to heavy bombers should have been spent on ground forces and tactical aircraft to support them. A 500-plane American bombing raid required 5,000 air crew, 30,000 ground crew, and at least 30,000 other support personnel.

The U.S. alone could easily have fielded another dozen ground combat divisions by redirecting production and personnel away from heavy bombers into tank and infantry divisions and tactical aircraft. Claims air power alone could have won the war are exaggerated. Nonetheless, the Anglo-American bombing campaign destroyed the German air force, which facilitated the Normandy landings and rapid Allied advance across France. It focused German attention and consumed a significant share of German military production. In the war's last year, Allied bombing became more accurate. Americans focused on Germany's railroads and a handful of oil refineries and synthetic oil plants. As a result, the German troops were critically short of gasoline and other supplies in the war's last months. By then, though, the war was almost won. Allied bombing hastened the end of the war, but did not end the war on its own, as air power advocates expected.

LIKE COMMAND OF THE sea, command of the air has proved difficult to achieve. Even as British and American bomber forces grew during World War II, Germany contested control of its air space with airplanes and ground-based defenses. Destroying German factories proved difficult. Aerial bombing wrecked buildings, but often left critical machinery only lightly damaged and easy to repair. The Germans hardened some factories and moved others underground. They also imported iron and other resources from neutral Sweden and Switzerland. Rather than cracking, bombing seemed to harden German civilian morale. A generation later, North Vietnam proved similarly difficult to bomb into submission.

The two Gulf Wars and NATO's 1999 intervention in Kosovo present rare cases in which one side achieved air supremacy. In all three of these wars, though, one side was hopelessly outnumbered and overmatched. Achieving command of the air in campaigns between equals, such as the Battle of Britain or the 1973 Arab-Israeli War, is more difficult. Unless one side has an overwhelming qualitative or quantitative advantage, the promise of air power remains fleeting.

Thus far, no one has managed to repeat Israel's stunning 1967 air attacks that destroyed Egypt's air force on the ground. It's also worth remembering that afterward Israel used its air force to support its ground forces, which in six days captured the Golan Heights, Sinai Peninsula, and West Bank. Israel did not try to bomb its enemies "back to the stone age," as former U.S. Air Force commander Curtis LeMay urged the U.S. to do in Vietnam.

Much as Julian Corbett emphasized that achieving local sea control was both more practical and more important than globe-spanning "command of the sea," local air superiority to facilitate ground or naval operations is generally all one needs. Israel never won command of the air in 1973, but it achieved the local air superiority needed to support offensives against Egypt and Syria that forced the war's conclusion.

It's also worth remembering Sun Tzu's advice. "The best policy is to take a state intact." Neither conqueror nor peacemaker benefits from bombing an enemy nation "back to the stone age." The vast destruction caused by bombing hampered the postwar reconstructions not only of heavily bombed Germany and Japan, but of Britain, France, Korea, and other members of the victorious allied coalition.

Many air power theories proved false. So far, civilian morale has yet to crack under sustained air attack. Governments proved similarly resilient in the face of sustained bombing. Nuclear weapons, though, changed that calculus by offering levels of destruction unparalleled in human history. Discussions of nuclear strategy, the subject of the next chapter, drew on theories of air power and took them to their logical and most horrific conclusion, the destruction of whole cities and civilizations.

Wiping out whole cities and civilizations is something only the worst of fictional villains would do. Nonetheless, sustained air campaigns offer interesting settings for writers. Connie Willis set several of her time travel stories during the Battle of Britain, forcing characters to deal with—and hopefully avoid—the random destruction of German bombing raids. Kurt Vonnegut's *Slaughterhouse-Five* addresses the Allied firebombing of Dresden. The exploits of bomber crews, such as the crew of the *Memphis Belle*, the first American bomber crew to complete the requisite 25 combat missions against Germany to allow the crew to rotate home, inspired numerous novels and movies. The best of these, such as the movie *Twelve O'Clock High* (1949) demonstrate the psychological strains of prolonged combat.

The ethical dilemmas and psychological pressures on bomber crews are central themes in many novels, including Len Deighton's *Bomber* (1970) and Joseph Heller's *Catch 22* (1961). Deighton's novel describes a fictitious British bombing raid on a German city in meticulous detail. He highlights the high casualties and fragile morale of British bomber crews, 55,000 of whom died during the war, the moral ambiguities of their mission of mass destruction, and the civilian death toll, particularly from firestorms, which feature in the novel but were actually quite rare during the war. Bomber crews faced the combined psychological pressures of executing dangerous, morally ambiguous missions over and over again. They risked their lives to kill defenseless civilians by the tens of thousands.

Joseph Heller flew 60 missions during the war and understood the pressures air crew faced. In *Catch 22*, he explores this psychological stress through the eyes of protagonist John Yossarian, a bombardier in an American bomber. As Yossarian notes, the air force grounded officers it considered crazy, and bombing missions were so dangerous you would have to be crazy to want to fly more of them. Yet, recognizing these dangers proved one's sanity. So, "if he flew them, he was crazy and didn't have to, but if he didn't want to, he was sane and had to" (Heller, Chapter 5).

John Yossarian is hardly the only fictional character who should have to deal with the twin problems of combat stress and the apparent illogic of military administration and bureaucracy.

Chapter Five: Nuclear Strategy and Game Theory

The development and use of nuclear weapons in World War II's closing days called into question the existing body of strategic thought. In the nuclear era's first years, strategists worked to integrate atomic weapons into existing military structures and war plans. Most soon found this impracticable. As Bernard Brodie noted in 1946, "thus far the chief purpose of our military establishment has been to win wars. From now on, its chief purpose must be to avert them. It can have almost no other purpose" (*The Absolute Weapon*, p. 76). Future science fiction luminary Arthur C. Clarke, then a Royal Air Force lieutenant, similarly concluded that in the nuclear age the primary goal of military forces must be to prevent wars ("The Rocket and the Future of Warfare").

The importance of deterrence became more evident in the 1950s following the development of hydrogen (thermonuclear) bombs. These weapons, exponentially more powerful than the two atomic bombs the United States dropped on Japan, made all-out nuclear war unthinkable. Following such a war, commentators noted it would be all but impossible to tell the winners from the losers. So, military planners focused on deterrence.

An effective deterrence, though, required the capability and willingness to wage nuclear war. As any number of firearms instructors have cautioned, "don't point a gun at someone if you're not willing to use it." The same applied to nuclear weapons.

Military forces needed the weapons, early warning radar and satellites, and other systems to effectively wage nuclear war. Civilians, in turn, required fallout shelters and other preparations to have any chance of surviving. So, planning for nuclear war consumed vast intellectual effort in the Cold War's first decades.

The novelty of nuclear weapons, the scientific expertise needed to develop them, and their amenability to mathematical analysis, opened the door to civilian strategists. While making strategy was never the exclusive work of military officers, more civilians than ever weighed in on strategic issues in the nuclear era.

Bernard Brodie, Herman Kahn, Albert Wohlstetter, and other civilian strategists grappled with the implications of nuclear war alongside military officers. Many of them worked for the newly formed RAND Corporation, a think tank created by the Douglas Aircraft Company, to do research and analysis (R and D) for the U.S. Air Force. When one Air Force general complained about this influx of civilians into what he considered an exclusive military preserve, Alain Enthoven, a RAND Corporation economist, famously quipped: "General, I've fought just as many nuclear wars as you have."

Unlike past strategic discussions, civilians assumed central roles both in developing nuclear strategy and in explaining it to the general public. While few people read Brodie or Wohlstetter, Kahn's alarmist and morbid *On Thermonuclear War* (1960) became a best-seller. Those who didn't read the book, heard about it in popular media or saw Walter Matthau portray a Kahn-like character urging an all-out nuclear strike in the movie *Fail Safe* (1964). Speculative fiction featured tales of nuclear war, while newspapers and national magazines terrified people with reports on the size of nuclear arsenals and the likely outcomes of nuclear war.

These fears provoked both anti-nuclear activists, who aimed to eliminate nuclear weapons, and so-called survivalists who prepared to survive nuclear war, among them science fiction authors Robert A. Heinlein and Jerry Pournelle.

Like the Webber family in the movie *Blast from the Past* (1999), several million Americans built backyard or basement fallout shelters in the 1950s and 1960s and stocked them with emergency supplies. Relatively few, though, were as elaborate as the Webbers', which contained food, power, and other supplies to sustain the family for 35 years.

Civilian analysts came to dominate nuclear planning for three reasons. First, nuclear strategy is the study of the non-use of nuclear weapons. So far. We have no body of historical literature or personal experience to inform nuclear strategy. It is an intellectual exercise in which civilians and military officers may engage equally.

Second, and related to the first, nuclear war is primarily about target selection on which economists and other civilian specialists are often better informed than military officers.

Third, nuclear weapons figure prominently in diplomatic crises. Since civilians determine foreign policy and guide grand strategy, they dominate discussions of nuclear strategy. Since using a single nuclear could instigate an apocalyptic thermonuclear exchange, nuclear weapons cannot be treated like other weapons. Civilian determination of their use is essential, and it is civilian leaders who determine if and when during international crises to make nuclear threats.

A Nuclear First Strike

WHILE SOME COMMENTATORS thought nuclear weapons invalidated past strategic wisdom, nuclear strategists actually built on the ideas of air power theorists, particularly Douhet. While the planes and bombs of Douhet's day could not deliver the devastating first strikes he promised, nuclear weapons could.

The possibility of a nuclear first strike, a "nuclear Pearl Harbor," as Americans called it, shaped nuclear strategy discussions. A well-executed surprise first strike could destroy a nation's nuclear arsenal, leaving it unable to deter follow-up strikes targeting its cities. Nuclear blackmail, what Lawrence Freedman labeled compellence, would surely follow. Give in to our demands or face mass death and the utter destruction of your civilization.

Bernard Brodie suggested the opposite might also work. In "Must We Shoot from the Hip?" he suggested only destroying part of Soviet industry in the first strike and retaining weapons for a follow-up strike, essentially holding Russia's remaining cities hostage to coerce a peace agreement.

Fears of a nuclear first strike increased in the late 1950s as the major powers developed ballistic missiles. Airplanes required many hours to travel between the Soviet Union and the United States. Intercontinental ballistic missiles (ICBMs) needed only a few dozen minutes. Short-range missiles based in nearby countries, such as American missiles in Turkey or Soviet missiles in Cuba, required even less time.

These fears focused attention on defense and survival. When even a single nuclear weapon could kill hundreds of thousands of people, defense would have to near perfection. Defending aircraft could intercept and shoot down enemy bombers. Defending against ballistic missiles, which in descent travel more than a mile per second, appeared impossible. Unlike bombers, missiles would "always get through."

Some nuclear strategists suggested the United States could win a nuclear war with the Soviets while suffering "acceptable losses" of only a few million deaths. Such talk horrified not only common citizens, but their leaders as well. During the 1962 Cuban Missile Crisis, President John F. Kennedy rejected suggestions to attack Soviet missiles in Cuba. A single surviving missile could devastate Atlanta, Miami, or other cities in range.

Originally published in 1965, the darkly humorous card game *Nuclear War* plays out this grim calculus. Players take turns firing nuclear missiles at one another. A player whose last people are killed gets to launch a retaliatory strike. This can trigger a cascade as that doomed player's retaliatory strike wipes out another player's population, triggering their retaliatory strike, and so on. Often, no one wins the game. Everyone dies. The same appeared true of nuclear war.

Deterring a First Strike

SINCE A FOOLPROOF DEFENSE against nuclear attack seemed impossible, strategists focused on deterring an enemy from executing a nuclear first strike.

Strategists define a first strike as an attack aimed at eliminating the enemy's nuclear weapons, not simply the first shots fired in a nuclear war. A second strike is the retaliatory attack fired against the enemy that launched the first strike. While first strikes aim at missiles and other nuclear weapons, second strikes target cities. They aim to punish the aggressor, devastating its cities and industries, and leaving it unable to wage war—or possibly survive as a civilization.

Executing a second strike requires possession of a large, survivable stockpile of nuclear weapons, along with secure communication to those weapons, to ensure a second strike so devastating that no rational person would risk launching a first strike.

A successful first strike requires accurate weapons that can destroy hardened missile silos and similar installations. More important, it requires locating the enemy's entire nuclear arsenal. The made-for-TV movie *The Day After* (1983) opened with a failed Soviet first strike. Soviet ICBMS strike American missile silos in Kansas, but the silos are empty. While unexplained in the movie, one assumes American early warning systems detected the incoming missiles. The United States launched its ICBMS before they were destroyed in their silos.

The movie highlighted another important point. Many military installations are in or near cities. One cannot launch a nuclear first strike that only hits military targets.

Several studies, including the 1957 Gaither Report and Wohlstetter's "The Delicate Balance of Terror" warned the U.S. was vulnerable to a Soviet first strike. U.S. leaders needed to harden missile silos, disperse aircraft, and take other steps to ensure they could retaliate against—and thus deter—a Soviet nuclear attack.

The United States and Soviet Union produced a variety of nuclear weapons and launch systems of various sizes to ensure their retaliatory capability. These included ICBMs, intermediate-range ballistic missiles, bombers, cruise missiles, and a host of short-range weapons scattered across hundreds of airbases, underground silos, and other sites. Submarines soon joined them, prowling the ocean with a dozen or more nuclear missiles each. No first strike could eliminate all these weapons.

Several commentators suggested creating doomsday weapons. These large, survivable nuclear weapons would detonate in the event one's civilization was destroyed—or communication with the device was severed. Parodied in the movie *Dr. Strangelove* (1964), both superpowers considered building such systems. The Soviet Union deployed a "dead hand" launch system that would transfer launch authority to individual nuclear missile commanders if the system lost communication with Soviet command centers. Such systems are inherently destabilizing. Also, as Dr. Strangelove explains, "the whole point of the doomsday machine is lost if you keep it a secret," which the Soviets did in both fiction and reality.

MILITARY STRATEGY FOR WRITERS 127

Deterrence depends not only on the ability to retaliate but also on the willingness to do so. Many scholars and writers have explored this conundrum, including science fiction author Theodore Sturgeon. In his story "Thunder and Roses" (1947), American leaders prepare to retaliate following a devastating nuclear attack on the United States even though radiation from American retaliatory strikes would spread and lay waste to the rest of the world.

Defending Against Nuclear Attack

FEARS OF NUCLEAR ATTACK, particularly a surprise first strike, encouraged both superpowers to develop anti-ballistic missiles (ABMs) to shoot down incoming ICBMS. In the late 1960s, the U.S. developed multiple independently targetable re-entry vehicles (MIRVs). These placed several—in some cases more than a dozen—warheads on a single ICBM or submarine-launched ballistic missile (SLBM). Intercepting all these incoming warheads would require a tremendous expenditure on thousands and thousands of defensive missiles. Neither superpower could afford that expenditure. In the 1980s, the United States experimented with space-based ABM systems as part of the Strategic Defense Initiative (SDI), soon nicknamed Star Wars, whose costs also seemed prohibitive.

The problem with any nuclear defense is that it would have to approach perfection. A system that achieved a 99% interception rate would be the most effective defensive system in human history. Yet, the Soviets could launch more than a thousand missiles, each with several warheads. Each of the two- or three-dozen warheads the almost perfect defense failed to intercept would destroy an American city and kill hundreds of thousands of people, perhaps millions, if it struck a high population city like New York or Houston. Most politicians found such losses unacceptable.

Another problem is that rivals could see effective defenses against nuclear attack as provocative. Leaders with effective defenses against nuclear attack would be more willing to launch a first strike, believing their ABM system would neutralize an enemy's second strike. Fearing that, an enemy might launch a first strike before the defender completed its ABM system. To prevent an unending arms race in both offensive and defensive missiles, the superpowers limited their development in a series of treaties in the 1970s and 1980s. Yet, both remained prepared to wage nuclear war.

Nuclear Proliferation

NUCLEAR STRATEGY EVOLVED in the 1950s and 1960s based on the cost and number of available bombs. At first few and expensive, improved technology, testing, and manufacturing techniques allowed both superpowers to assemble arsenals of hundreds and eventually thousands of nuclear weapons, moving from an era of scarcity to one of plenty and then superfluity. By the mid-1970s, both superpowers possessed enough weapons to devastate the world several times over. They achieved a state of mutual assured destruction (MAD). Even if struck by surprise, retaliation by the victim's surviving nuclear forces would destroy the aggressor.

Other nuclear powers, including Britain, France, and China, massed arsenals in the hundreds. In the 1970s and 1980s, India, Israel, and Pakistan joined the nuclear club and today probably have several dozen deployable nuclear weapons. These lesser nuclear powers also benefit from deterrence. Thus far, neither superpower has fought a nuclear-armed enemy. Both worked to limit the proliferation of nuclear weapons, as have some of the lesser nuclear powers, particularly Israel, which bombed nuclear weapons facilities in Iraq and Syria. Israel probably also worked with the United States to develop and unleash the Stuxnet computer virus, which set back Iran's nuclear weapons program many years.

Some commentators decried Israel's 1981 air attack on Iraq's Osirak nuclear reactor as unwarranted and a violation of international law. Others saw it as a legitimate example of preventative war. A nuclear-armed Iraq would have threatened not only Israel, but Saudi Arabia, Kuwait, and the other Gulf oil states, as well as Iran, with which Iraq was at war, having invaded the country six months earlier.

While the Israeli strike on Iraq's nuclear reactor derailed Iraq's nuclear program, it also encouraged other would-be nuclear powers to develop their nuclear capabilities more carefully and in greater secrecy. Preventing a potential opponent from developing nuclear weapons is quite difficult. Any nation with sufficient technical know-how and funding can do so. In 1965, for example, Pakistani President Zulfikar Ali Bhutto declared: "If India builds the bomb, we will eat grass or leaves, even go hungry, but we will get one of our own." India did, Pakistan followed, and in 1998 the two nations engaged in a series of provocative back-and-forth nuclear tests. North Korea likely has nuclear weapons. Other nations are close behind.

This is another reason to pursue nuclear weapons secretly. If your opponent is uncertain of your nuclear capabilities, they are less likely to attack. A first strike launched to eliminate an enemy's nuclear program could instead provoke a nuclear response from an enemy with a secret nuclear stockpile.

There is also the problem of international law and opinion. The circumstances justifying preventive war are unclear. In 1967, Egypt massed troops on Israel's border and closed the Red Sea to Israeli shipping, acts that signaled imminent hostilities and justified Israel's preemptive strike. In 1981, though, Israel faced no imminent threat from Iraq. Similarly, Israel faced no imminent threat from Syria a generation later when it attacked Syrian nuclear and chemical weapons facilities. In both cases, political leaders understood the point of Iraqi and Syrian nuclear weapons was to counter Israel's nuclear arsenal. Given the bellicose rhetoric from those nations, one could not rule out their willingness to execute a nuclear first strike.

The legalities of attacks on potential enemies' nuclear, chemical, or biological weapons programs are beyond the scope of this book. The more relevant question is, are they good strategy? Do the advantages of preventing or delaying an enemy's acquisition of nuclear weapons outweigh the risks of provoking that enemy's retaliation, either at the time or at some point in the future?

Nuclear Plans and Games

STRATEGIES OF AIR POWER depend on aircraft able to reach and destroy targets of strategic significance. Nuclear strategy similarly reflects the size and capabilities of one's nuclear arsenal. In 1947, the United States had only thirteen atomic bombs. At the time, they were expensive to build, had to be assembled just before use, and relied on planes like the B-29 to fight their way through enemy defenses to reach their targets. In this era of scarcity, strategists expected to use nuclear weapons only against the most important targets, such as major enemy cities or large troop concentrations.

During the 1950s and 1960s, the superpowers acquired more—and more powerful—nuclear weapons, which science fiction authors marked with a wave of apocalyptic novels, including *A Canticle for Leibowitz* (1957) by Walter M. Miller, Jr., Nevil Shute's *On the Beach* (1957), Mordecai Roshwald's *Level 7* (1959), and so many short stories that *Galaxy* magazine editor H. L. Gold complained "over 90% of stories submitted still nag away at atomic, hydrogen and bacteriological war."

Governments encouraged people to prepare for nuclear attack. The U.S. government published *Survival Under Atomic Attack* (1950), which warned people to shelter in subway tunnels or basements during a nuclear attack. Failing that, they should drop to the ground and shield their faces in their arms. After an attack, survivors should be wary of food and water contaminated by radiation, use the telephone only for emergencies, and avoid spreading rumors.

Other government publications explained how to safeguard one's home from fallout and build fallout shelters. *Popular Mechanics* offered plans for home shelters to suit a variety of budgets and do-it-yourself capabilities. While of uncertain effectiveness, Yale University psychologist Irving Janis suggested fallout shelters would mitigate people's fears of nuclear war ("Psychological Aspects of Vulnerability to Atomic Bomb Attacks").

The U.S. government abandoned civil defense efforts as nuclear arsenals increased in size and magnitude. Once the superpowers amassed arsenals sufficient to destroy every major city and military target several times over, effective civil defense became impossible. Weapon accuracy also improved, though with bombs tens or hundreds of times more powerful than those dropped on Hiroshima and Nagasaki, accuracy only mattered when targeting command centers, missile silos, and other hardened, underground installations.

An all-out nuclear war between the superpowers would have devastating consequences. Tens of millions of people would die in the initial attacks. Radiation would kill tens of millions more over the next days and weeks. Scientists warned of nuclear winters and other long-term aftereffects. Nuclear war would change the climate and devastate ecosystems.

Deterrence relied on the threat of the twin threats of genocide and ecocide. So, the superpowers maintained large, diverse, and survivable nuclear arsenals to ensure sufficient retaliatory capability to devastate any attacker. The personnel manning these arsenals drilled regularly to ensure they'd be ready when war came. Essentially, the major nuclear powers held their enemy's civilian population hostage. The certainty that all involved would lose a nuclear war preserved deterrence.

Yet, deterrence required a demonstrated willingness to fight this unwinnable war. Since no rational actor would start a nuclear war, American Secretary of State Henry Kissinger once suggested that it was important to appear irrational. One must demonstrate a willingness during foreign policy crises to push nuclear escalation to the brink of war, hence the term brinksmanship. Only then would an enemy take your threats seriously.

This apparently worked during the 1973 Arab-Israeli War. The Soviets threatened to intervene to support their Arab allies. The United States countered by ordering a nuclear alert and putting bombers in the air. The Soviets backed down. Threats of nuclear war played on fears of the unknown and incalculable. Once escalation began, leaders could lose control. Any panicked subordinate with a finger on "the button" could unleash nuclear Armageddon. Those fears encouraged caution among senior leaders.

Once war began, nuclear strikes would hit command centers, severing contact between senior political and military leaders and their subordinates in direct control of nuclear weapons, as well as with enemy leaders. Making peace would be impossible.

Equally worrisome was the prospect that a lesser nuclear power, like France, would take matters into its own hands, launch its own missiles, and trigger nuclear war between the superpowers.

Assorted analysts grappled with the twin problems of planning to fight nuclear wars and crisis management to prevent the outbreak of nuclear war.

When Robert S. McNamara became U.S. Secretary of Defense in 1961, senior military officers briefed him on the plan for nuclear war, the SIOP (Single Integrated Operational Plan). This involved launching every American missile and bomber at Soviet cities and industrial sites. Shocked, McNamara, an auto executive renowned for number crunching and long-term planning, responded: "General, you don't have a war plan. All you have is a kind of horrible spasm."

MILITARY STRATEGY FOR WRITERS

How then did people plan to fight a nuclear war? What were the strategic issues involved?

One option, discussed above, was to attack first, hoping to destroy most of an enemy's nuclear arsenal in a first strike. If this failed, though, what was the next step? How was an enemy likely to respond to a successful—or failed—first strike?

What if, rather than a massive first strike, the enemy used only one or a handful of nuclear weapons? What was the appropriate response? Was it possible to fight a limited nuclear war in which one employed only a few nuclear weapons? Could one confine the use of nuclear weapons to the battlefield with so-called tactical nuclear weapons? Or would the use of even a single nuclear weapon trigger a series of escalations leading to all-out nuclear war?

Political scientists and mathematicians applied game theory to these questions and the possibilities of nuclear war. They developed elaborate models to explore crisis management and the use of nuclear weapons. Yet, the answers to these questions remain unclear.

One might look at nuclear confrontation as a game of chicken. Two reckless teens drive their cars toward one another or toward some deadly obstacle. The one who swerves first, the "chicken," is declared the loser. The other wins, unless they die proving their bravery, as happens to "Buzz" in the movie *Rebel Without a Cause* (1955).

As a model for nuclear confrontation, chicken reinforces Kissinger's ideas of brinksmanship. The crazier and more suicidal you appear, the more likely your opponent is to back down. Except your opponent works to appear equally crazy and suicidal, returning us to the trial of wits between Vizzini and Wesley in *The Princess Bride*. It is a game of bluff and counter bluff with apocalyptic consequences.

Chicken is a two-person, zero-sum game. The outcome for one player is balanced by an equal but opposite outcome for the other. If one wins, the other loses. Or both lose by either swerving at the same time or colliding into one another.

Political scientists and mathematicians soon developed more elaborate models to simulate a variety of complex, multi-polar diplomatic crises and escalations toward nuclear war. John Von Neumann, a mathematician who pioneered the field of game theory and worked on the U.S. atomic bomb project during World War II, applied his skills to developing and targeting the U.S. nuclear arsenal in the 1950s. Among his propositions was that the U.S. and Soviet Union would reach a stable state of mutual assured destruction.

The person most associated with gaming nuclear war is Thomas Schelling, an economist whose works include the pioneering *The Strategy of Conflict* (1960). Schelling used game theory to explore how rivals maneuvered, bargained, and even cooperated in foreign policy crises involving nuclear weapons. How could one use threats of mutual nuclear annihilation to advance one's international interests while avoiding the actual outbreak of nuclear war? For Schelling, military threats—whether nuclear or conventional—were ways to signal one's intentions and determination to an enemy, real or potential. His ideas influenced the U.S. bombing campaign in Vietnam, Rolling Thunder, which aimed to force North Vietnam to the peace table.

Its failure highlights a problem with game theory. It is more descriptive than predictive. Enemies may doubt one's intentions or misread your signals. They may even be playing an entirely different game.

Prisoners Dilemma and other models developed by game theorists reflected the fears and risks of nuclear war, particularly once the superpowers reached a state of mutually assured destruction. They emphasized nuclear wars were unwinnable and thus fundamentally irrational. No sane person would escalate a crisis to the point nuclear war became likely. In that regard, game theory may have helped stabilize the Cold War and prevent the outbreak of nuclear war. Achieving that stability was the only rational strategy once the superpowers reached nuclear superfluity.

Cold War Containment and Deterrence

THE SOVIETS DETONATED their first nuclear weapon in a 1949 test, several years before most American analysts expected. Yet, despite determined efforts over the next decade, the Soviets remained well behind the U.S. in both numbers of nuclear weapons and the ability to deliver them, which required large aircraft, such as American B-47 and B-52 bombers.

Relying on their nuclear dominance in the 1950s, American leaders proclaimed a policy of massive retaliation to deter Soviet aggression. The U.S. would respond to Soviet attacks with overwhelming nuclear strikes at "places of our choosing." American leaders left it deliberately unclear what sort of aggression would trigger a nuclear response. Massive retaliation relied on this uncertainty. Enemies had no way to know when they crossed a threshold that triggered nuclear war.

As foreign policy and grand strategy, this was absurd. Would the United States respond to a communist revolution in an inconsequential country by nuking Moscow? Of course not. In the absence of an existential threat, such as a full-scale Soviet invasion of Western Europe, Japan, or another important U.S. ally, the threat of massive retaliation was hollow. This led the incoming administration of John F. Kennedy to introduce a policy of flexible response in 1961. The U.S. would respond with roughly equivalent and corresponding force to Soviet aggression. Kennedy and his advisors recognized that no single strategy, or weapons system, applies to all situations.

While poor policy in the real world, massive retaliation makes for a good game mechanic. Chris Crawford's groundbreaking computer game *Balance of Power* (1985) reduced every superpower dispute to nuclear threats in a deadly game of poker. At each crisis, superpowers increase the threat of nuclear war until one of them backs down or they trigger a nuclear war. In the latter case, the games ends with the famous text screen: "You have ignited a nuclear war. And no, there is no animated display or a mushroom cloud with parts of bodies flying through the air. We do not reward failure."

Twenty years later, Ananda Gupta and Jason Matthews adapted this idea to their award-winning board game, *Twilight Struggle* (2005). More nuanced than Crawford's game, it still pits the Cold War superpowers against one another as they seek allies and pursue regional influence around the world. Players win games by dominating the largest portion of the globe, though serious missteps may trigger a nuclear war. The player who triggers the nuclear exchange loses the game.

Game theory, along with games like *Nuclear War*, *Balance of Power*, and *Twilight Struggle*, model the horrific reality of nuclear war and illustrate the vital importance of deterrence. Unrestrained nuclear war would kill hundreds of millions of people, probably billions. But could one fight a limited nuclear war?

Limited Nuclear War, Escalation, and De-escalation

IN THE 1950S, MANY analysts, including Henry Kissinger, thought limited nuclear wars were possible. In "A Concise History of the Crostic Union War" (1962), Edward Teller, the "father of the H-Bomb," suggested the U.S. could win a limited nuclear war against the Soviet Union given a sufficiently determined president willing to suffer "acceptable losses." While fellow atomic scientist Robert Oppenheimer frequently disagreed with Teller, he, too, urged military planners to bring "battle back to the battlefield." They should focus on fighting and winning battles rather than annihilating cities and civilizations.

In the event of a Soviet invasion of Western Europe, or perhaps Yugoslavia or another non-aligned nation, NATO planned nuclear strikes against East Germany and other Soviet allies, but not the Soviet Union itself. NATO leaders hoped to keep the war limited even after they escalated to nuclear weapons. Some hoped to confine a prospective European war to tactical nuclear weapons, those between one-tenth and one-hundredth the power of the Hiroshima and Nagasaki bombs. The problem, as Bernard Brodie quipped, was that "people saved by us through our free use of nuclear weapons" would probably be the last people ever to ask the United States for help ("More about Limited War," 117).

Nonetheless, American and Soviet soldiers prepared to fight limited nuclear wars. The U.S. Army replaced the previous triangular organization of its divisions into three regiments with five battlegroups designed to disperse widely on nuclear battlefields. Highly mobile American troops with networked communications planned to engage attacking Soviet divisions by using tactical nuclear weapons. Absent the spaceships and powered combat armor, this is the war portrayed by Heinlein in *Starship Troopers*. His novel reflected military thought in the late 1950s.

Some planners assumed tactical nuclear weapons favored defenders. Massing attackers would present better targets than dispersed defenders. On the other hand, attackers might use nuclear weapons to blow holes in enemy defenses through which they advanced. A surprise attack and/or rapid movement could quickly intermingle enemy and friendly troops, making nuclear weapons difficult to use.

Other commentators suggested restricting nuclear war to tactical weapons would limit damage to major cities and other populated areas. Except that many cities occupy river crossings or other geographic chokepoints that make them military targets—even more so if a city contains military bases, airfields, or similar facilities. West German leaders were particularly concerned about this since a war between NATO and the Soviet Union and its Warsaw Pact allies would be fought mostly in Germany. As one German leader quipped, a tactical nuclear weapon was one that "detonated in Germany." Few Germans relished the idea of turning their country into a nuclear battlefield.

Ultimately, discussions of limited nuclear focused on keeping nuclear wars limited. How did you prevent the enemy from escalating? Once someone launched a nuke, how did you prevent tit-for-tat retaliation in which the antagonists fired more—and ever larger—nukes?

Many scholars have addressed the problem of escalation without resolving it. Herman Khan famously presented a "nuclear escalation ladder" composed of 44 rungs. These range from the start of a crisis and diplomatic posturing to various levels of nuclear war (starting at rung 15) culminating in a spasm in which the superpowers unleash their full nuclear arsenals. Kahn labeled this "insensate war," the point at which political leaders abandoned all restraint, unleashed their full arsenals, and lost control of the conflict.

Kahn suggested the first nuclear use would probably be a single weapon fired to warn an enemy against taking one step further. John Hackett posits this in his future war novel, *The Third World War* (1978). After their initial offensive fails and NATO's counterattacks make progress, the Soviets fire a nuclear missile at Great Britain, destroying Birmingham. NATO retaliates by nuking Kiev in Ukraine. Both superpowers step back from the brink before more cities are struck. In *Red Storm Rising* (1986), authors Tom Clancy and Larry

Bond similarly posit that a conventional war between the superpowers would lead them to escalate to nuclear war, but that they would step back from Armageddon after firing only a few nukes.

But once enemies fired a nuke or two, would one of them back down? Since nuclear deterrence had failed to prevent war, what chance was there that fears of nuclear escalation would halt a war already in progress? How do you prevent further escalation? How do you negotiate an end to a conflict that has gone nuclear before it escalates to Armageddon?

Bernard Brodie doubted one could. He also doubted nuclear powers would launch nukes in ones or twos. He assumed nuclear powers would use hundreds of weapons in their initial attacks to overwhelm the enemy. This made the decision for nuclear war "a race against annihilation," which the swiftest would win. If deterrence failed, he argued, it would fail catastrophically (*Strategy in the Missile Age*, 98).

Like the models of game theorists, Khan's escalation ladder is clearer in theory than in practice. Opponents would likely read signals differently and even envision different escalation ladders, opening the way to involuntary escalation as opponents misunderstood one another's actions and intentions. A huge 1983 NATO military exercise and wargame, for example, so alarmed Soviet leaders they put their forces on alert in anticipation of nuclear war. Uncertainty raised tensions between the superpowers but also fortified deterrence, and that deterrence kept the Cold War cold.

Case Study: The Cuban Missile Crisis

ON 14 OCTOBER 1962, American reconnaissance aircraft, which had monitored the Soviet miliary build-up in Cuba for several months, photographed the assembly of recently arrived Soviet nuclear missiles. Successive flights located more missile installations and related construction. Soviet leaders denied placing the missiles, escalating the crisis. Confronted with photographic evidence, the Soviets then claimed the nuclear missiles were for "defensive purposes."

Tense diplomatic conversions continued as American President John F. Kennedy discussed options with his senior advisors. These ranged from doing nothing to increasing diplomatic pressure on Cuba to military responses ranging from blockading Cuba, air strikes on the missiles, and a full-scale invasion to remove the missiles and topple Cuban dictator Fidel Castro.

At the time, the U.S. could hit the Soviet Union with about 5,000 nuclear warheads, delivered by aircraft or missiles. In contrast, the Soviets could only hit the United States with about 300 warheads plus the few dozen warheads Americans thought they had in Cuba. The latter could reach cities in the southern U.S. in a matter of minutes. The nuclear balance favored the United States. It could annihilate the Soviet Union while only, in the words of *Dr. Strangelove's* General Ripper, "getting its hair mussed."

Uncertain of allied support and worried about escalation, Kennedy ruled out an invasion, but placed American forces on nuclear alert. Bombers were ready to take-off at a moment's notice.

Following an emergency meeting of the United Nations Security Council, in which Soviet leaders again refused to admit they had placed nuclear missiles in Cuba, Kennedy ordered American bombers into the air and on continuous alert, the highest state of readiness short of outright war. A few days later, American warships halted Soviet cargo ships *en route* to Cuba. Other Soviet cargo ships turned back, but Soviet anti-aircraft missiles in Cuba shot down an American U-2 reconnaissance plane, killing its pilot.

Military leaders advocated immediate air strikes against Cuba, but Kennedy insisted on caution. He warned the Soviet ambassador that U.S. reconnaissance flights would continue. If they were fired on, it would mean war.

Meanwhile, a Soviet submarine crossed the blockade line. American warships tracked it and forced it to the surface with warning shots. That submarine carried nuclear torpedoes. A less cautious Soviet captain might well have started a nuclear war by firing tactical nuclear weapons at American warships.

Shortly afterward, Soviet and U.S. aircraft, some of the latter armed with nuclear missiles, almost clashed over the Bering Sea. With the superpowers at the brink of war, the Soviets "blinked" first. In exchange for a secret American promise to remove its nuclear missiles from Turkey, something it planned to do anyway, the Soviets withdrew their missiles from Cuba.

While unknown to Kennedy's advisors at the time, the Soviets actually had 162 nuclear warheads in Cuba. More important, Soviet officers in Cuba had the launch codes for them. They could have instigated a nuclear war on their own authority, which Fidel Castro, according to some accounts, urged them to do. Kennedy was right to be cautious.

The crisis underlined to everyone the dangers of nuclear war and how easily crises could escalate. In the aftermath, both superpowers stepped back from the brink and worked to ensure no future crisis brought them so close to nuclear war. Among other measures, they installed the famous hotline between the White House and the Kremlin.

OVER TIME, ASSESSMENTS of nuclear weapons moved from obsessions over surprise attacks and vulnerability to notions of stability and deterrence achieved through balance of power and effective diplomacy. The paradox of being ready to fight a war no one wanted endured, but in ways that usually reinforced rather than undermined deterrence.

Fears of nuclear war spawned an entire genre of post-apocalyptic fiction, but the tensions and contradictions of nuclear deterrence have proved equally rewarding topics for fiction writers. So, too, have the possibilities of nuclear disarmament and blackmail as featured in Robert Heinlein's "The Long Watch" and the film *The Day the Earth Stood Still* (1951).

Strategists developed elaborate plans for nuclear war while devoting equal efforts to ensuring that war never took place. Both American and Soviet grand strategy emphasized avoiding nuclear war. They understood what American President Dwight Eisenhower wrote a friend a few years before the Cuban Missile Crisis. "We are rapidly getting to the point that no war can be won." As he explained, "war implies a contest; when you get to the point that contest is no longer involved, and the outlook comes close to destruction of the enemy and suicide for ourselves," one must reassess the situation and step back from the brink. "Arguments as to the exact amount of available strength as compared to somebody else's are no longer the vital issues" (Jervis, *Meaning of the Nuclear Revolution*, 4-5).

Whenever nuclear-armed powers find themselves at war, escalation to nuclear war is a possibility. Novelists grappling with war in the contemporary world should consider this. Why doesn't the outbreak of war in Korea in Harold Coyle's novel *Team Yankee* (1987) lead to global thermonuclear war? How must characters behave to limit the prospect of nuclear escalation? Or perhaps the characters do something to provoke nuclear escalation?

Since the end of the Cold War, growing numbers of declassified documents show how close the United States and Soviet Union came to nuclear war. Whether in direct confrontation, as during the Cuban Missile Crisis, or during routine peacetime operations, individual air and naval commanders could have fired tactical nuclear weapons and begun the escalation to total thermonuclear war.

The issues raised in Sturgeon's "Thunder and Roses" are enduringly relevant as are the psychological stresses of people in prolonged combat, particularly when placed in morally ambiguous situations.

Chapter Six: The People in Arms, Strategies of Insurgency

While nuclear weapons dominated strategic thought in the generation after World War II, most of the wars fought in those years involved insurgencies. These included the Chinese Civil War (1927-1949) and numerous wars of national liberation in which colonized peoples from Algeria to Zimbabwe fought to expel foreign rulers. These asymmetric wars, what nineteenth century writers called small wars, pitted trained, regular armies against irregular forces.

Insurgencies were hardly a new phenomenon in the twentieth century. Alexander the Great battled insurgents in Afghanistan and other parts of the recently conquered Persian Empire. Julius Caesar grappled with both insurgents and conventional armies in Gaul. After his death, the Roman army fought insurgents in Britain, Judea, and other territories whose peoples resisted forced integration into the Roman Empire. Vietnamese insurgents resisted repeated Chinese invasions. Spanish insurgents bedeviled Napoleon's best generals.

While conventional operations proved important in determining the outcome of the American Revolution, particularly American victories at Saratoga and Yorktown, insurgents set the stage for these victories. Their operations forced Britain to scatter its army across the former colonies, and these garrisons were vulnerable to surprise attacks, such as George Washington's raids across the Delaware River against Trenton and Princeton in 1776.

Washington's strategy relied on these insurgents to exhaust Britain in a prolonged war and prevent Britain from massing its troops in overwhelming numbers against the regular soldiers of Washington's Continental Army. Constant insurgency raised the cost of reconquering and garrisoning Britain's 13 mainland colonies beyond what growing numbers of British politicians would pay.

Insurgency has featured in numerous novels, such as Jean Lartéguy's *The Centurions* (1960), which describes the contemporary operations of French legionnaires against Algerian insurgents. Like Americans in Vietnam, French soldiers struggled to distinguish between friend and foe. David Drake's *Hammer's Slammers*, Robert Asprin's *Phule's Company*, and other fictional mercenaries are similarly bedeviled by insurgents and struggle to target the enemy effectively without hurting innocent civilians.

Fictional protagonists, though, appear more often as insurgents rather than their enemies. In Cyril Kornbluth's "Not This August" (1955), Billy Justin leads American insurgents against communist invaders. A host of popular young actors do the same in the movie *Red Dawn* (1984). Lunar insurgents fight a tyrannical Earth in Heinlein's *The Moon is a Harsh Mistress*. Paul Atreides leads an insurgency in Frank Herbert's *Dune* (1965). C. S. Forester's Rifleman Dodd helps Spanish and Portuguese insurgents fight French invaders during the Napoleonic Wars in *Death to the French* (1932). The Envoys of Richard K. Morgan's *Altered Carbon* trilogy, spark insurgencies on worlds across the galaxy. Insurgency provides a setting and scope for protagonists to engage in the subterfuge, political machinations, and derring-do that hook readers.

At the core of any insurgency is motivation. What motivated average Americans to speak out against British rule and then take up arms to fight against it? What factors would drive a fictional character to become an insurgent? How do these factors influence that character's conduct? Do they kill indiscriminately, like many modern-day terrorists, or do they limit their attacks to military targets, as most American revolutionaries did? How do they cope with rigors of insurgent life? How do they treat civilians, both those sympathetic to their cause, and those opposed? How do they expect to win their insurgency? What is their theory of victory?

Defining Insurgency

SCHOLARS CONTINUE TO argue about exact definitions of insurgency. That, combined with the diversity of historical insurgencies and their inherent complexity, makes the topic difficult to analyze. For reasons of clarity, authors should differentiate between insurgency, a strategy, and guerrilla warfare, a tactical and operational approach to winning an insurgency.

Insurgents conduct guerrilla operations. They strike government targets by surprise and then retreat into the hinterland where they shelter in hidden bases and difficult terrain. But there is more to insurgency than ambushes and surprise attacks.

Long before American rebels fired at British redcoats at Lexington and Concord, they were on their way to winning the war. Samuel Adams, Paul Revere, and other American patriots laid the political foundation for a prolonged war of independence over the previous decade. Their political appeals convinced growing numbers of American colonists to sever their allegiance with Great Britain and eventually take up arms to fight for independence. While Americans eventually formed the Continental Army, which engaged British forces in conventional battles, the American Revolution began as an insurgency.

Winning an insurgency requires more than winning battles. It requires changing people's political allegiance. In some cases, such as communist insurgencies, this requires changing their political ideology, as well. As Mao Zedong later wrote, "people are decisive; weapons [and battles] are not."

In a conventional war, one usually wins by convincing an enemy government to surrender. Insurgents win by convincing the majority of people to abandon their existing government and instead support a new government established by the insurgents. Governments rejected by their own people inevitably fall. Insurgents win by winning the people's "hearts and minds."

It is also important to differentiate between regular military forces that engage in hit-and-run attacks and insurgents who often disperse, cache their weapons, and hide among the population. Both regular and irregular forces can operate by stealth, strike the enemy by surprise, and fall back, avoiding enemy forces or luring them into traps. Insurgents do not hold a monopoly on guerilla tactics. Nathanael Greene, George Washington's most able general, proved a master of them.

Greene, who assumed command of American forces in the Carolinas following several disastrous defeats, wore down British forces commanded by Charles Cornwallis in a series of skirmishes and larger battles, most of which he lost. Aggressively pursued by Cornwallis, Greene led the British on a long chase across the Carolinas and into Virginia. He regularly doubled back to strike the British, but each time denied Cornwallis the decisive battle he sought and evaded British pursuit. As Greene commented, "we fight, get beat, rise and fight again" (Weigley, *American Way of War*, 36).

Greene won often enough, though, that his force grew as volunteers arrived, while Cornwallis's army shrank. Eventually, Cornwallis had no choice but to retreat, leading his emaciated army to the coast to await rescue by the Royal Navy. That rescue, of course, never came. George Washington seized the opportunity, marched in force to support Greene, and forced the surrender of Cornwallis's outnumbered troops.

Greene's southern campaign shows not only the advantages of combining guerrilla and conventional operations, but also illustrates what Clausewitz called the "culminating point of victory." Greene lured Cornwallis past this point and wore out his army in prolonged pursuit and fighting. Greene knew his American soldiers, both regulars and irregulars, were better suited to this type of campaign than their British antagonists. He also understood Cornwallis's impetuous personality. Greene knew both his enemy and himself and used this knowledge to full advantage, luring Cornwallis to destruction

For French officer and scholar David Galula, "insurgency is the pursuit of the policy by a party, inside a country, by every means." Successful insurgents combine violence with normal political activities and popular appeals to the public. Unlike ordinary wars, insurgencies are not a "continuation of the policy by other means." Insurgencies begin "long before the insurgent resorts to the use of force" (Galula, *Counterinsurgency Warfare*, 1).

Sam Adams and the other Sons of Liberty understood this well. No one fired a single shot at the Boston Tea Party, yet it had great political influence, as did Thomas Paine's pamphlet "Common Sense." In insurgencies, Galula notes, a mimeograph machine is often more useful than a machine gun. Passion and political acumen trump military force and firepower.

Mao Zedong's Three Phases of People's War

THE MOST INFLUENTIAL thinker on insurgency is Mao Zedong, who led China's Communist Party to victory in a generation-long civil war against the Nationalists, led by Jiang Jieshi (Chiang Kai-shek). Building on Clausewitz, Mao suggests "politics is war without bloodshed while war is politics with bloodshed." War, he wrote, "is the highest form of struggle" to resolve conflicts among social classes, as well as nations and political groups. Mirroring Clausewitz, Mao emphasizes the inherent violence of class struggle and revolutionary warfare. "A revolution is not a dinner party, or writing an essay, or painting a picture, or doing embroidery; it cannot be so refined, so leisurely and gentle, so temperate, kind, courteous, restrained, and magnanimous. A revolution is an insurrection, an act of violence by which one class overthrows another."

Mao describes what became the standard approach to people's wars. These wars rely on the mass mobilization of people. Ideally, the insurgents win the "hearts and minds" of people who spurn their government and instead support the insurgents, providing the foundation for a prolonged war. If all goes well, the insurgents undermine, destroy, and replace the existing government with one of their own making.

Mao's ideas on strategy evolved over the course of China's long war, which lasted from 1927 to 1949 and continued despite Japan's invasion of China in 1937. At times, Mao's communist army seemed on the verge of defeat and annihilation, but each time it retreated, recovered, and grew stronger. This cycle of defeat and recovery influenced Mao's thought. He believed insurgencies progressed through several stages. He offered "Seven Steps to Fight a Foreign Occupier," any of which could provide an interesting story setting. They include:

1. Arousing and organizing the people
2. Achieving internal political unification
3. Establishing bases
4. Equipping forces
5. Building national strength
6. Destroying the enemy's national strength
7. Regaining lost territories

Mao soon refined these to the three phases commonly discussed today. He labeled them defense, equilibrium, and offense. In the first phase, an insurgency begins organizing. It focuses on strategic defense, winning over the population, and building up one's forces—political and military. Insurgents create a political base of support among the people. They educate (or indoctrinate, depending on your perspective) people politically and offer them inducements, such as land redistribution or other political reforms.

It is among the "rejected elite," Galula argues, that insurgents find their "indispensable leaders." These political leaders use propaganda to magnify people's perceptions of problems, spread the insurgents' message among the population, and build local political cadres. Exploiting local political grievances is critical in an insurgency's early stage, but their importance diminishes as an insurgency gains strength. As the tide of war turns against the government, people previously on the fence will gravitate toward the insurgents, hoping to wind up on the winning side (Galula, *Counterinsurgency Warfare*, 14-16).

As insurgents expand their political base, they also build a military apparatus to secure safe base areas for their supporters and troops. Within these liberated territories, the insurgents establish their own government, to which local people, willingly or not, pay taxes. To show their strength, insurgents strike carefully chosen government and military targets.

Insurgents operate like gnats, biting their targets both front and rear. They exhaust the enemy while growing steadily stronger. Insurgents work to weaken their enemies, and to deceive and confuse them. It is essential to "make the enemy blind and deaf by sealing his eyes and ears and drive his commanders to distraction by creating confusion in their minds." Paraphrasing Sun Tzu, Mao explained, "there can never be too much deception in war" (240).

Government forces must disperse to maintain control over large areas, scattering garrisons across disputed territory. So, Mao argued, even if outnumbered ten to one, insurgents could concentrate their forces to outnumber the enemy at places and times of their choosing. The enemy's garrisons and the supply lines to them, along with other government installations and infrastructure, provide ready targets for insurgents.

In this stage, avoiding defeat is more important than inflicting losses on the enemy. Guerrillas operate in the enemy's rear areas but have no rear areas of their own. As Mao wrote, insurgents should be "nowhere and everywhere." They attack when and where they choose and retreat from superior enemy forces. Ideally, they draw enemy forces deep into insurgent-friendly territory, past their "culminating point of victory" and to places where insurgents can attack them with advantage.

Insurgents operate within the populace "as little fishes in the ocean." Government efforts to strike insurgents hiding among the larger population inevitably hurt the innocent along with the guilty. In doing so, they foster resentment against the government that fuels insurgent recruitment. This makes winning support from the local population critical. Insurgents, Mao emphasized, are not bandits. They must remain true to their ideology and show they fight for the people. Actions that hurt local populations, such as taking food and supplies from them, undermine the insurgent cause.

In Mao's second phase, the insurgents expand through both political and military means. They grow their existing bases, establish new base areas, and become increasingly aggressive, achieving a military equilibrium with the enemy. Insurgents increase their military operations, aiming to both weaken government forces and expand the territory under insurgent control. If successful, these operations garner more civilian support and help recruit new fighters. Rather than abandoning their bases and retreating to avoid a catastrophic defeat, insurgents in this phase defend them vigorously. As their strength grows, they expand into new territories and establish new bases there.

In the first two phases, insurgents focus on popular opinion, both domestic and international, to win supporters. This, as Mao warned, required treating people with scrupulous correctness. One should be neither selfish nor unjust and never steal from people. "Replace the door when you leave the house, roll up the bedding on which you have slept, be courteous, be honest in your transactions, return what you borrow, replace what you break, do not bathe in the presence of women," and "do not without authority search the pocketbooks of those you arrest."

At the same time insurgents court the population's goodwill, they work to create a general climate of insecurity by attacking government targets. If successful, these attacks weaken public support for a government unable to protect them or even defend itself. These attacks may also provoke the government to respond with harsh measures that constrain civil life and harm innocents, further eroding government standing in public opinion.

Robert Heinlein portrays this in *The Moon is a Harsh Mistress*, a novel in which lunar settlers, called Loonies, rebel against the Earth. In a plot loosely patterned on the American Revolution, lunar insurgents provoke the ruling Earth-appointed warden into a series of overreactions resulting in riots and civilian deaths. The rebels publicize these atrocities in an adept propaganda campaign that wins them support and recruits, much as the Boston Massacre helped the Sons of Liberty win support against Great Britain. Later in the novel, the Loonies dispatch ambassadors to Earth to gain allies, much as American rebels dispatched Benjamin Franklin to France.

One of the insurgent leaders, Professor Bernardo de la Paz, has read Sun Tzu and paraphrases him regularly. Like the American revolutionaries, the Loonies understand they cannot take their war to

Earth. Their only prospect for victory lies in sapping the will of Earth to hold on to its lunar colony. The Loonies need to convince Earth to withdraw its forces by demonstrating the costs of garrisoning the Moon exceed the economic benefits of maintaining colonial rule. Like the American rebels, the Loonies want an amicable peace in which trade between the Earth and Moon continues. As Prof. de la Paz counsels, always "leave room for your enemy to become your friend." In other words, don't put him on "death ground."

The American insurgency against Britain quickly fielded large, conventional military forces, the Continental Army. Most insurgencies, though, take a long time to reach this stage, years or even decades. Some, like Heinlein's Loonies, never do. Insurgents must control substantial territory to provide the resources to build and sustain a conventional army, which also requires substantial influxes of military equipment, either captured from the enemy or supplied by friendly powers, since few insurgents can manufacture weapons in quantity.

Once adequately equipped, trained, and formed into conventional military units, the insurgents go on the offensive. This transition from insurgency to conventional war is Mao's third phase. Insurgent armies launch full-scale military offensives. They engage and pursue the enemy's primary military forces, destroy them, topple the enemy regime, and seize control of the country.

Even in Phase Three, the political war continues. Insurgents disseminate their ideology, recruit new members, and strike targets of opportunity. Political recruitment never stops. Should things go awry in Phase Two or Three, insurgents fall back to isolated base areas or scatter among the people to rebuild the insurgency, both politically and militarily.

This, of course, is what Mao did in the famous Long March. Communist insurgents proved unable to defend their base areas in Southern China. In 1933, led by Mao, they evaded pursuing Nationalist troops in a year-long, 4,000-mile trek. Afterward, they established new safe areas in northern China near the Mongolian border. There, they rebuilt their strength and grew the insurgency. Fifteen years later, Mao's armies drove the Nationalists from mainland China.

Maoist Insurgency in Vietnam

VIETNAMESE COMMUNISTS Ho Chi Minh and Vo Nguyen Giap proved Mao's most adept students. They followed his model to build a political base in Vietnam for their Viet Minh movement. Like Mao, they maintained strict control of their organization as it grew into a successful insurgency, while fragmenting, confusing, and disorganizing their enemies. Thanks to weapons shipments from newly Communist China, the Viet Minh eventually fielded large conventional forces. These steadily pushed back French garrisons and then defeated French paratroopers at the climactic Battle of Dien Bien Phu in 1954, which led France to withdraw from North Vietnam.

Over the next 20 years, Giap employed the same strategy against the government of South Vietnam and its American ally. Despite repeated defeats, such as their disastrous 1968 Tet Offensive, Vietnamese Communists eroded American support for the war in South Vietnam, which led to American withdrawal in 1973. The war continued, and in 1975, South Vietnam's government fell to conventional North Vietnamese offensives.

Giap diverged from Mao in some important respects. For Mao, an insurgency always aimed for Phase Three and a full-scale conventional war. This was much less important to Giap, who emphasized the primary importance of the first two phases. Rather than developing through Mao's three phases, Giap saw regular and guerilla warfare as continuous and happening all the time. Insurgencies were messy and need not develop in the clear stages demarcated by Mao.

Insurgents should execute whatever operations they were capable of, always keeping in mind the centrality of politics and winning over the people.

Even once he fielded large conventional forces, Giap argued insurgent units should continue to operate alongside conventional forces, harassing the enemy in guerilla and terror operations. Doing so gave Vietnamese Communists great resiliency and allowed them to recover from repeated, large-scale defeats in conventional operations. Despite heavy losses from American "search and destroy" operations, Communist political cadres remained active and effective throughout South Vietnam. The same proved true in the 1968 Tet Offensive in which Communist forces, both southern insurgents and North Vietnamese regulars, launched large, simultaneous attacks on several dozen cities and towns across South Vietnam. American and South Vietnamese forces inflicted catastrophic losses on these southern insurgents. Yet, most Communist political cadres remained untouched and soon resumed operations.

The United States and the government of South Vietnam proved unable to translate their military victories into political success, particularly at the village level. This, many analysts argue, is where insurgencies are lost or won, not in dozens of big battles, but in thousands of local village meetings. One can make a similar argument for the American Revolution. Britain lost the war in New England town meeting halls.

What Makes a Successful Insurgency?

IN *On War,* Clausewitz focused most of his attention on conventional wars and the pursuit of decisive battle, but he also studied insurgencies. Of particular interest to him was how Spanish insurgents whittled away at Napoleon's armies. Clausewitz noted five conditions that supported successful insurgencies:

1. The war must be fought in the interior of the country.
2. It must not be decided by a single stroke (a decisive battle).
3. The theater of operations must be large.
4. The national character must be suited to that type of war.
5. The country must be rough and inaccessible, because of mountains or forests, marshes, or the local methods of cultivation (*On War*, 480).

A century later, during the First World War, British officer T. E. Lawrence, better known as Lawrence of Arabia, organized and led the Arab Revolt against the Ottoman Empire. Operating from what is today Saudi Arabia, Arab irregulars raided Ottoman positions and sabotaged railroads and other facilities. This forced the Ottomans to spread garrisons across the region, which limited their ability to halt British offensives launched from Egypt and the Persian Gulf. Arab irregulars fought their way into Syria, supported the advance of British armies, and helped transform the Middle East. After the war, Lawrence described his campaign and its strategy, making him one of the first writers to discuss insurgency from the perspective of the insurgent rather than the counterinsurgent.

A successful insurgency, Lawrence wrote in *Seven Pillars of Wisdom* (1926), required a sympathetic population. Only two percent of people need to take up arms and actively involve themselves in the fighting. The vast majority, though, must sympathize with the insurgents and at least passively support them. "More than half the battle," he wrote, takes place behind the front lines in the minds of the local people. While relatively few Arabs joined Lawrence's insurgents, most resented Ottoman rule, and many sympathized with and supported the rebels. They fed them, sheltered them, and provided them with invaluable information on Turkish troop movements.

Insurgents must also be quick on their feet and possess an "unassailable base" from which to operate. Exploiting their advantages of endurance, speed, and ubiquity, they strike isolated enemy garrisons and their lines of communication and supply. They attack "where the enemy is not," nibbling away at the enemy's strength while slowly growing strong themselves. As Lawrence noted, insurgents, especially at the outset, face "many humiliating material limits, but no moral impossibilities." They may strike whatever targets they choose. Insurgents who maintained their advantages of mobility, security, and popular support, would, Lawrence argued, inevitably win their war (Chapter 33).

As Lawrence understood, insurgents need incremental victories. These needn't be large, but insurgents must show they can—at least occasionally—win battles. These small tactical victories win them recruits, popular support, and even foreign allies.

George Washington exemplified this. Defeated and driven out of New York, Washington's army barely survived a grueling retreat through New Jersey. Once their British pursuers settled into winter quarters, though, Washington doubled back and overwhelmed British garrisons in Trenton and Princeton. In a matter of weeks, these victories over small British forces reversed the strategic situation in New Jersey. Militia units and individual recruits arrived to bolster the Continental Army. So, too, did food and other supplies, along with secret military aid from France.

Fearing further attacks, Britain withdrew its remaining garrisons from New Jersey. Loyalists fled. Patriots regained control of the state. Victory over a large British army the following year at Saratoga convinced the French government to formally ally with the United States and enter the war.

Similarly, in David Brin's novel *Uplift War* (1987) neo-chimp insurgents lured the invading Gubru aliens into carefully prepared ambushes to win their first victories. These successes boost morale and win the rebels recruits. They also give civilians hope, leading more civilians to passively—and over time to actively—support the insurgency.

Praised by Winston Churchill, Lawrence's *Seven Pillars of Wisdom* influenced many writers, among them award-winning science fiction author Lois McMaster Bujold. Read at the suggestion of her publisher, Jim Baen, Bujold credits Lawrence's book with helping clarify her strategic ideas. Lawrence's influence is visible in several of her stories featuring mercenary commander Miles Vorkosigan. A thoughtful strategist, Miles avoids direct battle and seeks indirect approaches against his enemies, both large and small. He undermines their support, wins local allies, outmaneuvers and/or outwits them.

Miles's grandfather, Piotr, helped lead a successful insurgency against the Cetegandan Empire, which had occupied his planet, Barrayar. Like American and Vietnamese insurgents, the Barrayarans raised the costs of prolonged war beyond what the Cetegandan Empire proved willing to pay. So, like the French and Americans in Vietnam, the Cetagandans left. Unfortunately, Bujold has yet to write much about Piotr's early life, his successful military career, or the Cetegandan occupation of Barrayar and the Barrayaran Insurgency.

Frank Herbert similarly drew on Lawrence for his award-winning novel *Dune*. Like Lawrence, Paul Atreides organizes desert warriors, the Fremen, into a successful insurgency that wears down occupying Harkonnen troops and draws others into the struggle because "the spice must flow."

While Sun Tzu argued no nation ever benefits from a prolonged war, strategists of people's war disagree. In fact, prolonging a war is usually central to their theory of victory. Mao, who drew on Sun Tzu and Clausewitz, argued prolonged conflict provided the opportunity to reshape political thought and eliminate those whose thought could not be reshaped. Insurgents needed to wear down the enemy while simultaneously reshaping their society and its political structures.

For Mao, insurgencies are necessarily protracted wars. They require many years, even decades to win. "There is no magic shortcut" to victory; no decisive battle to end them suddenly and dramatically (219). They are prolonged, painful struggles that require patience, sacrifice, and enormous commitment to the cause. Mao repeatedly argued against those who advocated premature offensives against Nationalist forces. "In the end, he warned, "Mr. Reality will come and pour a bucket of cold water over these chatterers, showing them up as mere windbags who want to get things on the cheap, to have gains without pains" (218). Winning an insurgency is usually a prolonged, painful, and bloody process.

Several near disasters proved Mao correct. Afterward, he assumed leadership of the insurgency during the Long March. Afterward, Mao avoided large-scale battles with Nationalist forces, and later the Japanese, husbanding and growing his forces until the time was right to strike in force. He never rushed into battle unprepared.

If a government is particularly unpopular, several insurgencies may emerge to contest its right to rule. One of the interesting results in these situations is that insurgents fight both one another and the government. During World War II, rival Yugoslavian insurgencies, the royalist Chetniks and Josip Broz Tito's Communists, fought each other and their country's Axis occupiers. Both periodically arranged truces with Germany or Italy so they could focus their attention on one another. In Algeria, the FLN ruthlessly eliminated rival insurgent groups. In what became Israel, the mainstream Haganah paramilitary defeated and forcibly absorbed Irgun, whose leaders wished to wage a more violent insurgency against both the British and Palestinians. In Cyril M. Kornbluth's novel *Not This August* (1955), Soviet and Chinese armies eliminate the Communist insurgents who helped them conquer the United States and Canada.

Insurgency for Limited Political Objectives

MAO FOCUSED HIS ATTENTION on people's wars that aimed to overthrow the state and transform society. One can, though, launch an insurgency for limited political objectives. Unlike Mao, the American revolutionaries sought little change in the colonial social order. They simply wanted independence from Britain. As numerous historians have underlined, most of the leading revolutionaries hailed from economically and politically successful families. They dominated colonial social and political life before the American Revolution and continued to do so afterwards.

Following the American Civil War, violent racist organizations like the KKK terrorized African Americans in the southern states and suppressed their voting. Over the next two generations, they helped racist politicians impose systems of segregation that deprived African Americans of their full rights as American citizens. While Confederate leaders failed to preserve slavery, this postwar insurgency ended Reconstruction and helped preserve much of the old racial hierarchy in the American South.

One can analyze any number of social and political movements as insurgencies, albeit nonviolent ones. Civil War historian Mark Grimsley offers the long struggle for African American civil rights as an example. Despite the emphasis on non-violent struggle by Martin Luther King Jr. and other leaders, civil rights activists engaged in many of the political actions common to insurgencies in their first phase. They dramatized the social and political inequities of American society and worked to gain media attention through sit-ins, marches, and other demonstrations. As their movement grew, they attracted allies, shaped public opinion, and won important judicial and legislative victories, culminating in the 1964 Civil Rights and 1965 Voting Rights Act. Arguably, the movement gained moral authority by remaining peaceful in the face of increasing violence against its members and leaders. The movement's hard fought political successes in the 1950s and 1960s, silenced extremists within the movement who called for violence.

Case Study: The Chinese Civil War

FIGHTING IN CHINA BETWEEN Nationalist forces led by Jiang Jieshi (Chiang Kai-shek) and Communists, eventually led by Mao Zedong, increased in the 1920s as Jiang sought to reunify China under a central government. While Jiang's Nationalist Party (the Kuomintang or KMT) gained control of China's major cities and important transportation routes, various warlords continued to rule much of the countryside. It was there the Communist Party flourished after Mao redirected its recruitment efforts from industrial workers to peasant farmers.

In July 1931, Jiang launched a major effort to destroy the Communist forces once and for all. Jiang's best troops launched concentric attacks on the Communist stronghold in Jianxi Province. Communist armies responded with a scorched earth campaign. They burned fields, poisoned wells, and evacuated local peasants with their retreating armies.

Nonetheless, Jiang's armies advanced steadily. In successive annual campaigns, they whittled down Communist forces and ruthlessly eliminated Communist political cadres. By mid-1934, the Communists had lost 60,000 soldiers and half their territory. Defeat seemed inevitably. Yet, 100,000 Communist soldiers fought their way out of Jiang's encirclement and began the 6,000-mile Long March that saved Chinese communists and established Mao as their undisputed leader.

Only about a third of those who began the march survived to reach Yenan in the north, a territory conveniently close to the Soviet Union, where Mao began rebuilding Communist political and military forces by appealing to China's oppressed peasants. Mao avoided fixed battles against Jiang's armies and instead adopted guerilla tactics, attacking where Nationalist forces or local warlords were weak and retreating when hard-pressed. As Mao later wrote:

> The enemy advances, we retreat;
> The enemy camps, we harass;
> The enemy tires, we attack;
> The enemy retreats, we pursue.

More important, Mao linked strategy and tactics to politics. The goal, he explained, was to "arouse the largest number of the masses in the shortest possible time and by the best possible methods."

Jiang planned a major offensive to root out Mao's Communists in their new haven, but Japan's invasion of China forced him to redeploy forces against that threat. Whether Jiang's offensive would have eliminated the Communist insurgency is much debated. What is certain is that Japan's invasion helped the Communists. This is one of the great ironies of World War II. The Anti-Comintern Pact, signed by the Axis powers in 1936, pledged them to fight Communism. Yet, their invasions of China, Eastern Europe, France, Greece, and other countries actually facilitated Communist expansion.

During World War II, Communist insurgencies around the world thrived, particularly in China, Vietnam, and Yugoslavia. In China, Mao's forces steadily gained adherents and territory. They harassed both Japanese and Nationalist forces, but avoided large battles, instead emphasizing the political nature of the struggle. When Japan surrendered and began evacuating its troops from China, the Communists were positioned to fill the power vacuum Japan left in northern China and Manchuria.

Jiang's American advisors encouraged him to consolidate his control of southern China and build up his strength, both political and military, before renewing the war against the Communists. Instead, Jiang committed his best troops to aggressive campaigns against the heart of Communist territory. He feared China divided between Communist and Nationalist halves and hoped to secure key strategic areas and win the war quickly. To do that, he scattered his troops in garrisons across territories strongly held by enemy insurgents.

Jiang's defeat came quickly. Mao's forces isolated and destroyed Nationalist garrisons one by one in northern China and Manchuria and then launched offensives that drove the Nationalists back. Entire divisions of Jiang's army changed sides, and the Nationalist position collapsed. Jiang and the remnants of his army fled from mainland China to Taiwan. Like most insurgents, Mao's forces lacked a navy and could not pursue them.

Jiang made a host of military mistakes, and Japan's invasion significantly helped the Communists. Jiang's political mistakes compounded his problems. As Mao realized, victory lay with the peasants who bitterly resented their landlords and politicians like Jiang who supported them. Absent substantial reforms, Jiang had little hope of winning popular support for his corrupt and ineffective government. This meant he had to defeat the Communist insurgency through purely military means. A return to his slow, methodical campaigns of the late 1920s and early 1930s might have worked. It would, though, have required many years and continuing American economic support. Instead, Jiang gambled. His bid to win a quick, decisive victory over the Communists ended in disaster.

MILITARY STRATEGY FOR WRITERS

MAO'S STRATEGIC WRITINGS became a template for insurgents around the world, whether communist or not. Insurgents emphasize political over military operations and use both to wear down the enemy in a prolonged campaign that builds to climactic military battles. While not every Maoist insurgency succeeded, enough did—such as the Viet Minh insurgency against France—to cement Mao's reputation as the foremost exponent of insurgent strategy.

Insurgencies provide ready fodder for fiction writers. What motivates their protagonist to join—or even launch—an insurgency? How popular is the insurgency? Is its popularity waxing or waning? Who joins the protagonist in fighting the government or colonial oppressor? What are their motivations? Is the government response to insurgency careful and measured or harsh and brutal like the Harkonnens in *Dune* or the Empire in the original *Star Wars* trilogy? Is this a bipolar struggle between an insurgent group and the government it seeks to unseat, or are other insurgent groups or nations involved? If the latter, what motivates these other participants in the struggle? What issues divide the insurgents?

In terms of strategy, what government weaknesses can the insurgents exploit? What insurgent weaknesses can the government attack? What stage has the insurgency reached? Has the struggle reached a critical turning point, such as a transition between two of Mao's three phases? Are the insurgents following Mao's playbook or do they favor some other path to victory? Is one side or the other on "death ground?" If so, how do its leaders respond to this crisis? What role does technology (or magic, if writing fantasy) play in the struggle?

Chapter Seven: Fighting Insurgents, Counterinsurgency

Counterinsurgency, nicknamed COIN, is a much debated—and sometimes ridiculed—field of study. Unsurprisingly, given recent American wars in Afghanistan and Iraq, counterinsurgency has again captured public attention. Army-Marine Field Manual 3-24, *Counterinsurgency* (2006), written by a team led by Generals David Petraeus and James Mattis, is the only U.S. military manual ever published and distributed by a civilian press. It is probably also the only one ever read by and quoted at length by civilian analysts.

Arguments about counterinsurgency hinge on the uniqueness of insurgency, and hence, counterinsurgency. Are these wars so unique they require special military units and unique approaches to strategy? Or, have counterinsurgency experts, nicknamed COINdinistas by their detractors, overemphasized the uniqueness of insurgency, and by extension their own special knowledge of how to fight them? Can, as one U.S. Marine general commented during the Vietnam War, any good army defeat insurgents?

Thankfully, discussing strategies of counterinsurgency does not require resolving this debate.

Over the last century, scholars and military officers developed a robust body of work analyzing unconventional conflicts featuring insurgency and, in some cases, terrorism. Important works include Roger Trinquier, *Modern Warfare: A French View of Counterinsurgency* (1961) and David Galula, *Counterinsurgency Warfare: Theory and Practice* (1964). Both draw from the French experience in Algeria, as does Jean Larteguy's novel *The Centurions* (1960). The Vietnam War provoked similar reflections among American scholars and military officers, such as Andrew Krepinevich's *The Army and Vietnam* (1986) and Eric Bergerud's *The Dynamics of Defeat* (1993). These works showcase one of the unusual aspects of counterinsurgency literature. Whether French scholars writing about Algeria or Americans about Vietnam, they are overwhelmingly written by the losers rather than the winners of these wars.

COIN strategists focus on denying insurgents their essential needs. To do this, counterinsurgents must attack insurgent base areas and develop light, mobile forces to pursue insurgents through difficult terrain, hounding them to destruction. To win hearts and minds, they must counter insurgent propaganda by circulating their own political appeals, perhaps sweetened with land grants and political reforms. Effective counterinsurgency also requires holding and effectively defending territory, especially cities and other strategically important areas. Doing all these at once is challenging, and often impossible. This forces the counterinsurgent to prioritize. Which of these are most important?

Fictional characters, too, must assess an insurgency's strengths and weaknesses and determine the best ways to combat it. Will protagonists focus on political reform and nation building, as in Harry Harrison's story "Commando Raid," or will they seek battle, hoping to bring superior firepower to bear on the enemy, the preferred approach in most of David Drake's "Hammer's Slammers" stories. Which approach is more likely to bring the war to a satisfactory conclusion?

Schoolbooks and Krags

THE COUNTERINSURGENT must choose between "schoolbooks and krags." The term derives from the United States' war in the Philippines following its acquisition of the islands in the 1898 Spanish-American War, when American soldiers carried Krag-Jorgensen rifles (nicknamed krags). American troops quickly defeated conventional Philippine forces, but then faced a popular insurgency led by Emilio Aguinaldo. The average Filipino had no wish to exchange Spanish for American colonial rule. They wanted independence.

American leaders soon realized defeating the insurgency required an appropriate balance between political reform (schoolbooks) and military force (krags). What resources should they devote to building schools, improving infrastructure, and reforming government institutions? Could they win Filipino "hearts and minds" by improving their quality of life?

On the other hand, how much military force was required to protect this new infrastructure, expand American territorial control, and safeguard those who accepted U.S. rule? How many troops (if any) did that leave to pursue insurgent forces through the Philippines' many islands and difficult terrain? What was the appropriate balance between offense and defense, between political and military action?

Every military action in an insurgency can produce political results that outweigh its tactical implications. Through both action and inaction, insurgent and counterinsurgent can win friends, create enemies, alienate parts of the population, or all three. The tension between winning hearts and minds and applying military force against insurgent makes counterinsurgency among the most difficult military tasks. Should counterinsurgents pursue an army-centric (destroy the insurgents) or population-centric (win hearts and minds) strategy? Traditional strategists favor the former; counterinsurgency specialists argue for the latter.

Both, of course, are important. The choice between these—and the relative priority of all the subsidiary operations to support them—plagues counterinsurgents. If they could do everything noted above effectively and simultaneously, they probably wouldn't be facing an insurgency in the first place. Limited resources—resources are always limited—force counterinsurgents to make difficult choices among these priorities.

Law, Morality, Insurgency, and Counterinsurgency

IN CONTRAST TO COUNTERINSURGENTS, who must tread lightly to avoid alienating people, insurgents have a multiplicity of options. Disrupting normal civil life is surprisingly easy and requires few resources. Disorder "is cheap to create and very costly to prevent" (Galula, *Counterinsurgency Warfare*, 8). Insurgents require few resources to spread chaos.

Defending against insurgents, though, is expensive. Counterinsurgents must devote great resources to achieve relatively little (34). Whiles insurgents strike targets of opportunity of their choice, government forces must defend everything. They need to be everywhere to prevent insurgent success.

There is also, Galula argues, an asymmetry of morality in these wars. Insurgents can do things that states, as upholders of law and order, cannot. When governments resort to terror and torture, they lose credibility and popular support. Insurgents often do not. This is particularly true if they choose their targets carefully, striking only those who "deserve" it.

MILITARY STRATEGY FOR WRITERS   171

During the Vietnam War, one American officer memorably explained to journalists why his unit burned down a South Vietnamese village. "We destroyed the village in order to save it," he said. Since U.S. forces could not protect the villagers from Communist insurgents, they destroyed villages and relocated the villagers. During World War II, Stalin relocated ethnic groups suspected of pro-German sympathies to Siberia where they couldn't cause any trouble. Counterinsurgents often move populations to "safe zones" to separate insurgents from the population in which they hide and whose support the insurgents require.

While sometimes effective, forced relocation is never popular, particularly when poorly handled, as in three counterinsurgency campaigns in the late 19th and early 20th century: Spain in Cuba, the Americans in the Philippines, and Britain in South Africa. In each case, the counterinsurgent forcibly relocated tens of thousands of civilians into crowded concentration camps where many of them died of disease and malnourishment.

Galula suggests resettlement is the last resort of a weak counterinsurgent, one incapable of executing any other strategy. Moving people not only antagonizes them but also makes it impossible to use them as a source of intelligence against the insurgents.

Some counterinsurgents don't bother to relocate civilians and simply bomb or otherwise destroy villages believed to shelter or actively support insurgents. The first *Star Wars* movie, *Episode Four: A New Hope* (1977), offers the ultimate application of this policy. Faced with an insurgency of unknown size and popularity, the Empire's rulers decide to suppress it by destroying whole planets, beginning with Alderaan, home to insurgent leader Princess Leia Organa. The Empire's apparent strategy was to eliminate the insurgents' bases of support and terrorize the Empire's population into loyalty—or at least passive acceptance of Emperor Palpatine's rule. As Galula would have predicted, the Empire's campaign of terror failed.

Since World War II, several insurgencies benefited from base areas outside the country for which they fought. These unassailable base areas proved particularly frustrating for counterinsurgents. Insurgents often operate freely across international borders. When counterinsurgents pursue them or strike these cross-border safe areas with artillery or air attacks, as the French did FLN bases in Tunisia, other nations, international organizations, and segments of their populations often condemn them.

During the Vietnam War, cross-border havens and supply routes in Cambodia and Laos allowed North Vietnamese forces to maneuver and strike targets in South Vietnam at will. A belated American invasion of Cambodia to destroy North Vietnamese bases and supply dumps, while militarily successful, provoked mass protests in the United States against this "expansion" of the war. The Ohio National Guard overreacted to protests at Kent State University, opened fire, and killed four people and injured many more. Police at Jackson State College in Mississippi also fired on protesting students, killing two and injuring 12 others.

Since then, nations have been more cautious about crossing international borders. The United States has conducted drone and air strikes in a host of countries with which it is not at war. Yet, following the American invasion of Afghanistan, American troops refrained from pursuing retreating Al Qaeda and Taliban forces into neighboring Pakistan. Safe havens in Pakistan saved the Taliban. It rebuilt its military forces and soon resumed the war against the United States—a war it won 20 years later.

Despite its friendly relations with the United States and dependence on American military aid and equipment, Pakistan's government similarly sheltered Osama bin Laden and other Al-Qaeda leaders and helped prevent the destruction of that terrorist organization. Muammar Gaddafi, Saddam Hussein, and other dictators have sheltered assorted insurgents and terrorists.

Clausewitz's Trinity and the Vietnam War

CLAUSEWITZ'S "PARADOXICAL trinity" offers the best way to examine insurgencies. To succeed, insurgents must exploit and exacerbate tensions among their target's government, military, and people. They need to discredit the government, gain popular support among the people, and defeat, neutralize, or coopt enemy military forces. The counterinsurgent, of course, must prevent this by isolating and/or discrediting the insurgents, destroying their military forces, and winning back popular support.

The Vietnam War provides an excellent example of this. The strain of a large, prolonged, and expensive war fractured trust among the American people, their government, and military forces. Military leaders resented political interference in their conduct of the war. Political leaders resented the military for its inability to deliver on repeated promises of success and continuing requests for more and more troops and resources. False claims by both military and political leaders that victory was at hand alienated the American public. Nightly coverage of seemingly futile American military operations and growing American casualties exacerbated this alienation.

By 1968, increasing numbers of Americans, including leading journalists like Walter Cronkite, who previously supported the war, recognized there was no "light at the end of the tunnel." Claims to the contrary by General William Westmoreland, the U.S. commander in Vietnam, seemed overly optimistic at best, downright lies at worst. American victory, if at all possible, clearly required more years of fighting, more lives lost, and emptying more of the nation's treasury into Vietnam.

Arguably, the American people proved better able to make the essential cost/benefit analyses for rational prosecution of the war than their military and political leaders. After 1968, polls showed a clear majority of Americans favored ending the war. A vocal minority demanded escalation. Some even talked about "nuking Hanoi."

Most Americans, though, simply wanted out. The cost of the war in blood and money far exceeded any possible benefit from victory. Continuing to fight would be irrational.

Members of Richard Nixon's incoming administration reached the same conclusion. Yet, it took them four more years—and many more American deaths—to withdraw U.S. forces from Vietnam. In fact, more Americans died in Vietnam in the four years after the 1968 Tet Offensive, as U.S. diplomats sought to negotiate an "honorable peace" and exit from Vietnam, than in the four years leading up to and including Tet.

There is no shortage of critics of U.S. strategy in Vietnam. Some argue the U.S. should have conducted more operations and more aggressive conventional operations. More bombing of North Vietnam with fewer restrictions, they suggest, would have forced North Vietnam's leaders to make peace. Others argue an invasion and occupation of Laos to cut the Ho Chi Minh Trail would have starved communist troops in South Vietnam of vital supplies and reinforcements. Particularly aggressive analysts suggest the U.S. should have invaded North Vietnam itself, an action that could have triggered overt Chinese or Soviet intervention in the war with all the risks of nuclear escalation that entailed.

Most critics, though, take the opposite tack. They argue the U.S. overemphasized conventional operations and starved counterinsurgency and nation building efforts of the resources needed for success. Galula, for example, argues "conventional operations by themselves have no more effect than a fly swatter." They catch some insurgents, but "new recruits replace them as fast as they are lost" (*Counterinsurgency Warfare*, 51). This certainly describes the U.S. experience in Vietnam. The US had to maintain counterinsurgent operations in particular regions for months to prevent insurgents from replacing their losses through new recruitment and to root out the insurgent political infrastructure. American troops rarely did this. They had too many other fires to put out and soon hopped aboard their helicopters to fly to the next one.

More important, as Eric Bergerud adroitly argues in *Dynamics of Defeat*, the United States could hammer Communist military forces and substantially weaken them, but it could not strengthen the government of South Vietnam or win popular support for it among its people (Bergerud, 5). Here, too, Communist forces effectively applied the ideas of Clausewitz's paradoxical trinity. They effectively discredited South Vietnam's government and fomented distrust and suspicion among the government, population, and military. They not only unraveled linkages among them but also between South Vietnam and its essential ally, the United States. Once Americans withdrew, South Vietnam's collapse became inevitable.

Defeating Insurgents

IN A CONVENTIONAL WAR you know you've won when the enemy government or its primary military forces surrender. On 7 May 1945, Alfred Jodl, Chief of Staff of the German army, surrendered to Allied forces on the instruction of Karl Doenitz, Adolf Hitler's designated successor as head of state. On 9 April 1865, Robert E. Lee surrendered the remnants of the Army of Virginia to Ulysses S. Grant. Afterward, the Confederacy collapsed as Jefferson Davis and the other members of his government fled home to their plantations. This ended any possibility of continued Confederate conventional military resistance.

Insurgent leaders, though, rarely surrender. Even when they do, some successor often picks up their mantel and continues the struggle. American soldiers and their Philippine allies captured insurgent leader Emilio Aguinaldo on 23 March 1901, but the war officially continued for another year, and unofficially for several more years after that as a succession of new insurgent leaders emerged.

The same is often true of negotiated settlements. Just because some insurgents agree to peace, such as the 2016 peace agreement between the government of Colombia and the Revolutionary Armed Forces of Colombia (FARC) doesn't mean everyone agrees. Some insurgents may continue the war and new insurgent organizations and leaders may arise to lead it. So, how do counterinsurgents know when they've won?

For Galula, the test is simple. "Victory is won, and pacification ends when most of the counterinsurgent forces can safely be withdrawn, leaving the population to take care of itself with the help of a normal contingent of police and army forces" (*Pacification in Algeria*, 244).

By this standard, those who argue the United States won the Vietnam War and then abandoned their ally are wrong. If South Vietnam could only stand while U.S. troops remained, then the insurgency was far from over. That insurgency forced South Vietnam to scatter its troops in garrisons to hold the countryside, which left it vulnerable to a conventional invasion by North Vietnamese regulars spearheaded by tanks and heavy artillery. Without American troops, South Vietnam could not simultaneously fight both communist insurgents and North Vietnamese regulars.

To succeed, a counterinsurgent must break the insurgent's military power and ensure people's safety. Galula argues, counterinsurgents have two options:

1. Build up their strength in areas with little insurgent activity and expand from there, executing what strategists have labeled a spreading "ink blot" or "oil spot" strategy; or
2. Aggressively attack the areas of greatest insurgent control, hoping to break enemy strength at its source and then mop the insurgency's remnants.

The correct choice depends on the relative strength of antagonists and is hard to judge. Ink blot strategies are necessarily slow and allow insurgents to build up strength in hard-to-reach strongholds, perhaps to the point where defeating them is costly or even impossible. On the other hand, committing the bulk of one's military power to distant or difficult to access territories is risky. That's how the Nationalists lost China to the Communists. The French similarly tried this in Vietnam, hoping to reverse what most recognized as a losing war. Instead, their defeat at Dien Bien Phu in 1954 accelerated their departure from Vietnam.

Seventy years earlier, though, French General Joseph Simon Galliéni, after being denied the additional troops he requested to conquer central Vietnam, proceeded slowly and methodically, securing one province at a time. He later did the same in Madagascar. Hubert Lyautey, who served with him, refined Galliéni's ideas and compared them to a spreading "oil spot." Counterinsurgents, he argued, should first thoroughly secure a small area. Once that's done, they may gradually expand from that secure base. When this strategy works, people voluntarily relocate to secure areas for safety, trade and other economic opportunities, and whatever incentives the government offers. Voluntary relocation combined with military and political action expands the oil spot. As the war turns against them, insurgents offered amnesty defect to the government, which helps expand the oil spot.

During the American Revolution, British leaders rejected a methodical, oil spot strategy and instead sought to rapidly seize control of the New England colonies. When that effort failed at the Battle of Saratoga, they dispatched a large army to the southern colonies and tried again. That effort, too, ended in disaster, as Americans regulars and insurgents whittled away Cornwallis's army and rendered it vulnerable to George Washington's *coup de grace* at Yorktown. A different strategy, one focused on careful, methodical counterinsurgency coupled with political reforms might have won Britain the war.

Galula's Eight-Step Model

REGARDLESS OF THE OPTION they choose, Galula suggests counterinsurgents must follow an eight-step plan in which military and political efforts complement and reinforce one another.

1. Destroy/expel insurgents from territory.
2. Deploy garrisons to protect the population and civil action teams to build/improve infrastructure.
3. Isolate/control/seduce the population.
4. Destroy insurgent political organization.
5. Hold elections.
6. Test new local leaders.
7. Organize political parties under tested leaders.
8. Win over/suppress the last insurgents.

Galula's first two steps focus on eliminating insurgent military forces. Even in this phase though, military action should be subordinated to political goals. So, one should attack insurgent forces with the minimal amount of firepower needed for success. Galula argues the political advantages of any military operation must exceed social and psychological costs, such as killing civilians or damaging their property. Effective military operations require both cultural awareness and the ability to gather and act rapidly on intelligence information about enemy forces. Counterinsurgents must engage with local populations and form effective and cooperative relationships with them.

Counterinsurgent victory requires "the permanent isolation" of insurgents from the population. This isolation, Galula clarifies, must not be "enforced on the population," but rather "maintained by and with the population" (*Counterinsurgency Warfare,* 54). Defeating insurgents requires the active support of local populations. So, it is better to have a small, active base of local support than a large, passive one. Like Lawrence, Galula argues, one should delegate as much responsibility for the war to the local population as possible. They need to have agency and be free to exercise their initiative.

In contrast to recent American interventions in Afghanistan and Iraq where American advisors sought to establish strong, centralized governments, Galula argues counterinsurgents win local support by building (or rebuilding) political systems "from the population upward" (*Counterinsurgency Warfare,* 95). Insurgencies are "bottom-to-top" movements. Successful counterinsurgencies must be as well. They need to have "boots on the ground," as Americans like to say, and work with local leaders. Political corruption plays into insurgent hands and must be eliminated, as must incompetent or ineffective government officials and bureaucrats. Rather than developing a strong, centralizing government in Kabul, Afghanistan's capital, Americans needed to encourage the emergence of local democracy in thousands of rural Afghani villages.

Effective counterinsurgency requires improvement of people's quality of life and their involvement in the political process. They need to see rapid, visible progress in improving/rebuilding their nation's infrastructure as well as progress in social and political reforms. This requires the work of civilian agencies in addition to military forces. People who have agency are more likely to commit to the struggle against the insurgency. Just as one isolates and destroys insurgent military forces, one must do the same to the insurgent political apparatus. This requires both traditional military and police actions to locate and eliminate insurgent operatives, as well as silencing their means of communication and countering their propaganda with one's own media.

As scholars like David Edelstein note, it is critical when supporting a friendly government's counterinsurgency effort for local people to understand the need for foreign troops, so they support them. For that to happen, foreigners must provide local populations a "credible guarantee" they have no interest in prolonged occupation and will depart as soon as possible (*Occupational Hazards*, 51).

On the other hand, Galula warns, winning over the people requires not only continuing evidence of progress but also a commitment to victory. The population needs evidence the counterinsurgent is in it for the long haul and will not abandon them if the going gets tough or the war is too expensive. As recent American experience shows, demonstrating a commitment to victory while simultaneously promising—and preparing for—a rapid departure is far from easy.

Once the insurgent political apparatus weakens and counter-insurgent forces win over significant parts of the local population, they must hold elections. This begins the final steps of Galula's sequence. After that, it is a matter of building a functioning democracy, eliminating corrupt, ineffective, or pro-insurgent politicians—preferably through elections and voting—and winning over the last of the insurgents, perhaps through amnesty programs that reintegrate them into society. The emphasis on democracy, elections, and voting, of course, reflects the political cultures of most counterinsurgency theorists who tend to be American, British, or French.

Non-democratic powers have, of course, fought insurgencies, but their record of success is underwhelming. While Nazi Germany effectively stifled domestic opposition, it eliminated none of the many insurgencies it faced across its European conquests. Soviet counterinsurgency efforts in Afghanistan proved a dismal failure despite, or perhaps because of, their brutality. Russia's even more brutal counterinsurgency campaigns in Chechnya exemplify Tacitus's observation about laying waste a land and calling it peace. It is hardly a counterinsurgency campaign that elicits admiration. The same could be said of the counterinsurgents in James Cameron's film *Avatar* (2009).

Dictatorial states cannot and will not grant their subjects local political autonomy. Doing so undermines the very nature of their regimes. So, Galula and other Western theorists may well be right. Democracy is probably an essential component of successful counterinsurgency in the modern era.

At the end of the nineteenth century, Europe's colonial powers brutally—and sometimes genocidally—stamped out insurgencies across their empires without granting their subjects even the semblance of local rule. They did so when they had tremendous technological advantages, not just in weaponry, such as machine guns, but also in communication and transportation, thanks to the telegraph, railroads, and steamships. Thanks to diplomatic agreements culminating the 1884 Berlin Conference they fought against isolated enemies. No European power would help indigenous people fight off a fellow European power.

Ethiopia, a mountainous country whose leaders purchased modern weapons, proved the only African nation to defeat and expel a European army in the late nineteenth century. It did so with a combination of both conventional forces and irregulars who operated in the rear of invading Italian armies.

Case Study: The Surge

SCHOLARS OFTEN POINT to the Malayan Insurgency, which pitted the communist insurgents of the Malayan National Liberation Army (MNLA) against British colonial rule in Malaya from 1948 to 1960, as an exemplar of counterinsurgent success. The centerpiece of British strategy involved the forced relocation into internment camps of about 500,000 civilians, many of them ethnic Chinese from whom the insurgents drew their primary support. British military forces then attacked insurgent-held territories, burning crops, destroying villages, and laying waste to large areas with defoliants like Agent Orange. These actions, combined with aggressive search and destroy missions, intelligence gathering and penetration of insurgent units, and a host of reforms to win "hearts and minds" brought success. Most importantly, Britain ended its colonial rule and facilitated the emergence of Malaysia as an independent state in 1957.

While much studied, British success in Malaya proved difficult to emulate. In many ways, the Malayan insurgency is an outlier. The MNLA proved uniquely vulnerable because its members were easily isolated. Its leadership and most of its rank and file were Chinese, but ethnic Chinese accounted for only about 10% of Malaysia's population. Unlike other communist insurgents at the time, the MNLA received no foreign support. Communism proved an unpopular ideology in Malaysia and independence from Britain deprived the insurgents of their primary rallying cry. After independence, the insurgency faltered. New communist leaders renewed the war a generation later and again lost the war.

A more useful—and more recent—example is the so-called "Surge" in Iraq, which neutralized what previously had been a popular and successful insurgency. In 2003, the United States led a coalition of allies in a successful invasion of Iraq that toppled long-ruling dictator Saddam Hussein. The 160,000 coalition troops proved more than sufficient to smash the Iraqi army but were inadequate to secure the country and facilitate the transition to a new, democratic government. Numerous scholars and strategists warned of this before the war.

A succession of missteps followed, such as demobilizing Iraqi military and police forces, which could have helped the American-led multinational coalition maintain law and order and stabilize Iraq. American military operations against the insurgency were clumsy, heavy-handed, and failed to consider local culture—mistakes dramatically compounded by the revelations of prisoner mistreatment at Abu Ghraib prison.

Resentment against American occupation and the new, Shia-majority Iraqi government, festered. This fed several anti-American insurgent movements, including al Qaeda in Iraq, a newly formed branch of the organization that committed the 11 September 2001 attacks on the World Trade Center and Pentagon. Casualties soared as coalition and Iraqi government forces lost control of growing territory including parts of Baghdad and other important cities.

By 2006, American leaders recognized disaster loomed. There followed a dramatic reshuffling of senior command and the deployment of 20,000 additional U.S. troops, the so-called "Surge" to Iraq. The new American commander, General David Petraeus, advised by a staff of remarkably capable and well-educated officers, nicknamed Jedi Knights, transformed American strategy. While additional troops helped stabilize the situation, victory depended on this new strategy, which involved winning the "hearts and minds" of Iraq's disaffected Sunni population from which al Qaeda in Iraq received most of its support—so much support that al Qaeda leader Osama bin Laden repeatedly asked al Qaeda in Iraq leader Abu Musab al-Zarqawi to send him money.

American troops focused on Anbar Province the center of al Qaeda in Iraq's strength. They increased their presence, patrolled more often, changed how they patrolled to avoid alienating local people, and capitalized on missteps by al Qaeda in Iraq. The latter's overconfident leaders expanded their operations too widely, while promoting religious extremism, persecuting local imams, and executing indiscriminate attacks that alienated people. The rise of independent Iraqi media outlets who reported on these atrocities, helped counter al Qaeda propaganda. As Field Manual 3–24, *Counterinsurgency* notes, "the information environment is a critical dimension of such internal wars."

Before the Surge, more than three-quarters of local Iraqis had never met an American, let alone talked to one. That changed. Americans engaged more directly with local leaders who increasingly perceived al Qaeda as a threat to their own social and political positions. American and local Iraqi leaders met regularly to discuss problems and iron out their differences. Americans involved local leaders in political decisions.

As relations improved, Americans spent lavishly to recruit individual sheikhs and other opinion influencers and arm local self-defense forces. By the end of 2007, more than 100,000 Iraqis were on the American payroll and had joined organizations like Concerned Local Citizens or Sons of Iraq to defend their communities alongside U.S. troops. This "Anbar Awakening," undermined support for al Qaeda in Iraq. Meanwhile, a surge in local intelligence sources helped American forces target al Qaeda command centers, weapons stockpiles, and leaders, including Abu Musab al-Zarqawi, killed on 7 June 2006 by an American air strike on his safe house. Al Qaeda in Iraq was soon starved of funds, munitions, and recruits. Its membership fragmented into rival factions and insurgent activity plummeted.

AS GALULA EXPLAINS and the American Surge in Iraq demonstrates, no single factor produces counterinsurgent victory. American efforts to win hearts and minds, recruit supporters among local elites, and raise and equip local defense forces operated synergistically with traditional military operations and intelligence gathering to undermine al Qaeda's political operatives and whittle away its military forces. American officers needed to establish rapport and build trust with local Iraqi leaders before they would accept money from Americans, let alone fight alongside them. Similarly, al Qaeda religious intolerance and brutality helped Americans demonstrate the alignment of interests between the American-supported Iraqi government and local Iraqi leaders.

The British could likely have ended the American Revolution, or at least substantially eroded support for it, by giving Americans direct representation in Parliament in the early 1770s. By the time Britain's leaders seriously considered this dramatic step, though, the Revolution had spread across the thirteen colonies and confined British rule to a handful of coastal enclaves, such as New York City.

This underlines one of the problems of fighting insurgency. It is usually difficult to recognize an insurgency until it's too late to settle the issues fueling it easily and peacefully. A government's unwillingness or inability to address people's political demands allows an insurgency to grow, which government missteps may further fuel. This is why most counterinsurgent theorists emphasize political over military measures.

However, implementing political reforms requires military forces to protect reformers from insurgent attack. Without that protection, reform is impossible since insurgents specifically target reformers, aid workers, and government officials.

Fictional characters will face this same dilemma. How do they prevent insurgents from disrupting their political reforms—and perhaps killing the reformers? How do they gather intelligence about insurgents? How do they pursue and destroy insurgent fighters without alienating the local population, as Americans did in Vietnam, with lavish displays of firepower that inevitably effect civilian life?

How do they disrupt insurgent political networks, counteract insurgent propaganda, and hinder insurgent political and military recruitment?

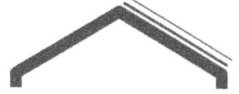

Chapter Eight: Strategies of Terror

Terrorism is not a new phenomenon. While the term dates to the late eighteenth century and the Reign of Terror during the French Revolution, terrorism, like insurgency, has ancient roots. Jewish sicarii resisted Roman rule in Judea by assassinating Roman officials and their Jewish collaborators. In the medieval era, the Nizaris, a Shiite Muslim sect, founded a small state and protected it for 200 years by dispatching specially trained agents to eliminate or terrorize their enemies. Nicknamed assassins by their enemies, the term may derive from assassins' use of hashish. Regardless, terrorism can be an effective strategy.

Terrorism is a strategy of the weak, one adopted by organizations that lack popular support and/or military power. Like insurgents, terrorists seek to leverage minimal resources for great results. They hope to spread their message, gain support for their cause, and cow their enemies through public acts of mass violence. Well-resourced organizations generally avoid terrorism. They have other options.

Some terrorists are nationalists, with purely local or regional interests and objectives. Others have global ambitions. Even those with purely regional goals, though, may choose to act globally to gain attention for their cause. Assorted terror groups with purely local grievances, such as the Irish Republican Army (IRA) and the Popular Front for the Liberation of Palestine (PFLP) have conducted attacks in other parts of the world to publicize their cause.

Some terrorists are state sponsored. The Soviet Union funded a host of terrorist organizations in its heyday. For many years, Syria provided the PFLP with funds, training, and safe base areas. The level of control these nations have over the terrorists they fund varies considerably. Some are very tightly controlled, essentially operating as arms of their sponsor's intelligence agencies. Others, such as Hamas in Gaza and Hezbollah in Lebanon, both funded by Iran, operate with great independence.

Terrorists without generous state sponsors need other sources of funding. Joseph Stalin robbed banks to fund Communist Party operations in Tsarist Russia. The Taliban in Afghanistan and FARC (Revolutionary Armed Forces of Colombia) profit from selling opium and other narcotics. Other terrorists rely on kidnapping for ransom. Some conceal themselves as charitable organizations, benefitting from international donations. Hamas did this for many years until its links to terror became too obvious to hide. A Pakistani charity, Jamat al Tabligh, facilitated the travel of al Qaeda operatives. Since the 11 September 2001 al Qaeda terrorist attacks on the United States, more than two-dozen international charities have been accused of funneling funds to terrorist organizations.

Defining Terrorism

TERRORISM IS FUNDAMENTALLY a political act. Its practitioners aim to change a government policy or overthrow the government itself. Apart from that, there is no agreed upon definition for terrorism. Around the world, government agencies and international organizations floated their own definitions. At their core, these disputed definitions reflect the old (and generally inaccurate) saw that "one person's terrorist is another person's freedom fighter." The obverse, of course, is patently false. Not all revolutionaries engage in terrorism. Similarly, the "freedom" and other causes for which many terrorists commit their atrocities rarely achieve universal acceptance and adherence.

Some insurgents reject terrorism, as George Washington did. Others incorporate terrorism into their larger strategy, as the Viet Minh did. For yet other insurgents, such as the FLN (National Liberation Front) in Algeria in the 1960s or Shining Path (Sendero Luminoso) in Peru in more recent years, terrorism becomes their primary strategy. Sometimes this is a deliberate choice, as in the case of Shining Path. More often, insurgent leaders embrace terrorism because they have no effective alternative. Conventional FLN operations against the French in Algeria regularly ended in disaster. So, too, did their efforts to cultivate a successful rural insurgency. In contrast, urban terrorism proved politically and militarily effective.

Similarly, several Palestinian organizations, such as Black September and the PFLP, embraced terrorism after being denied safe and effective base areas in nations bordering Israel. They murdered Israeli athletes at the 1972 Olympics, hijacked airplanes, and conducted other bloody attacks far from the Middle East to publicize their political demands and because direct attacks on Israel had proved difficult.

People offer dozens of different definitions for terrorism, none of which have attained universal acceptance. In 1998, the U.S. State Department defined terrorism as "premeditated politically motivated violence perpetrated against noncombatant targets by subnational groups or clandestine state agents, normally intended to influence an audience." This definition starts well but ends poorly with the vague goal to "influence an audience," which is just a means to end. Terrorists have specific political and/or social goals.

In 1979, Israel's Jonathan Institute defined terrorism as: "the deliberate and systematic murder, maiming, and menacing of the innocent to inspire fear for political ends." This is one of the broadest definitions and specifically includes states that terrorize their own populations, such as the French Revolution's Reign of Terror or the governments of Idi Amin, Saddam Hussein, and Joseph Stalin. It would also include the strategic bombing campaigns advocated by Douhet, Trenchard, and other theorists discussed in this book's air power chapter, since in addition to destroying enemy industrial and military facilities their advocates hoped to terrorize enemy populations into surrender. The definition's weakness is that "menacing the innocent" is vague.

What constitutes menacing and who is innocent? The leaders of Hamas and other anti-Israel organizations have repeatedly stated that no Israeli, even a child, is innocent. All are legitimate targets. FLN leaders similarly rejected the innocence of French teenagers who they deliberately targeted by bombing soda shops and dance clubs.

Terrorist organizations differ dramatically from one another in funding, goals, methodology, and organization. Fortunately, winning agreement on a broad definition of terrorism is not essential for discussing strategies of terrorism. For simplicity and to maintain its focus, this chapter uses the most common definition of terrorism: sub-national actors who attack civilian targets to advance their political goals. Terrorism is a violent political act aimed primarily at civilians.

In general, terrorists aim to disrupt normal civil society, capture media attention, create a climate of fear, erode popular support for a government, and weaken that government's security forces. As David Galula notes, disorder "is cheap to create and very costly to prevent" (*Counterinsurgency Warfare*, 8). Terrorists rely on this. They seek to exploit the tensions inherent to Clausewitz's Paradoxical Trinity, fueling passions and exacerbating differences among the people, government, and military. Because terrorists need media attention, they often attack targets of symbolic importance.

Some terrorist organizations have limited goals. They seek to win through psychological means, terrorizing governments to change a policy, rescind a law, or coerce individuals into ceasing behavior deemed objectionable. Examples of these include bombing clinics that offer abortions, sabotage of oil, timber, and other companies perceived as harmful to the environment, and attacks on women and minorities designed to exclude them from full and equal participation in civil society, such as the routine violence visited on African Americans during the Jim Crow era and contemporary attacks on gay bars.

Other terrorists have grander ambitions. They seek to build popular support through acts of terror to attract funding and recruits to grow their organization large enough to topple a government or drive out an "occupying" or "imperialist" power. In these cases, terrorists hope their deeds recruit sufficient adherents to lay the foundation for an insurgency that could then follow Mao's three stage model, eventually fielding conventional military forces. Examples of these groups include the Baader-Meinhof Gang and other Red Brigades of the 1970s and 1980s, Algeria's FLN, the Irish Republican Army, and the PFLP.

Terrorist acts aim to produce specific reactions in specific audiences. They aim to:

- Intimidate their immediate targets.
- Publicize their cause and win sympathy from others.
- Attract funds and recruits from both domestic and international sources.

The reaction to terrorism is often more important than the damage caused by specific acts of terror.

Terror attacks may influence elections, as the 2004 Madrid train bombings did in Spain, or simply disrupt normal life by making us take off our shoes in airports. They may discourage foreign investment and aid, as terror attacks in Iraq did in the immediate aftermath of the 2003 American invasion. If government forces overreact to terror attacks, as they often do, that too, may win the terrorists public sympathy. Heavy-handed or indiscriminate government force that harms the innocent along with the guilty can alienate people otherwise horrified by the terrorism that sparked the government's reprisal. This, in turn, often may produce surges in terrorist funding and recruiting. Terrorist leaders know this and hope to provoke government overreactions, believing notoriety will help their cause.

As a result, many terrorists explicitly target the innocent. They attack schools and other places children congregate, and even use children to deliver their bombs. Everyone is a legitimate target. Attacking innocents not only intimidates their enemies (not even your children are safe) but garners more publicity.

Other terrorists are more discriminating in their targets. Russian anarchists in the late nineteenth century specifically targeted politicians and wealthy members of the upper class. They believed killing enough of them would provoke a popular revolt and usher in a more enlightened society. They killed Tsar Alexander II and many others but failed to galvanize a popular revolution.

Yet, their highly publicized assassinations encouraged similar campaigns around the world, including in the United States, where anarchist Leon Czolgosz assassinated President William McKinley in 1901.

Che Guevara similarly believed a handful of disciplined insurgents, which he termed *foco,* could use terror to build popular support and create the conditions needed for sustained insurgency. He tried out his strategy in Bolivia, but the average Bolivian rejected terrorism. Without a friendly populace to shelter them Guevara and his insurgents were soon captured or killed by government forces assisted by the United States.

Timothy McVeigh and the other perpetrators of the 1995 Oklahoma City bombing believed terrorism and attacks on government targets would ignite a racist insurgency that toppled the U.S. government, perceived by these terrorists as dominated by African Americans, Jews, and other undesirables. In its place, they planned to create a white ethno-state. Their Oklahoma City attack killed 168 people in the Murrah Federal Building, including 19 children who died in the building's childcare center. Rather than imitation, the attack evoked horror and a short-lived crackdown on domestic terrorism by the U.S. government, which ended when the 11 September 2001 attacks redirected attention to overseas terrorists.

George Washington and most of his fellow American revolutionaries explicitly rejected terrorism. They did not target the wives and children of British officers, plant bombs in marketplaces, or otherwise broadly target civilian society. Nonetheless, tarring and feathering outspoken Loyalists was hardly a humane practice, since hot pine tar could cause blisters, burns, and other injuries.

To sum up, there are five elements to terrorism:

1. It is a planned, premeditated act of violence, often against symbolic targets.
2. Terrorists seek to capture media attention to promote their ideas and attract local and international support and recruits.
3. They aim particularly at civilian targets and public opinion.
4. It is a political, rather than criminal, act that seeks specific political and/or social change.
5. While nations may aid terrorists, as Serbia supported the Black Hand or Pakistan the Taliban, terrorists themselves are sub-national actors with a specific agenda. They are often bound by ethnicity, ideology, religion, or other

common identity.

In general, terrorists target five audiences: the government, members of their organization, a domestic constituency they claim to represent (cultural, ethnic, ideological, religious, social, etc.), members of that constituency living in other countries, and world opinion. One way to examine terrorist strategies is by analyzing how they target these five audiences.

Targeting the Government

TERRORISTS MIGHT TRY to push a government to implement some reform. They might convince political leaders that the terrorist group reflects actual social or political grievances that must be addressed. More likely, attacks on the government, such as targeted assassinations of senior politicians, could either paralyze the government, demonstrating its ineffectiveness, or panic the government into ill-considered or reckless action, such as imposing martial law, which alienates the general population. The 1998 movie *The Siege* plays out this scenario, and Osama bin Laden did, in fact, expect the U.S. government to implement martial law after the September 11 attacks.

Some terrorists commit atrocities to provoke government retaliation. The more outrageous the atrocity, the more severe (and indiscriminate) the government response is likely to be. Increasing government repression, terrorists hope, will polarize the civilian population, strengthening their movement and weakening support for the government. Or the terrorists may hope to change a government's foreign policy.

Many terrorists attack the United States because the United States supports the terrorist's enemy, either indirectly, through diplomacy and monetary aid, or directly with military support and even "boots on the ground." These terrorist attacks aim to convince a government to abandon an ally, regional presence, colonial mission, or similar commitment. By raising the costs of that support, terrorists hope governments will do the appropriate cost-benefit analysis, decide the commitment is too expensive (in money, troops, or simply attention) and withdraw.

Terrorist Membership

TERRORISTS RECRUIT new members by committing acts of terror. This is why today's terrorists record and post videos of their attacks on the Internet. These are part of the terrorists' advertising campaigns. They both recruit new members and provide tangible evidence of success to existing members to keep them loyal and active. They also garner support and funding for the terrorists.

Even small-scale operations can boost terrorist morale and win new recruits. Like any belligerent, terrorists need incremental dividends to keep their cause alive. Successful attacks build group cohesion. They offer the prospect of eventual victory that keeps terrorist organizations' rank and file committed to their cause. Conversely, inaction or failed attacks depress morale and reduce recruitment. Historically, most terrorist organizations have failed and faded away, like the Bader-Meinhof Gang.

A Constituent Population

TERRORISTS HOPE TO appeal to some constituent population, often within a particular nation or region, though some, such as the Red Brigades and Al-Qaeda, operate transnationally or even globally. The terrorists' constituency might be a particular religious or ethnic group, such as the Tamils in Sri Lanka for whom the Tamil Tigers fight. Or they might focus on a social or economic class, such as communists proclaiming, "Workers of the world unite!" Regardless, terrorists claim to fight in their name, to secure their freedom, restore their rights, or otherwise defend their interests.

Just because terrorists claim to fight for a particular constituency does not mean that constituency welcomes their support or approves of their actions. Terrorists need to win this constituency's support and allegiance, which is almost always a terrorist organization's primary audience. They need to capture their attention, excite them, and win them over to achieve mass political mobilization. To do that, they pose as their champions and attack the government and others seen as their oppressors.

Ideally, terrorists erode the government's reputation and standing and then assume its mantle of authority. So, in addition to targeting civilians, terrorists assassinate government officials, attack police stations, and sabotage military installations. When successful, these attacks undermine a government's authority and reveal it as incapable of defending the people it claims to represent. This, in turn, opens the way for terrorists or insurgents to win over the people and supplant the government.

Non-Constituent Populations

TERRORISTS ALSO SEEK to influence other people. These non-constituent populations could be the citizens of another country, particularly a colonial or imperial power, or people likely to sympathize with the plight of the terrorists' constituent population. Targeting the former is particularly important in anti-colonial or anti-imperial struggles. Terrorists seek to drive a wedge between a colonial government and its own home population. The idea is to deprive the target government of the domestic political base it needs to wage war against the terrorists.

The FLN did this in its war with France. They protracted the war, whose growing costs forced the French government to borrow funds and raise taxes. Constant news about the war—much of it bad—wore people out. Increasingly fatigued, their commitment to retaining Algeria, France's last major colony, faded away.

The FLN also brought the war to France, threatening its population. They provoked France's government into waging war with such brutality that it alienated its citizens, who were horrified by their army's actions, which included routine torture and execution of prisoners. French citizens turned against the war and eventually their government, which collapsed. The FLN effectively attacked all aspects of Clausewitz's paradoxical trinity.

The collapse of France's government, the Fourth Republic, brought Charles de Gaulle to power, who despite previous declarations to the contrary, recognized the economic, political, and social costs of the prolonged war were such that he had no choice but to end it. Continuing the war threatened France's political stability.

International Institutions and Opinion

FINALLY, SOME TERRORISTS seek international support for their cause. They court international institutions and work to sway world opinion to their point of view. The FLN effectively cultivated support from the United Nations, as well as garnering the support of Senator John F. Kennedy and other American politicians who sympathized with their cause. Egypt and other Arab states supported the FLN, as did the Arab League.

Another example is the Palestine Liberation Organization (PLO), which despite supporting terrorist attacks against Israel and Jewish institutions around the world, was recognized by the United Nations in 1974 as the legitimate representative of the Palestinian people. Ali Hassan Salameh, a member of the PLO's first United Nations delegation, helped plan and execute the Munich Olympics terror attacks two years earlier.

Recognition by world organizations helped a host of terrorist organizations and their sponsors spread their message, garnering support and funding. While this international support is not essential to terrorist victory, it certainly helps. Terrorist organizations unable to internationalize their appeal and win supporters beyond their immediate constituency often wither away. While terrorism may be "the weapon of the weak," it still requires support and funding.

Analysis: Five Audiences of Terrorism

NOT EVERY TERRORIST organization targets all five of these audiences. Though, the more ambitious a terrorist's goals, the more likely they are to address all five. A problem, of course, is that appealing to one audience may alienate another. Brutal massacres of government adherents may win terrorist's support at home, particularly if people perceive the attacks as legitimate reprisals for government brutality and oppression, but alienate people in other countries who are appalled by the bloodshed. Despite hundreds of successful, headline-grabbing attacks by a host of different terrorist organizations claiming to represent them, it's hard to see how terrorist attacks have furthered the cause of Palestinian statehood. Particularly in the 1960s, 1970s, and 1980s, whatever sympathy the Palestinians gained for their plight was offset by the violence and number of terror attacks conducted by Palestinian organizations—so many that Palestinian and terrorist became synonyms in some people's minds.

Similarly, Palestinian leaders were among the most outspoken supporters of Iraq during the 1990 Gulf War. Saddam Hussein claimed to be fighting for the Palestinians (and other marginalized and exploited Arabs). Palestinian leaders encouraged Palestinian volunteers to fight for Saddam Hussein's regime, and Palestinian oil workers in Kuwait cooperated with Saddam Hussein's invasion and helped loot the country. On the Israeli-occupied West Bank, Palestinian leaders organized mass demonstrations against Israel and the American-led coalition fighting to liberate Kuwait. Demonstrators cheered scud missile attacks on Israel and Saudi Arabia, which at the time many believed contained chemical warheads.

As popular as Saddam Hussein was among average Palestinians—and he seems to have been quite popular given the size of Palestinian demonstrations—these pro-Saddam displays alienated many Palestinian supporters in the United States and the Arab world, particularly in Kuwait, which Saddam Hussein invaded. Financial and diplomatic support from Kuwait and other Gulf states, previously among the top funders of Palestinian organizations, dried up.

The end of this funding, which coincided with the collapse of the Soviet Union and the end of its funding, forced Palestinian leaders to change strategy. They recognized Israel's right to exist and, for the first time, seriously sought a peaceful, negotiated, two-state settlement. Their efforts produced the Oslo Accords (1993) and other agreements, which outlined a promising path to peace. Unfortunately, the emergence of Hamas, which quickly and violently displaced existing Palestinian authority in Gaza, along with the assassination of Israeli Prime Minister Yitzhak Rabin by an Israeli terrorist, derailed the peace process, which has foundered ever since.

Case Study: The FLN in Algeria

THE FLN'S WAR TO LIBERATE Algeria from a century of French rule presents an excellent example of an effective terror campaign. In fact, the FLN became a model for later terrorist organizations, in part because of its positive portrayal in the film *Battle for Algiers* (1966) by Italian writer and director Gillo Pontecorvo, an FLN sympathizer.

By the late 1950s, roughly 11% of Algeria's population of ten million were colons, that is immigrants from Europe or their descendants. They occupied all the senior government positions and dominated the local economy. Rather than improving in the twentieth century, the economic gulf between them and the majority of Algerians, mostly Arabs and Berbers, widened. In the aftermath of World War II, growing numbers of Algerians, some of whom fought in the French army during the war, demanded a greater say in government. Some demanded independence, but many would have accepted greater autonomy for Algeria within some form of French union.

Like the British government in the decade before the American Revolution, France's post-war government failed to recognize the seriousness of Algerian discontent. French troops brutally crushed demonstrations in Setif and other cities in 1945 and arrested their leaders. A decade later, Algeria exploded in violence as the FLN, and other organizations launched an insurgency against French colonial rule.

The French army, though, quickly mastered the insurgency. It built elaborate fortifications along Algeria's borders with Tunisia and Morocco. Supported by rapid response teams, some in helicopters, the French prevented any significant infiltration of FLN troops from these countries into Algeria to support the insurgents. French naval and air patrols similarly blocked most supplies from reaching Algerian insurgents from overseas.

In province after province, the French army, supported by locally raised Muslim troops, effectively isolated local populations from the insurgents and pursued and destroyed them. Unlike its war in Indochina, fought mostly by elite units and the French Foreign Legion, France committed large numbers of troops to Algeria, eventually more than 400,000. These allowed it to effectively control large parts of the country and stifle the insurgency in the countryside. The insurgency's failure forced the FLN to change its strategy.

MILITARY STRATEGY FOR WRITERS   201

As the rural insurgency collapsed, the FLN adopted a strategy of urban terrorism. There were several advantages to this. Most of Algeria's European population lived in Algiers and other large cities, as did many of the Muslims most closely associated with French rule. This made cities a target rich environment for terrorists. Algeria's densely populated cities were also difficult to police and easy to hide in. This was particularly true of the Casbah, the oldest part of Algiers. Adding hiding places to its ancient, but frequently repaired and updated buildings proved easy. Its narrow, twisting streets and alleys made spotting and avoiding (or ambushing) police easy.

FLN terrorists struck both the Muslim and European populations, targeting police stations and government buildings. They soon expanded this campaign to purely civilian targets, particularly soda shops and dance clubs catering to teenagers and young adults. Muslim women who could pass as European slipped through French checkpoints and planted bombs in these clubs, which killed hundreds and maimed many more. Increasingly indiscriminate terrorist bombings provoked increasingly vicious French reprisals. Terror spread in a worsening cycle.

As the situation worsened, France imposed martial law on Algiers. French paratroopers took control of the city and effectively rooted out the FLN's terror network in a systematic campaign that relied on a heavy troop presence, numerous checkpoints, aggressive patrolling of city streets, paid informants, and intelligence extracted from captured and suspected FLN operatives through torture. Their campaign, as described and justified by French second-in-command Paul Aussaresses in *Battle of the Casbah* (2004), was brutal and effective. Yet, France lost the war. Within a few years, it evacuated Algeria's European population and abandoned its colony and the local Muslim troops who had fought for France.

This is one of the great ironies of the war. The French valued their Algerian colony so much they made it a department of France, an official part of the French nation. They committed a substantial army to retain control of Algeria and recruited tens of thousands of Algerian Muslims (*harkis*) who fought bravely and effectively for France. French troops never lost a significant engagement against the FLN. Throughout the conflict, French troops maintained control of every city and strategically important area of the country. The FLN never won a major battle or controlled any significant part of Algeria for more than a few months. How then did the FLN win the war?

Part of the problem, Galula notes, is that France employed lots of sticks, but too few carrots. The counterinsurgent needs to achieve pacification without a constant military presence. France never managed this. More importantly, the FLN's leaders out-thought the French. They were better strategists and proved better able to wage a protracted war.

The FLN leaders who began the war were ridiculously optimistic. They made two false assumptions. First, that a few large-scale attacks on French installations and French civilians would spark a popular uprising against France. Second, that France, weakened and humiliated by its recent defeat in Vietnam, would quickly concede and abandon Algeria.

Instead, France reacted effectively and in force. In addition to quickly securing Algeria's major cities and towns, the French captured most of the FLN's senior leaders.

New leaders, though, quickly emerged to take their place, and the FLN's new leaders proved flexible and adaptable. Constantly searching for an asymmetrical response to French initiatives, they sought out and exploited French weaknesses. The FLN maintained constant pressure on France. Its conventional forces (the ALN) in friendly Tunisia regularly attacked France's border defenses while insurgents and terrorists operated inside Algeria. Unlike the French, the FLN's leaders regularly reassessed the strategic situation and changed their strategy accordingly, all the while exploiting French political weakness and building international support for Algerian independence.

Like many counterinsurgents, France belatedly implemented reforms to appease the Algerian population. These included generous land grants and other incentives. The FLN, in turn, neutralized many of these efforts by murdering Muslims who benefitted from French largesse. The FLN also targeted the families of *harkis* serving in the French army.

French forces effectively suppressed insurgent bands as they formed but had great difficulty tracking down small terrorist cells.

Along with targeting those associated with the French regime, the FLN effectively eliminated what they referred to as "third forces." The FLN targeted any Muslim Algerians who sought a middle road between insurgency and acceptance of French rule. By killing these moderates, the FLN left the average Algerian only two choices: the FLN or French colonialism.

Average French citizens also came to believe their choices were limited. They could either accept a seemingly endless war in Algeria fought in ways anathema to them or allow Algerians to go their own way. Increasing reports of French atrocities and the torture and execution of FLN prisoners proved particularly problematic. While no society wishes its military to behave barbarously, memories of the Nazi occupation of France were fresh in the 1960s. Many French politicians had fought in the resistance. Most French civilians had experienced the brutality of Nazi rule. Many had lost friends to Gestapo torture and Nazi concentration camps. For French soldiers to behave like the hated Nazis was unacceptable, though perhaps not surprising, since several hundred Nazi soldiers escaped prosecution for war crimes by joining the French Foreign Legion. While effective in suppressing the FLN, French strategy and tactics undermined support for the war at home.

Torture was tactically effective for the French but a strategic failure. Even as French paratroopers and Foreign Legionnaires caught and imprisoned or killed FLN leaders, new ones took their place. As Machiavelli warned centuries earlier, brutality was only effective in the short term. As long as the causes of a revolt persist, new revolutionaries will appear. A conqueror, he suggests, has only two options. Either treat conquered peoples well to win their loyalty or drive them from the territory entirely.

The combination of increasing FLN terror and the growing sense among civilians and soldiers that France would soon abandon Algeria produced two interesting events. Parts of the French army in Algeria mutinied, vowing to continue to fight for a French Algeria. Loyal troops quickly suppressed the mutiny, but the mutineers weren't done. Supported by many European Algerians, they formed the OAS (Secret Army Organization), a terror group that claimed to represent the European victims of FLN terrorism. In essence, Algeria's European population was so terrorized it spawned its own terror organization to fight back. The OAS launched about 3,000 terror attacks in the last months of 1961.

This made the last year of the Algerian War, 1962, a three-sided struggle among the FLN, the new OAS, and a French army whose leaders were reluctant to risk the lives of their troops for a land their government planned to give away. OAS members and sympathizers launched a wave of attacks against the FLN, suspected FLN sympathizers, and French politicians favoring accommodation with the FLN. They repeatedly tried to assassinate Charles de Gaulle, who they accused of betraying them.

From the perspective of the FLN, this was great. They had the French killing each other. Terrorism had already spread from Algeria to metropolitan France, and incidents increased in the war's last years. The FLN targeted pro-French Algerians hiding in France, along with hardline politicians who favored continuing the war. The OAS attacked politicians, intellectuals, and others perceived as sympathetic to the FLN or Algerian independence. And of course, the FLN and OAS targeted one another. Numerous innocents died in the crossfire.

Continued Algerian resistance eroded French support for the war. In 1962, France recognized Algeria's independence and evacuated its troops along with roughly a million Algerian residents of European descent. France abandoned several hundred thousand *harkis*, along with their families, to the FLN, which killed many of them.

FEW DEMOCRATIC GOVERNMENTS emerge from terrorism, and the FLN was no exception. For a few years, FLN leader Ben Bella ruled a corrupt and oppressive government. In 1965, Houari Boumediene, wartime commander of the ALN, seized power in a military coup. He ruled through force of arms until his death in 1978. Military rule continued afterward, compounding economic and social problems that fueled discontent. In 1991, the Islamic Salvation Front (ISF) seemed poised to win long-delayed national elections. Fearing this militant Islamist party, the ruling military junta canceled the election. The ISF launched a campaign of insurgency and terror, and the government responded with vicious reprisal. More than a 100,000 Algerians died by violence over the next decade.

The Algerian War, particularly the Battle of the Casbah, remains a model other terrorists hope to emulate. The bombs are often bigger, and increasingly carried by suicide bombers, but today's terrorists follow the basic tactics and strategy of the Algerian campaign. They attack and kill innocents to expose the government's weakness and people's vulnerability, hoping these attacks will also provoke a heavy-handed and/or indiscriminate government response that inspires more people to become terrorists. Terrorists succeed by eroding the will of the people and government. Some governments eventually accede to terrorist demands, as France did in Algeria and Great Britain did in Ireland. A few governments have collapsed entirely when faced with terrorism. In other cases, terrorism provides a base from which an insurgency can grow.

More often, though, terrorism fails. History is littered with failed terror organizations. Yet, terrorists appear regularly in thrillers and spy novels. They make excellent villains.

SPECTRE, perhaps fiction's best-known terror organization, features in many James Bond novels and movies. Following the dictates of their name (Special Executive for Counter-intelligence, Terrorism, Revenge and Extortion), SPECTRE has kidnapped people for ransom, blackmailed and extorted politicians and business people, stolen and sold state secrets, and threatened mass destruction with nuclear weapons.

Unlike most historic terrorist organizations, though, SPECTRE—at least as conceived by Ian Fleming—operated for profit. Its leaders sought money rather than any specific national objective, such as changing a government or liberating some territory from foreign oppression. In *Thunderball* (1961), for example, SPECTRE steals two nuclear weapons and threatens to use them unless they're paid an enormous ransom. A few years later, in the movie *You Only*

Live Twice (1967), SPECTRE works with the People's Republic of China, to instigate war between the United States and the Soviet Union from which it expects to profit.

As with insurgents, authors should consider terrorists' motives and goals. What led a character to become a terrorist? What do they expect their terrorism to accomplish? Are they only in it for the money like SPECTRE? Are they nihilists hoping to incite an apocalypse like Japan's Aum Shinrikyo, who released nerve gas on trains? Do they wish to promote some ideology, like the communist red brigades of the 1970s? Or, like most terrorists, do they seek some national or territorial objective, such as freeing Palestine from Israeli (or British) rule, Algeria from French rule, or Ireland from British rule?

The latter make the most realistic terrorists, but this forces authors to inject themselves into contemporary political debates. While authors might avoid choosing sides in a conflict, they must confront the oft-deployed canard that "one man's terrorist is another's freedom fighter." This, perhaps, is why Fleming invented SPECTRE and made it a for-profit operation. No one could ever confuse SPECTRE operatives with freedom fighters.

Whether motivated by ideology, nationalism, or greed, terrorists have a theory of victory. They expect their vile deeds to produce some positive result, at least for themselves. Do they expect to achieve their goal through terrorism alone, or is terrorism just the first step in a prolonged struggle? Are they more like Mao or Giap, who saw terrorism as just one of many tools to employ in a prolonged ideological struggle that moved through several phases culminating in conventional military operations, or are they more like the racist author of the *Turner Diaries* who expects terrorism to provoke all-out civil war?

Are they reluctant terrorists who see no other way to strike at a powerful and implacable enemy, or do they revel in wanton violence and destruction? What is their vision for the post-war world? What sort of society do they expect to build on the wreckage of the old? How does this vision inform their choice of targets? Assuming they achieve their goals and displace the existing political and/or social order, will they be able to establish a stable, peaceful, popular government? Or will they face a new wave of terrorism aimed at them?

Chapter Nine: War in the Far Future and Strategy in Space

Developing effective strategies for a science fiction universe requires answering a much-debated question. At what point does new technology affect strategy? Or does it? Are strategic principles fixed and enduring, or do they change over time due to technological advances and other factors?

More than a century ago, at a time of rapid technological change, Alfred Thayer Mahan argued strategic principles were universal and unchanging. Many of today's strategists agree. Michael Handel, for example, insists the basic logic of war is consistent and eternal: the primacy of politics, importance of alliances, correlating ends and means, knowing your enemy and yourself, discerning your enemy's plans while concealing your own, deceiving the enemy, pursuing asymmetric advantages, and coping with friction and uncertainty.

In contrast, many popular authors, particularly those writing techno-thrillers and science fiction, are technological determinists. They imbue new technologies with tremendous agency and the power to transform war and whole societies. At their most extreme, they resemble Wile E. Coyote who substitutes advanced technology for strategic thought in his unending pursuit of the Road Runner.

From giant magnets to rocket-powered running shoes, Coyote's repeated failures with cutting-edge Acme technology reflect reality. Advanced technology alone rarely wins wars. Only a handful of technologies, such as steam power, have ushered in revolutionary social change. In *The Dynamics of Military Revolution, 1300-2050* (2001), MacGregor Knox and Williamson Murray, identify only five developments in the last thousand years that fundamentally changed "the framework of war" (6). They are:

1. The seventeenth century emergence of modern nation-states capable of deploying large, disciplined military forces.
2. The late eighteenth-century French Revolution, which merged mass politics and warfare.
3. The industrial revolutions of the late eighteenth and nineteenth centuries, which made it possible to arm, equip, move, and sustain armies of unprecedented size.
4. The First World War, which "combined the legacies of the French and Industrial Revolutions."
5. The advent of nuclear weapons.

New technologies figured in all of these, but only in the case of nuclear weapons was technology the sole factor involved. In the others, a host of administrative, political, and social changes—often facilitated by new technologies—transformed societies and the wars they fought.

Technology is important, but it cannot be removed from its social context. In World War II, the United States fielded the most motorized military force in history. This reflected its emergence over the previous 20 years as the world's most motorized nation. By 1939, almost every American family owned an automobile (or two), compared to only about one-fifth of families in Western Europe. Similarly, British and American airlines dominated commercial aviation before World War II. This provided the foundation to build air forces that dominated the skies of World War II and bombed enemy cities to rubble. Military forces and the technologies they use reflect the societies that produce them.

Technology affects tactics much more dramatically than strategy. Tactics developed for the wood and canvas biplanes of the First World War proved ineffective when applied to faster, low wing metal monoplanes in the Second World War. Supersonic jets and guided missiles forced new tactical changes a generation later. The same is true of infantry tactics following the development of gunpowder. Across several centuries, soldiers changed their organization and tactics to adapt to ever more lethal and longer-ranged weapons.

Operationally, full-rigged sailing ships, steam power, and internal combustion engines increased the reach of armies and fleets. These and other technologies allowed them to travel farther and faster, stay in the field or at sea longer, and conduct and coordinate more complex maneuvers.

Yet, as *Star Trek's* Mr. Spock once noted, military technologies are the most fleeting secrets of all. Technological advantages are usually short lived. The Soviet Union detonated its first atomic bomb just four years after the United States dropped atomic bombs on Hiroshima and Nagasaki, far sooner than most pundits predicted. Enemies either adopt new technologies themselves or find ways to adapt to them.

While tactics and technology change, strategic concepts remain broadly applicable. Given a particular enemy, is a quick decisive victory possible? If not, are you or your enemy more likely to win a prolonged war of attrition? Is the enemy's economy vulnerable to attack? Is yours? Can you disrupt your enemy's alliances, subvert their home front, or otherwise undermine their war effort through political or diplomatic means? Interior lines, culminating points of victory, and similar concepts are as useful today as when Clausewitz and Jomini articulated them 200 years ago.

Strategic discussions between British leaders and their allies on defeating Germany in the First World War differ little from those of the Second World War—or from the war against Napoleon a century earlier. Where to focus the bulk of their military forces? What is the war's primary theater? When should one open a new theater of war? How best to apply naval and air power against a continental enemy?

Similarly, strategies of insurgency and counterinsurgency remain unchanged. Whether it's Roman legionnaires pursuing Jewish rebels through Jerusalem's streets or French paratroopers tracking FLN operatives through the back alleys of Algiers, fundamental principles endure.

Frank Herbert's science fiction novel *Dune* illustrates this. Despite space travel, force fields, and a variety of exotic weapons, the antagonists employ familiar strategies. The Harkonnens invade the planet Arrakis and catch the defending Atreides clan by surprise, thanks to effective intelligence and a well-placed spy. While initially successful, the Harkonnens' bid for quick decisive victory fails. A growing insurgency by Arrakis's indigenous population, the Fremen, bedevils the Harkonnens and forces them to deploy more troops to Arrakis, straining their finances. Paul Atreides, whose path to victory resembles that of Lawrence of Arabia, leads Fremen attacks of increasing daring and size on Harkonnen installations.

The Harkonnens respond with a brutal, indiscriminate counterinsurgency campaign that makes practically every mistake highlighted by counterinsurgency theorists like David Galula. They fail to isolate the insurgents, neutralize their base areas, or win over significant segments of the local population. Barred from political participation, the people of Arrakis look to the insurgents for help.

In contrast to the Harkonnens, Paul Atreides and the Fremen insurgents follow Lawrence's and Mao's playbooks. They slowly wear down the Harkonnens while building popular support. The "desert power" of the Fremen neutralizes superior Harkonnen technology. Driven from the open desert, the Harkonnen fall back to a handful of cities and fortified outposts. This undermines the Harkonnens' finances, which depend on the spice melange, harvested only in the desert. As Vladimir Harkonnen understands, the person "who controls the spice, controls the universe," and he loses that control.

While the Harkonen military weakens, the Atreides-Fremen alliance grows steadily in numbers as well as financial and military power. When the time is right, the Atreides-Fremen insurgency transitions to Mao's third phase and launches a major offensive against the center of Harkonnen power on Arrakis to force decisive battle.

Muddled Strategies of the Far Future

SO, HOW DO YOU APPLY strategic principles in a science fiction or fantasy setting?

Given Arthur C. Clarke's oft-quoted remark that sufficiently advanced technology is indistinguishable from magic, you can analyze the two together. Magic, after all, is just another kind of technology, as long as its results are predictable. You can't plan strategy if you don't know whether your wizardly spell will kill a gnat or level a city. If magical results follow consistent natural laws, though, it matters little for strategic planning whether one destroys cities with wizardly fireballs or B-17 bombers dropping incendiary bombs. The essential strategic issues remain the same. How best to apply your strengths against an enemy's weaknesses?

Science fiction and fantasy authors often draw on their own history and heritage. Tolkien, for example, drew on his personal experience and understanding of the First World War to write *The Lord of the Rings*. One can even see that war's propaganda, which portrayed the conflict as an apocalyptic struggle between civilization and barbarism, reflected in Tolkien's depiction of the struggle of civilized dwarves, elves, hobbits, and humans against Sauron and his throngs of barbaric orcs.

Science fiction, particularly "space opera" draws from our nautical heritage. Since E.E. "Doc" Smith's Lensmen novels in the 1950s and the television show *Star Trek* a decade later, fictional space forces predominantly used naval ranks and terminology. Spaceships are captained and belong to fleets commanded by commodores and admirals. Science fiction's interstellar wars similarly draw on our long history of naval warfare. They feature commerce raiding, pirates, blockades, and seemingly decisive battles between enormous space fleets. Planetary invasions resemble the amphibious invasions of World War II and require landing craft and other specialized equipment.

Some authors obscure the strategic decisions guiding their protagonists. Others resort to the most obvious strategies, such as direct assaults on enemy strongholds or superweapons, such as *Star Wars'* Death Star. In neither iteration of *Battlestar Galactica* do the Cylons evince any strategic acumen after their initial devastating strike on humanity. In E.E. "Doc" Smith's *Galactic Patrol* (1937), the rival fleets of Boskone and the Galactic Patrol brawl without any strategy other than seeking a decisive fleet battle. When this fails, the Galactic Patrol sends an operative to assassinate the Boskonian leader.

Strategies of assassination often work in novels, but they have few historical exemplars. Even on the rare occasions of successful assassinations, dead leaders are easily replaced. In World War II, American fighter planes intercepted and shot down Japanese Admiral Yamamoto's plane, killing him. His death didn't change Japanese strategy or operational planning in the least. His successors planned and fought much as Yamamoto had.

The Serbian assassination of Archduke Franz Ferdinand is a rather unique occurrence. The Serbian assassins who killed the archduke did not hope to spark a world war and certainly didn't want to provoke a massive Austrian invasion of Serbia. The assassination set off a chain of events that might well have led to Serbia's destruction.

Instead, the First World War destroyed the Austro-Hungarian Empire, liberated Bosnia, and led to the creation of Yugoslavia, a Serbian-dominated Balkan state. None of that was predictable, though, and things might well have turned out differently.

Despite Admiral David Glasgow Farragut's order to "damn the torpedoes" and steam "full speed ahead," most historical admirals are reluctant to risk their fleets. Capital ships, whether Nelson's ships-of-the-line, First World War battleships, or Second World War aircraft carriers, are "lumpy capital." They are expensive, take years to construct, and are difficult to replace. Admirals do not risk them lightly.

There are two primary exceptions to this. First, when one has an overwhelming numerical advantage over the enemy, as Farragut's fleet had over the Confederate defenders of Mobile Bay. Second, in science fiction where vast fleet battles are practically the norm. The Death Star, in fact, may be the lumpiest capital ship ever produced. Many fans have questioned how the Empire can afford to keep building them as the Rebel Alliance destroys each in turn.

It's not essential for fictional protagonists to be strategists. In James A. Corey's *Tiamat's Wrath* (2019), Martian marine Sergeant Bobbie Draper readily admits she's "not a grand strategist." Her shipmate Naomi Nagata, though, has a solid grasp of strategy. She launches a surprise strike that cripples an enemy shipyard, understanding that warships are expensive and difficult to replace. Crippling an enemy's shipbuilding capability can win a war.

Similarly, *Star Trek's* Captains Kirk, Picard, and Pike may lack strategic insight, but the strategic wisdom of Star Fleet admirals should guide their missions. If not, how can one address Eric Larrabee's question of "the reason why?" Why is Captain Kirk in the Romulan Neutral Zone? What strategic purpose does his mission serve?

Conversely, why, in the original series episode *Balance of Terror* have the Romulans dispatched a stealth ship to attack Federation space stations guarding the Neutral Zone? What do they hope to achieve? What is their policy and strategy?

Strategic Education

THE MUDDLED, OBSCURED, or simplistic strategies undergirding many science fiction tales highlight a glaring absence: professional military education. *Star Trek's* Star Fleet officers attend Star Fleet Academy, an undergraduate institution resembling Britain's Royal Military Academy at Sandhurst, the U.S. Naval Academy at Annapolis, the U.S. Military Academy at West Point, and the U.S. Air Force Academy in Colorado Springs. After that Star Fleet officers do not pursue post-graduate education and have no continuing education requirement. The same appears true of Earthforce officers in *Babylon 5,* the Barrayaran Empire of Lois McMaster Bujold's Vorkosigan novels, "Doc" Smith's Galactic Patrol, and a host of other science fiction franchises.

That still puts them ahead of the Jedi Knights of *Star Wars* whose sole education is hands-on training and an apprenticeship system better suited to the Middle Ages than the far future. The Jedi Knights' ignorance serves a narrative purpose, though. Their strategic incompetence precipitates the Republic's fall.

This educational void is strikingly unrealistic. For more than a century, the military officers of Earth's major powers have received substantial post-graduate education, just like doctors, lawyers, and other important professions.

The U.S. Naval War College, founded in 1884, was the first institution aimed at mid-career officers. Others soon followed. Today, American officers may choose from a host of graduate programs, including the Naval War College, Air War College, Army Command and Staff College, School of Advanced Military Studies, National

Defense University, and many others. Norway has a national defense college for senior officers, as does Sweden. Nigeria has six post-graduate institutions for officer education, including Air, Army, and Naval war colleges. All these institutions offer substantial instruction in strategy, which is usually taught through historical case studies.

The U.S. military strongly encourages higher education. Currently, it expects mid-grade officers to complete three graduate-level courses. For the navy, these are Strategy and Policy, National Security Decision Making, and Joint Maritime Operations. Other services have similar requirements. Officers who fail to meet them are often restricted from promotion to higher ranks.

Officers can earn a master's degree from the Naval War College and similar institutions. Over the course of their careers, roughly 90% of American officers who reach senior ranks earn master's degrees; 10% earn doctorates, as General David Petraeus did. Why then are science fiction's military officers so poorly educated?

Part of the answer, of course, is that many—probably most—authors simply don't know about today's educational requirements of military officers.

Perhaps equally important is the fondness of many science fiction authors for outdated political institutions. Beloved writers of science fiction's "golden era" like Isaac Asimov recast ancient empires and medieval feudalism into interstellar polities. Since military organizations reflect the societies that produce them, the imperial military organizations in Asimov's *Foundation* trilogy and Poul Anderson's Dominic Flandry series are as archaic as the political entities guiding them. They don't have war colleges because their ancient antecedents, the Chinese or Persian or Roman Empires, didn't have them.

That's both unfortunate and illogical. Our modern, technological society requires millions of people with graduate degrees. They account for roughly 10% of the American population. That's unlikely to change in the future, even in cyberpunk dystopias. Like most admirals and generals in today's world, senior officers in science fictional universes should attend war colleges and earn graduate degrees. Their actions should reflect this learning.

Technology, Innovation, and Military Superiority

SCIENCE FICTION NECESSARILY involves new technology and SF authors are generally optimistic about the opportunities new technologies offer. Their fictional superweapons are far more likely to produce the German blitzkriegs of the first years of World War II than the tactical stalemates of the First World War or the nuclear stalemate of the Cold War. In fiction, technology produces wondrous results.

This is partly because authors often focus on the weapons themselves rather than their essential supporting systems, such as reconnaissance and intelligence to locate and identify targets, communications systems to convey that information in time to be militarily useful, and whatever supply and logistics arrangements the superweapon requires.

The problems of First World War battles directly resulted from the era's communications technology. Commanders communicated via field telephone, which required physical transmission wires between headquarters and the frontline. These systems proved inadequate to manage the war's million-man armies. Once attacking soldiers left their own trenches and "went over the top," they lost communication with higher command. Even if their assault succeeded, by the time they communicated this to higher command—through messengers, flares, or other simple signals—enemy reinforcements would have arrived. Their commanders could not maintain a continuous assessment of the situation, make correct and timely decisions, and commit troops at times and places essential to sustain their offensive.

Defenders had a shorter decision cycle, which allowed them to quickly reinforce critical areas, effectively mass artillery fire, and successfully counterattack at times and places of their choosing.

Mary Robinette Kowal offers an interesting solution to this problem in her novel *Ghost Talkers* (2016). Unfortunately, extracting tactical information from the ghosts of recently slain soldiers proves both cumbersome and time consuming. Rather than spiritual advisors, First World War soldiers needed portable radios, which would not arrive until the Second World War.

Once can easily imagine similar problems when dealing with interstellar distances. In the absence of a radio-like device providing instantaneous communication, an ansible in science fiction terms, communication and intelligence information will necessarily lag the developing military situation, perhaps by weeks or even months, mirroring the situation in the age of sail.

In *The Strategy of Technology: Winning the Decisive War* (1970), Stefan Possony and Jerry Pournelle argue: "other things being equal, battles are won by superior technology."

There are several problems with this statement. First, "other things" are never equal. Second, no single technology is superior in all circumstances. Third, how exactly is one to judge technological superiority? People still argue the relative merits of the Soviet AK-47 and American M-16 assault rifles. The former is more rugged, reliable, and easier to maintain; the latter is lighter, both the weapon and its ammunition, allowing soldiers to carry more ammunition and fire with greater accuracy.

The development of any weapon system involves a host of trade-offs, which different military organizations assess differently. Israeli tanks prioritize first shot accuracy and crew survivability. The Soviets prioritized cross-country mobility and low cost, which allowed them to manufacture tanks in greater quantity than their likely enemies. "Quantity has a quality all its own," as Stalin reputedly liked to say.

West Germany favored fast tanks for tactical mobility; their British allies thought heavy armor more important. Americans, as always, wanted it all, but still had to make many compromises to produce the M1 Abrams tank.

Understanding and integrating new technologies into existing military forces is far from easy. On the eve of the Franco-Prussian War, the French army deployed a new weapon, the mitrailleuse. Like contemporary American Gatling guns, the weapon used multiple barrels to fire 100 bullets per minute. Had the French deployed them with their forward infantry units, the mitrailleuse would have made a tremendous difference in the war's opening battles. Instead, French officers thought of them as artillery pieces. They deployed them to the rear where they failed to influence any of the war's major engagements, all of which the French lost.

American technological superiority was all but useless in Vietnam, where communist insurgents and North Vietnamese regulars found easy solutions to circumvent complex technologies. Communist forces hid themselves with camouflage, moved at night or in poor weather, and protected their most important assets in deep tunnels and underground bases. When American planes dropped "people sniffers" along the Ho Chi Minh Trail to track their movements, communist soldiers found they could spoof them with urine-soaked rags, or simply by peeing on them.

During the First Gulf War, the United States made a concerted effort to locate and destroy Iraq's scud missile launchers, which bombarded cities in Israel and Saudi Arabia. Despite the deployment of spy satellites, reconnaissance aircraft, and special forces troops on the ground, the U.S. failed to destroy a single scud launcher, instead wasting its effort blowing up decoy after decoy.

Arthur C. Clarke's story "Superiority" (1951) nicely illustrates several of these points. Its protagonist, a senior military leader awaiting court martial, explains how his nation lost a war due to the enemy's "inferior science." Instead of incrementally improving existing weapons, the protagonist invested heavily in developing new weapons "totally different from" their predecessors. The slow development of these systems, along with the need to train personnel in their use, surrendered the initiative to the enemy. The protagonist's nation also lost its numerical superiority as factories transitioned to building innovative new spaceships and weapons systems, while their enemies incrementally improved tried-and-true systems.

Following several military reversals, the protagonist realizes these superweapons, originally seen as a luxury, had become their only hope for victory. So, he doubled down on his investment in cutting-edge technology, which only compounded the problem. As he laments, "our magnificent fleet" was "crippled by our own science." Over-investment in new technologies lost a war to an enemy who better managed technological innovation.

Clarke's story offers an extreme case of what Nazi Germany did in the Second World War. The Nazis over-invested in new technologies to create a handful of superweapons, including ballistic missiles and jet aircraft. They could have built tens of thousands of conventional aircraft and other weapons with the same funds—probably not enough to win the war, but certainly sufficient to stave off defeat another year or two.

In Gordon Dickson's *Dorsai* series, military organizations take the opposite approach. The increasing complexity of infantry weapons increased maintenance time and made them vulnerable to enemy countermeasures. So, militaries reverted to simpler weapons. Dickson suggests "the trick with modern warfare was not to outgun the enemy but carry weapons he could not gimmick." Since "chemical and radiation armament" were "easily put out of action," soldiers adopted spring-rifles, which used non-metallic mechanisms to fire tiny projectiles from their 5,000 round magazines (*Dorsai!*).

Too many authors assume a linear progression of technology across cultures. Many also assume new technologies automatically and necessarily displace older ones. For a cogent, readable refutation of this, see David Edgerton's *The Shock of the Old* (2006).

Look at the history of transportation. Ninety percent of world trade still moves by sea, and it does so at speeds not significantly faster than clipper ships 200 years ago. People today rely on a host of vehicles to get around: bicycles, roller skates, scooters, cars, trains, planes, helicopters, and more. We've had bicycles for more than a century, trains for almost twice as long. Yet, both remain in common use. Note also, that given virtually identical technological bases, Europeans and Japanese walk and take trains while most Americans and Canadians drive cars. Culture, geography, and other factors help determine the technologies people adopt.

Adopting new technologies also takes time. Roughly a decade passed between the Wright Brothers' first flight and the development of militarily useful airplanes. In 1848, Prussia adopted the breechloading Dreyse needle gun as its standard infantry rifle. This revolutionary weapon helped Prussia defeat Austria a generation later, in 1866. It required almost the entirety of those 18 years to manufacture enough needle guns to equip the Prussian army (342,000 soldiers in 1866). Designing a new weapon is one thing. Manufacturing it in quantity, developing doctrine for it, getting it into the hands of soldiers, and training them to use it all require time.

Too often, authors of time travel stories elide these difficulties. Despite the example of L. Sprague de Camp's *Lest Darkness Fall* (1941), which highlights the difficulties of introducing future technologies into past societies, time traveling protagonists produce startling technological revolutions overnight.

Eric Flint grapples with this in his 1632 series of novels, but still has technological innovation, as well as social and political change, proceed at an unusually rapid pace. The French army in his stories, for example, re-equips its soldiers with breechloading rifles at a faster rate in the 1630s than Prussia historically managed in the 1850s. Flint probably recognized this and deliberately accelerated technological and social change to drive the plots of his novels at paces readers expect and enjoy.

Sufficiently advanced technology, such as that employed by the Martians in H. G. Wells' *War of the Worlds* (1897), limits the need for strategy. Rather than a clash of wills "resolved through bloodshed," war better resembles insect eradication, a simile Wells uses repeatedly to describe the Martians' technological slaughter of Earth's defenders. In doing so, Wells implicitly critiques his era's brutal colonial wars, which featured similar technological mismatches and genocidal campaigns, such as Germany's campaign against the Herrero in Namibia.

Culture, Technology, and War

JUST AS SOCIETY AND culture shape military organization and technological developments, they also shape strategic choices. Japanese officers in World War II were assiduous students of Sun Tzu and developed complex strategic plans that relied on deception, misdirection, and stealth. Their German allies embraced a military heritage dating to Frederick the Great and emphasized maneuver and decisive battle. Their American opponents leaned into their industrial, logistical, scientific, and technological superiority.

In Poul Anderson's *The High Crusade* (1960) Sir Roger, an English knight assembling troops to fight France in the Hundred Years' War, captures an alien warship that lands in his fief. Despite his acquisition of new technology, Sir Roger's conceptions of war and strategy remain the same. Finding himself in an alien interstellar empire ruled by the Wersgorix, he launches a chevauchée, raiding enemy settlements to live off the plunder, undermine Wersgorix rule, and rally disaffected Wersgorix subjects to his cause. Henry V would have been proud.

While cultures differ, the sources of conflict and reasons for war may also be universal. Poul Anderson's spacefaring merchant Nicholas van Rijn has an unerring ability to learn about local cultures, exacerbate their conflicts, and profit from them. The same could be said of *Star Trek's* Captain Kirk.

Thucydides' fear, honor, and interest are as relevant for analyzing future wars as they are for the past and present. Technologies change, but the reasons people go to war will endure, as will the strategic principles guiding the conduct of war.

Frictional Futures

SINCE THE FIRST GULF War, various analysts have suggested computers, satellites, advanced sensors, and similar systems enabling real time intelligence and "network-centric warfare" will provide commanders with enough intelligence to eradicate uncertainty and fog of war. Thus far, their predictions have failed. The vastness of space will compound the difficulties of command, communication, and intelligence gathering. Given the sheer volume of space, one may not need a Romulan cloaking device to evade whatever sophisticated sensors the future offers to hide in space.

Gordon R. Dickson is almost unique in his consideration of friction, chance, and uncertainty in his military science fiction. At their worst, Dickson explains in *Dorsai!* (1960), mistaken orders and navigational errors may cause warships to collide or even fire on one another, as has repeatedly happened in historical battles. Future technologies may reduce friction, but the human element, and its uncertainty, will remain.

Distance increases friction. Future commanders may be far from the action and equally far from senior military and civilian leaders. Gaining, maintaining, and communicating accurate assessments of military situations requires substantial and continuing effort, which interstellar distances impede. New technologies mitigate some friction, but as Clark and Dickson suggest, advanced technologies produce problems of their own.

What happens when the enemy learns to jam your faster-than-light communications, disrupt your warp drive, or otherwise counteract technologies critical to your operational plan? What if the enemy makes better use of new technologies than you do?

This was the case in May 1940 when Nazi Germany invaded France. The Germans did not possess any significant technological advantages. They won the ensuing battles due to a better understanding of how war had changed, incredibly stupid French war plans, and the immense friction within the France's senior leadership, which slowed decision making.

War in Space

FICTIONAL PORTRAYALS of space wars generally draw from Earth's nautical heritage. *Starship Troopers* and *Star Wars* draw on the Pacific Theater of World War II for inspiration, emulating its amphibious invasions and aircraft carrier battles. Like their terrestrial predecessors, fictional space wars feature battles between fleets of spaceships, along with commerce raiding, blockades, smuggling, and planetary bombardments and invasions.

Isaac Asimov famously called *Star Wars* to account for the absurdity of close-range dogfights and eagle-eyed pilots pressing home attacks on enemy ships at point-blank range. Guided missiles, drones, and other technologies were already eliminating such things from contemporary warfare. Somehow, weapons in "a galaxy far, far away" are so inaccurate that the hero, Luke Skywalker, is forced to use the mystical powers of the Force to accurately target the Death Star's vulnerable exhaust port. That mission could have been accomplished with an equivalent of today's Predator drones armed with Hellfire missiles. These, though, are issues of technology and tactics. What about strategy?

Despite recent technological advances, such as deep-sea drilling, most food, resources, and other goods in today's economy are produced on land. That's where almost everyone lives and works. Sea power is important because of how it influences events on the land. As a result, most sea battles take place near land. In fact, every sea battle before the nineteenth century took place within sight of land.

The situation will probably be similar for future space fleets. Space power will be important because it influences planets (and perhaps asteroids and space stations) where most people will live. So, space battles, too, will probably occur near planets or locations of strategic importance, such as wormhole nexuses and other imagined interstellar equivalents of crossroads, trade routes, and maritime chokepoints. The vastness of space will be even harder to control than the Earth's seas. Winning uncontested command of space will be difficult, perhaps even impossible.

Space Blockades and Commerce Raiding

LIKE THEIR MARITIME ancestors, future space admirals will debate the advantages and disadvantages of close and distant blockades. A close blockade requires fewer ships, but these ships are more exposed to sudden sorties by enemy ships and defensive weapons. Maintaining a naval blockade in the age of sail was difficult because contrary winds could blow a blockading fleet off station. Storms could scatter its ships, leaving some isolated, damaged, and vulnerable. Steam power solved this problem, but the development of mines and submarines in the late 19th century made close blockades dangerous. On the other hand, the development of radar, spy satellites, and GPS in the twentieth century made it easier for blockaders to track the comings and goings of ships from enemy ports. Whatever weapons the future offers, planets will have room for lots of them, as will moons and large asteroids.

Space blockades will likely be distant. This substantially raises their cost and makes it easier for smugglers and blockade runners to circumvent the blockade. In addition to defensive weaponry and spaceships, blockaded planets would offer bonuses to smugglers and perhaps subsidize the construction of fast or stealthy blockade runners like the *Millennium Falcon* in *Star Wars* or *Serenity* in the *Firefly* television series.

As in the past, larger fleets will blockade an enemy planet. Admirals lacking sufficient ships to establish a blockade could instead scatter their ships among trade routes to attack enemy commerce. Planets facing a blockade would likely do the same, scattering their warships to raid enemy commerce.

The vastness of space and speeds at which starships must travel to reach their destinations will make commerce raiding difficult. Settings like *Star Trek,* in which space travel is unconstrained by warp points or similar factors, much as winds, currents, and seasons did in the era of sailing ships, will compound these problems. *Star Trek's* Orion Pirates seem to catch their prey through spies, sabotage, and traps, rather than awaiting and ambushing them at common trade routes, as Earth's pirates still do.

Blockades and commerce raiding aim to constrain the enemy's economy to force concessions or even surrender. They rely on the defender's dependence on trade, particularly on imported goods. During World War II, Japan not only imported most of its petroleum and iron, but roughly half the food its people consumed. It was exceptionally vulnerable to blockade and attacks on its trade. The United States might well have starved Japan into submission without bombing its cities to rubble.

Nazi Germany, on the other hand, was more self-sufficient thanks to its early war conquests and alliance with Romania, which had large oil fields. Conquering Ukraine and parts of Russia further bolstered the German economy. The Allied blockade hurt Germany, cutting off supplies of rubber and various alloying metals. It was insufficient, though, to force Germany to surrender, and the Germans found alternatives and workarounds for most of their scarcities.

The greater a target's dependence on imports for its survival, the more vulnerable it will be to blockade or other disruptions to its economy. A planet being terraformed might be vulnerable to disruptions of this process, which could wipe away decades or centuries of work. Asteroid colonies, space stations, and planetary settlements that depend on vital imports like oxygen, water, and food or fertilizers would be particularly vulnerable to attacks on its commerce. Planets that profit from exports will also be good targets.

On the other hand, blockading a self-sufficient planet to force concessions will require many years. Given sufficient political will, a habitable planet that produces food and other goods in quantity could survive a blockade indefinitely. In contrast, blockading fleets rely on supplies shipped at great expense. These expenses will mount over time, perhaps to the point that it may no longer be cost effective. Like a medieval siege, the besieged may outlast the besieger, as the Earth seems poised to do in Gordon R. Dickson's *Chantry Guild* (1988).

Commerce raiders in space will face the same issues and need to make the same decisions as historical commerce raiders on Earth. The campaign might resemble Germany's U-boat campaigns and aim to destroy enemy commerce. Or it could emulate privateering and commerce raiding from the sailing era. Privateering was a business enterprise from which captains, crews, and ship owners expected to profit by selling captured enemy ships and cargoes. Even naval officers and crews profited from capturing enemy commerce and warships.

The point of both a blockade and commerce raiding are to coerce an enemy without destroying them. To be effective, they must reduce enemy commerce or inflict such damage to it that vital trade shrinks below levels enemy leaders can tolerate. Increasing shipping and insurance costs may drive some enemy commerce from the space lanes, but commerce raiding ultimately depends on capturing or destroying an economically ruinous quantity of enemy shipping. Neither American nor French privateers ever managed to do this to Great Britain, nor did German U-boats a century later.

Planetary Invasions

GIVEN THE EXPENSE OF prolonged blockades, why not just invade an enemy planet like Heinlein's starship troopers?

Planetary invasions will suffer from the same problems as blockades. Planets are large. Any planet with a significant population can field large military forces—potentially so large the costs of an invasion are prohibitive. How does one transport and land the millions of troops needed to capture and secure an inhabited planet? Much as Sun Tzu warned against attacking cities, future strategists will warn about the costs of invading densely populated planets.

Logistics matter. Despite numerous novels to the contrary, Japan could not have invaded Hawaii during World War II. Its navy lacked the sealift to transport sufficient troops across the Pacific, as well as the cargo shipping to keep those troops supplied after a successful invasion. Planetary invasions are orders of magnitude more difficult. They would require substantial numerical superiority or technological advantage, perhaps both.

Another factor to consider is that the damage inflicted on planets by mass invasion and prolonged fighting will reduce their value, perhaps to the point conquest becomes economically unfeasible. Even biological weapons and enhanced radiation weapons like neutron bombs will leave dangerous residues in their wake. To paraphrase Sun Tzu, it's best to capture planets intact.

Harry Harrison's character Slippery Jim diGriz explores these problems in *The Stainless Steel Rat's Revenge* (1970). It might work, diGriz suggests, in a solar system with several inhabited planets. "If one planet is backward and the other advanced industrially the primitive one might be invaded successfully." If they managed "a real defense," though, the distance-time relationships make planetary invasions impractical. "When every soldier and weapon and ration has to be lifted from the gravity well of a planet and carried across space, the energy expenditure is considerable, the transport demands incredible and the cost unbelievable," even within "a solar system where the planets are practically touching on a galactic scale." Interstellar distances compound these problems, making warfare between planets in different star systems "even more impossible" (Chapter 3).

The most obvious military trend over the last two centuries is the high rate of ammunition expenditure and equipment loss. In the first months of World War I, all the major powers exhausted their ammunition stocks. Shortages persisted for more than a year. Egyptians, Israelis, and Syrians similarly exhausted pre-war stockpiles in the 1973 war. Desperate, they called on their Soviet or American backers who airlifted supplies to them (and whose crossing flight paths sparked nuclear threats against one another). In the First Gulf War, Americans expended all their smart munitions in a matter of days.

There is no reason to expect this trend to change. It may even accelerate, making planetary invasions even more expensive.

Yet, Slippery Jim notes, "nothing is basically impossible if people want to tackle it hard enough." That is, after all, how he approaches his criminal enterprises.

One option is local support. Hidden spies or fifth columnists among the target's population could support the invaders. Vidkun Quisling, Norway's former defense minister, assisted Nazi Germany's invasion of Narvik. Slippery Jim's antagonists similarly use quislings and spies to support their planetary invasions.

Another option is biological warfare. In Hayford Pierce's story "Unlimited Warfare" (1974), Britain unleashes a bioweapon that kills French grape vines, forcing the French to important and consume "inferior" wines from Algeria, California, and Italy. France retaliates by unleashing a deadly virus against the world's tea crop, depriving the British of their essential afternoon tea.

Pierce plays the situation for laughs, but specialized crop destroying agents would spread across national borders and infect other crops. The infiltration and mutation of biological agents is all but impossible to stop. Their use in Earthly wars has been limited due both to technological complexities and the near certainty that biological agents would inevitably redound on whoever unleashed them. During its invasion of China in the 1930s, the Japanese army spread anthrax and cholera, which killed some of its own soldiers in addition to thousands of Chinese civilians. Terrorists might employ bioweapons, but they would have to be particularly nihilistic. Even terrorists need to breathe and eat.

If one has a spare planet or space station or two, though, bioagents may become attractive weapons for patient aggressors. One could introduce them to an enemy planet, blockade the planet to prevent their spread, and wait for them to devastate the planet's population and/or ecosystem. In David Brin's *The Uplift War* (1987), invading aliens plan to introduce bioagents targeting all hemoglobin-using life. Since the aliens lack hemoglobin, they would be immune. Unless, of course, their bioagent mutated.

Cyber war offers a similar, and thus far safer, option. Attacks on enemy computer networks to steal and/or destroy data have become common. So, too, have acts of sabotage. These small-scale attacks raise a host of questions. Are they acts of war? What forms of retaliation are valid? Most importantly, what is their strategic effect?

Can one so degrade enemy computers and networks that it leaves them open to attack? Can one execute a computer attack as sophisticated and thorough as the Cylon cyberattack in the *Battlestar Galactica* reboot? Russia seems to have managed that in its 2008 war with Georgia, but Russian cyberattacks failed to dent Ukrainian defenses in 2022. As Martin Libicki points out, "the difference between a great and a merely good hacker can be orders of magnitude." Success in cyberwarfare requires "finding and growing the great ones" (*Cyberspace in Peace and War*, 158). Like bioagents, though, computer viruses can spread—and perhaps mutate—beyond the bounds established by their creators.

Superior technology is practically a requirement for successful planetary conquest. In Dickson's *Way of the Pilgrim* (1987) the alien Aalaag conquer Earth thanks to tremendous technological advantages. Their soldiers are invulnerable to human weapons. Wells's Martians possess similar technological advantages, as do invading aliens in *Independence Day* (1996) and similar films that draw on his novel.

If one's technological advantage is not insurmountable, though, effective defense may prove possible. Defenders may adapt to—or adopt—the invader's weapons. While other African states fell to European colonizers in the late nineteenth century, Ethiopia scattered invading Italian armies despite their superior technology and firepower. Even if the invader eventually wins, the cost can be prohibitive.

Nuclear War, Planetary Bombardment, and Deterrence

WHY NOT JUST NUKE THE planet from orbit? Given sufficiently advanced technology, any planet is vulnerable to nuclear attack, asteroid bombardment, and similar mass destruction. Threats of planetary bombardment could coerce the surrender of a planet unable to respond in kind, such as the Narn homeworld in *Babylon 5*.

Historically, most politicians and military strategists concluded nuclear wars were unwinnable. Science fiction authors, though, explored their possibilities, both on Earth, as in Nevil Shute's *On the Beach* (1957), and in interplanetary conflicts.

C.M. Kornbluth's story "The Luckiest Man in Denv" plays out a scenario of ongoing nuclear war between Denver and Los Angeles over rights to the Colorado River. Thanks to sophisticated defensive missiles, the war lasts for many generations, during which Denver's leaders fortify their city and militarize their society. Since the land above their city is a radioactive wasteland, the people of future Denver live entirely underground.

Philip K. Dick and other authors posited similar continuing nuclear wars fought over a devastated Earth by nations whose populations had burrowed underground for protection. They epitomize what Clausewitz called absolute war and Khan labeled insensate war. No cost-benefit analysis can justify them.

Most science fiction authors took their nuclear wars to the stars. Given the universe's infinity of planets, wrecking a few seems a small price to pay for winning wars against encroaching alien menaces or carving out intergalactic empires. In science fiction, planet killing became acceptable. Jack Williamson wrecks the entire solar system in a few stories. Smith's Galactic Patrol devastates whole planets by orbital bombardment. Later, it destroyed the home planet of their Eddorian enemies by slamming another planet into it.

Most science fiction authors are content to use asteroids to wreck planets, such as the 12-kilometer-wide asteroid that triggered an ice age and killed the dinosaurs 66 million years ago. In Corey's *Expanse* series, terrorists pepper the Earth with several asteroids, killing billions, and rendering large parts of the planet uninhabitable. Led by a narcissistic megalomaniac and lacking a planet of their own, the terrorists did not fear of retaliation.

This reflects contemporary fears of terrorists with nuclear weapons. Preventing nuclear war relies on deterrence, which is only practicable among nation-states. If you wreck my homeland, I'll wreck yours. So far, no one's managed to deter conventionally armed terrorists. How then, could one deter nuclear-armed terrorists?

This is the plot to Tom Clancy's *The Sum of All Fears* (1991). The PFLP (Popular Front for the Liberation of Palestine) acquires a lost Israeli atomic bomb. Working with East German terrorists, the PFLP plots to instigate a nuclear war between the United States and the Soviet Union by detonating their bomb in Denver during the Super Bowl while German terrorists disguised as Soviet soldiers attack American troops in West Berlin.

While frightening, the scenario is also strategically obtuse. How would instigating a nuclear war between the superpower benefit Palestinians? Nothing connects their strategy (start a nuclear war) to their goal (liberate Palestine). The situation is even worse for East Germany, which would suffer direct nuclear attack when the superpowers started lobbing ICBMS at one another. Fortunately, protagonist Jack Ryan foils the senseless evil scheme.

Much like nuclear deterrence on Earth today, many science fiction authors posit similar systems of deterrence involving planet killing weapons. In the *Expanse* series, Earth and Mars go to war with one another but refrain from bombarding one another's planets. They fight within agreed upon rules and confine their fighting to the asteroid belt and farther reaches of the Solar System.

Similarly, in the television series *Babylon 5,* the galaxy's major civilizations have outlawed the use of mass drivers to slam asteroids into planets. The Centauri, though, violate this agreement. Following the destruction of the Narn space fleet by Centauri allies, the Centauri bombard the Narn home world with asteroids to force its surrender. The Centauri felt free to do this because the Narn lacked allies and were no longer capable of responding in kind following their fleet's destruction. Deterrence only works when retaliation is possible.

Star Wars' Emperor Palpatine is similarly unconstrained. The Rebel Alliance lacks planet-destroying weapons. Even if it had them, its leaders were unlikely to use them since planetary genocide would undermine the morality of their cause. Even in galaxies "far, far away" insurgents need popular support.

The ethics and morality of weapons of mass destruction remain the ultimate check on their use. The American decision to employ atomic weapons against Japan remains hotly debated and cannot be settled here. The important point is that the United States did not use them in any future conflict, even during the brief years it enjoyed a nuclear monopoly. American leaders believed using nuclear weapons would undermine their nation's place as the leader of the free world. The costs of nuclear use outweighed any likely military benefits.

Omniscience, Genetic Generals, and Super-Soldiers

MILITARY SCIENCE FICTION often focuses on the search for military advantage. At the tactical level this usually involves technological solutions, such as the powered armor of Heinlein's starship troopers, enormous fighting machines like Keith Laumer's bolos, or efforts to breed, create, or train super-soldiers, such as Marvel's Captain America, *Dune's* elite Sardaukar, and *Star Wars'* cloned soldiers.

Similar efforts at the strategic level involve finding or creating military geniuses or developing ways to predict the future for military advantage. In *Dune,* Paul Atreides combines both abilities. Most authors, though, are content to endow their protagonists with just one of these traits. Orson Scott Card's Ender Wiggin is a military genius produced by selective breeding, social programming, and harsh education.

Dickson's Dorsai stories (more properly called the Childe Cycle) offer an entire culture, the Dorsai, whose members seek to perfect their military skills. His landmark novel *Dorsai!* (1959), originally titled *The Genetic General*, chronicles the successive military victories of Dorsai mercenary Donal Graeme. Yet, it's an accident of birth that produces military genius Donal Graeme, a "genetic general" of mixed Dorsai and Exotic heritage. The later culture emphasizes the arts, philosophy, and intellectual pursuits.

Donal's great grandfather, Cletus Graeme, was also a military genius. He developed the unique Dorsai command structure, which split military planning and execution between a combat commander and a "battle operator," who despite the name is "a theoretical strategist whose job is to consider "the strategical situation and problem and lay out a campaign plan," which the combat commander executes after making "any and all alterations to it he thinks it needs" (*Tactics of Mistake*). Both Graemes win near bloodless victories, exactly as Sun Tzu advocates.

The allure of genius, precognition, and scientific mechanisms to accurately predict the future attracts many science fiction authors. While George Kennan famously predicted the Soviet Union's collapse, his prediction derived as much from hope as reason. It lacked the specificity and determinism common to science fiction. Asimov's Hari Seldon develops the field of psychohistory and uses it to accurately predict the rise and fall of empires in his *Foundation* novels. In Poul Anderson's story "Marius," Professor Eino Valti's "sociosymbolic logic" guided strategic planning. His "matrices were not concerned with a man's heart. They simply told you that given such-and-such conditions, this and that would probably happen."

Overdependence on charismatic leaders, regardless of their genius or omniscience, is problematic. Frank Herbert warned against this in *Dune* and its sequels, and these warnings resonate with the works of Sun Tzu and Clausewitz.

War is an innately human experience. It cannot be reduced to mathematical equations. People's hearts matter. Perhaps that's why science fiction's machine intelligences, whether *Battlestar Galactica's* Cylons, Fred Saberhagen's Berserkers, or the many computers plaguing *Star Trek's* Kirk and Spock, always come up short.

Clausewitz recognized the role genius plays in war. One never knows when a military genius like Alexander the Great or Napoleon Bonaparte or Donal Graeme or Ender Wiggin will emerge. Whether accidents or the products of genetic engineering and/or intense training, these people think circles around their opponents. They seem to operate outside the norms of war.

Clausewitz's answer to them was education. The point of military education is not to produce a genius. It aims to broadly educate large numbers of officers to become collectively smart—smart enough to counter Napoleon, whose exploits haunt *On War's* pages, and any future equivalent. Education matters. It grounds strategic thought.

IN JACK CAMPBELL'S *Lost Fleet* series, the space navy has largely eliminated professional military education, an absence sorely felt by protagonist John Geary who must regularly explain basic strategic—and even tactical—principles to his ship and squadron commanders. It's a clever device that shines a spotlight on Campbell's protagonist but is unlikely to occur. The admirals and generals who led the U.S. to victory in World War II all received substantial, postgraduate military education. Admirals Halsey, King, Nimitz, and Spruance all attended the Naval War College. Bradley, Eisenhower, MacArthur, Marshall, Patton, and other successful generals attended the Army War College, the Army Command and General Staff College, or both. While a few programs closed during the war, most continued to educate and graduate officers through accelerated programs. Professional military education is essential to a modern (and future) military force. Military victory requires military education.

The point of professional military education is to produce a large body of educated officers. Modern war is too complex for a single genius to master and manage. Crafting a successful policy and strategy to win a war requires the collective effort of civilian and military leaders. Today's senior military leaders rely on large staffs like General Petraeus's "Jedi Knights" who developed the strategy behind the "Surge" in Iraq. Allied victory in World War II similarly derived from the efforts of numerous American, British, and Soviet officers who collectively out-thought, out-strategized, and eventually outfought Nazi Germany.

Guided by enduring strategic principles, senior civilian and military leaders seek allies, assess enemy strengths and weaknesses, and direct military force to execute any of the number of strategies discussed in this book. Military victory results from this collective effort by educated, experienced officers, not the schemes of lone geniuses, however brilliant.

There will always be a role for dynamic leaders like Patton at the tactical and operational levels of war, but these commanders, too, rely on staff officers to transform their brilliant ideas into battlefield victory.

The more technology changes, the more important it is for military institutions to rapidly adjust to the situations they confront. The French army failed this test in 1940. The Israelis, despite initial defeats, adapted to the changed battle space of the 1973 war and successfully counterattacked both the Syrians and Egyptians. Future armies will face similar challenges involving increasingly more complex military technologies.

Yet, increasingly complex weapons systems take longer to build. As U.S. Secretary of Defense Donald Rumsfeld noted, "you go to war with the army you have, not the army you might want or wish to have at a later time." Regardless of the nature of a particular war, you fight it with the weapons you have. Only rarely—and usually only in prolonged, total wars during which the antagonists devote substantial resources to research and development—will dramatically new technologies appear and force changes in the conduct of war.

Similarly, technology (or magic) may enhance one's combat capabilities, but only in extreme cases will technology alone win wars. Harnessed to a poor strategy, superior technology may prove useless. It may even become a detriment or distraction, as it did for the United States in Vietnam. Overreliance on technology distracted American commanders from the essential elements of effective counterinsurgency.

Whether close to home in our own solar system or in galaxies "far, far, away," enduring principles will guide strategic decision making. When should one risk the space fleet or armada of dragons or other magical creatures? When is the correct time to open a new theater of war? Should one invade an enemy planet, nuke it from orbit, or simply blockade it? Is the enemy economically vulnerable? Can one win without fighting? When do the costs of war exceed its likely benefits? How does one successfully end a war and create a lasting peace? No matter the time or place, whether wars are fought with swords, spells, or plasma cannons, superior strategy wins wars.

Questions to Ask as You Write

Ultimately, strategy is the search for comparative advantage. While politics, technology, and other factors will differ from war to war and story to story, basic strategic principles endure and remain broadly applicable.

Strategy should drive the plots of stories centered on military matters.

- How do you use military force, and/or other means, to achieve your political goals? Will the threat of force suffice, or must you go to war?
- How do you apply your strengths against an enemy's weaknesses?
- How do you force an enemy's surrender?
- How do you establish an international environment more favorable to you than your former enemy or enemies?

Whether a story's protagonists are lowly privates, commanding generals, or some rank in between, strategy provides "the reason why."

- Why are a story's characters at a specific place at a specific time?
- What is their mission? Does it rely on deception or misdirection?

- Is their information on enemy dispositions accurate?
- Does the strategy guiding their actions result from careful planning or is it a last-minute improvisation?
- Is it cautious or reckless? A desperate gamble or a calm, assured strike?
- Do the commanders assume a long war or a short one?
- Do they hope for a quick, decisive battlefield victory?
- On what other operations does the strategy rely for success?
- Does the strategy reflect the norm for this nation, society, or military institution?
- Is it something enemies should expect or is it unusual in some way?

It's not essential for protagonists to understand or even be aware of the strategy their actions serve. Nonetheless, that strategy establishes the context for their actions.

- How will the protagonist's victory or defeat undermine or advance the villain's schemes?
- How will victory or defeat affect the story?
- Is it a turning point? If so, to what?
- Is the strategy sound?
- Can it continue to unfold, or is it flawed?
- Does the strategy need to change to advance the story?
- How does the strategy align with the protagonist's and villain's goals?
- Does it advance or hinder them?

Strategy is particularly important for villains and should always guide their actions.

- What is your villain's goal?

- What strategy will they use to achieve it?
- On what classical strategists do they draw?
- How does their personality inform their strategic choices?
- What weaknesses in their enemies do they perceive and intend to exploit?
- Are they aware of their own weaknesses? If so, how do they plan to conceal or protect them?
- How does the villain plan to conquer a territory, subdue recalcitrant rebels, or shatter an enemy alliance?
- Does the villain prefer direct action, or do they seek subtler paths to victory?
- Do they rely on deception and misdirection?
- Do they favor a direct or indirect approach to their objective?
- To what strategic errors might they fall prey?
- Does the villain stay the course like Emperor Palpatine in *Star Wars* or change goals and/or strategies to suit changing circumstances? Perhaps, like Miles Vorkosigan's nemesis Commander Cavilo, they're distracted by new opportunities or their own whims to change their goals and strategy?
- What flaws in the villain's strategy can the story's heroes exploit?

REGARDLESS OF THE STRATEGIES guiding antagonists and protagonists, uncertainty, chance, and friction will impede their plans. As Clausewitz said, everything in war is uncertain. This should be as true for fictional wars as it is for actual ones.

Planning reduces friction, but cannot eliminate it entirely. No matter how carefully a campaign is planned, friction will intervene in unexpected ways, creating opportunities for one's opponents. Similarly, chance occurrences stymie every strategist. Ships with vital supplies are delayed, food spoils, gunpowder is soaked by rain, officers misread maps, and so on. The best commanders find ways around these unexpected obstacles. Others may panic or make rash decisions, which war's inherent uncertainty will compound.

Commonly, villains' plans succeed in a novel's first half, while heroes seize the initiative and develop new plans that pave the way for their success in a novel's second half. Strategic decisions should anticipate and inform this turning point. As heroes learn more about the villain's goals and strategy, they should develop new strategies of their own.

The hero's ultimate victory should result not from blundering into battle, but from out-thinking and out-strategizing the enemy. Heroes might exploit a flaw in the villain's strategy, seize an unexpected opportunity, or employ deceptions that leave their enemies confused and vulnerable. Daring operations supporting unexpected strategies produce more satisfying victories than direct approaches and brute force. Hopefully, this book has given you some ideas to do just that.

A Guide to Quick Military History Research

When heroes assault or defend a castle, it's best to know what castles looked like and how they functioned. How were they normally assaulted and defended? Why did round towers replace square towers on castles? Why did arrow-head bastions replace round towers in the sixteenth century? Where did defenders normally emplace catapults or cannon? How effective were they? Learning these answers is critical for any novel featuring medieval or renaissance warfare.

Gaining a similar knowledge of modern weapons and warfare is equally important for a contemporary military novel or technothriller. Nonetheless, one does not have to emulate Tom Clancy, who reputedly enjoyed reading *Janes Defense Weekly* and similar publications and spent considerable time doing so.

A certain amount of research is essential for military fiction, particularly stories grounded in history. Yet, the drive to read one more book, consult one more archive, or interview yet another subject is the primary reason many history PhD candidates fail to complete their dissertations, and why novelists trunk half-finished stories. Research is an endless lure that eventually offers diminishing returns. Each additional article and book read provides less and less new or useful information.

Time spent researching is time not spent writing. So, what are the best ways to target your historical research to get "the most bang for the buck" and quickly return to writing your novel?

Issues with Wikipedia and AI

WIKIPEDIA IS MANY PEOPLE'S first stop when researching a topic. It can be great for simple fact checking, such as names, dates, and major events. It's also a good place to double-check basic facts, so you don't confuse Herodotus and Thucydides as one well-known science fiction author did in an otherwise well-regarded short story.

For more in-depth research, though, Wikipedia is problematic. Contrary to the pronouncements of its founders, allowing just about anyone to write and edit for Wikipedia does not guarantee accuracy. Like the old adage about "too many cooks" spoiling a meal, too many writers—particularly when unconstrained by any editorial norms—can spoil an encyclopedia. There may be wisdom in crowds, but there's also a lot of stupidity.

Wikipedia is rife with errors and contradictions. One naval battle I checked a few years ago had the wrong numbers of ships for both antagonists and incorrectly listed one ship as involved in the battle that was actually in port undergoing repair. Different Wikipedia articles on related subjects, such as military commanders, important battles and campaigns, or the history and relative merits of your favorite musical group, often contradict one another.

That's just simple carelessness or poor research. Unfortunately, Wikipedia has more egregious—and in some cases deliberate—errors and omissions. A few years ago, some Wiki editors began removing or reducing references to the atrocities various Nazi generals, such Erich von Manstein, committed or oversaw during World War II. When questioned, these editors claimed wartime atrocities were not relevant. Rather, articles on senior German officers should focus solely on their battlefield performance, which these editors found surprisingly praiseworthy given the long list of German military failings that led to their defeat.

Various academic historians discussed pushing back, but none of those involved in these early discussions had (or have now) time to police the Internet. Thankfully, Ksenia Coffman and a few others stepped into the breach. They worked to remind people of the Nazi affiliations of Germany's generals and the numerous war crimes they committed or deliberately ignored. They've worked tirelessly to correct the shocking amount of misinformation on Nazi Germany on Wikipedia, which ranges from whitewashing Holocaust perpetrators to glorifying the Nazi military and its leaders. It's an endless task that brought Coffman and her colleagues no end of harassment and hate mail.

My point is not to excoriate Wikipedia and similar Internet sources for their failings, but rather to point out that Wikipedia entries are contested terrain. They are subject to change at the whims of the editors who oversee them and the writers who contribute to them. Few of these people are experts in their fields. At best, most are dedicated amateurs.

I've authored two substantial Wikipedia entries and corrected a few others. In most cases, I had to explain and justify my work to Wikipedia editors who know little or nothing about the topic involved and who kept trying to "correct" what I wrote. Constantly checking my own entries and correcting those of others is simply not worth the effort. Most of my academic colleagues feel similarly.

A Wikipedia entry on a relatively obscure subject might be very good and authored by an expert in the field. On the other hand, it might be the rushed work of someone only casually familiar with the topic, or an enthusiast obsessed with minutia who misses the big picture. I suggest the following rule: the more obscure a Wikipedia entry, the more likely it is to either be very good or seriously problematic since fewer eyes will have looked at it.

At the opposite extreme, popular topics evoking controversy have their controversies mirrored in Wikipedia. Editors and writers fight over them and make back-and-forth changes. Sometimes these involve big issues, such as the nature and causes of the Cold War. Others involve seemingly trivial topics, such as falafel. Many Middle Eastern peoples claim this as their traditional cuisine and these claims and counterclaims ignited bitter arguments and editing wars among Wikipedia contributors. These editing wars keep Wikipedia's coverage of controversial topics bland and inoffensive, and thus less useful for writers.

It is beyond the scope of this book to enter the raging debates on using generative AI in one's writing. Nonetheless, you should be aware of its problems for research. Generative AI invents facts and evidence, portrays fictional characters as real, and muddles the biographies of actual people. On any given day, ChatGPT thinks I specialize in a different historical field, all of them wrong. It thinks one of my colleagues helped found the U.S. Naval Institute 150 years ago. (He doesn't look a day over 60.)

When generative AI produces grammatically correct nonsense, its errors are easy to spot. Often, though, ChatGPT and its ilk blend fiction and reality in ways difficult for non-experts to detect. A colleague recently asked ChatGPT to write an essay about how combat between rowed war galleys changed in the sixteenth century.

ChatGPT correctly noted two important changes. First, Mediterranean war galleys became much larger. Second, they added cannon in the bows. Then Chat GPT messed up. It argued that galleys got faster in these years, and that combat range increased because of the cannon. Both these points are superficially logical but dead wrong. Sixteenth century cannon took so long to reload that captains held their fire until they reached point-blank range. There was no advantage to firing early. In fact, the cannon didn't even have carriages to facilitate combat reloading.

Galleys actually became slower in these years for two reasons. First, the cannon made them heavier, but they didn't add more rowers to compensate for the added weight. Second, the major powers replaced free, well-fed rowers with poorly fed slaves and convicts who lacked the energy and motivation to row as strongly as their free predecessors.

An allied issue is AI bots scraping the internet to create historical databases. Often, they confuse fiction and reality and put the two things side by side as if they are of equal veracity. One recent example of this was a fictional WWII military officer from a popular boardgame that ended up in an automatically generated historical database next to historical figures.

While generative AI may be useful for some things, it is terrible at writing and researching history. You cannot trust it.

You don't need to spend weeks in dusty archives to effectively research a topic for your next novel. On the other hand, relying on Wikipedia and similar sources for more than simple fact-checking is a mistake. Just as a military organization would never rely on a single source of information when planning a major operation, you shouldn't rely on a single anonymous source for information critical to your story.

Finding Reliable Sources

MANY GRADUATE PROGRAMS list the books they expect their PhD candidates to read, along with other materials. You don't need to become a graduate student to benefit from these resources, which identify the most important scholars, ideas, and readings in particular fields. Take a look at what the top programs in military history, such as Duke, Ohio State, and Temple, are assigning their students and consult those relevant to your novel.

Course syllabi are readily available online. If someone's teaching a course on the topic you're writing about, why not check out the assigned readings on their syllabus? They often have links to important articles that will quickly get you up to speed.

Specialized encyclopedias, such as those published by ABC-CLIO, Greenwood Press, Routledge, Sage, and other academic publishers, are excellent resources. Among the best of these are the many encyclopedias on particular wars edited by Spencer Tucker for ABC-CLIO. A well-regarded scholar himself, he assembled and directed teams of top scholars to write them.

Entries in specialized encyclopedias invariably list the most important books on their topic. They're also a good place to locate experts you can consult directly. Most will be happy to answer questions about their specialties via email or point you in the right direction to find your answer.

A good library, particularly a college library, will either have the encyclopedias themselves or digital subscriptions to them. If not, you can probably request the encyclopedia entries you need (not the whole encyclopedia) through Interlibrary Loan from your local library.

National archives and specialized libraries, such as presidential libraries in the United States, are putting more and more material online, including important speeches, diplomatic documents, and correspondence among senior leaders. Does your hero (or villain) need to make a speech? Why not look at what historical figures in similar circumstances had to say?

The British Library hosts a growing collection of ancient Greek manuscripts. The websites of the historical branches of military organizations, such as the U.S. Navy's History and Heritage Command

MILITARY STRATEGY FOR WRITERS   251

and the U.S. Army's Center for Military History, host a wealth of data, documents, photographs, and other materials. Among them is the entire 78-volume official history of the *U.S. Army in World War II*. You can't do better than that. Most military institutions in democratic countries offer similar resources.

Consulting high quality sources at your project's outset will save you time and effort down the road, provide the depth, detail, and verisimilitude to draw your readers into your story, and help you write the best possible book.

Ten Indispensable Books

The body of work on military history and strategy is vast and growing daily. Listed below are ten books that will get you up to speed quickly. They offer nice overviews of particular subjects and will point you to other important works.

Azar Gat, *War in Human Civilization* (2006). A masterful, intellectually nuanced discussion of war from the dawn of history to the present. Gat explores the roots of war and why we fight, how military systems developed over time, and provides an overview of major conflicts through the end of the twentieth century.

John Keegan, *The Face of Battle* (1976). In this immensely influential work, Keegan applied ideas from the then relatively new field of social history to military history. Using three famous battles, Agincourt, Waterloo, and the Somme, Keegan examined the experience of battle from the soldier's viewpoint. He looked at military events from the bottom up, as social historians say. Instead of carefully drawn maps with lines showing the movement of troops, he presents the visceral realities of battle and the struggles of soldiers and junior officers to overcome their fears, make sense of the chaos around them, and face and fight their enemies.

Geoffrey Parker, *The Cambridge History of Warfare* (2020, 2nd ed.). While focused on the West and its rise, each chapter of Parker's book offers a useful survey of military developments from the ancient Greeks and Romans, through the Middle Ages, and into the modern era. It's particularly useful as a reference for topical books to deepen your knowledge on particular eras, and major events and wars.

Wayne E. Lee, *Warfare and Culture in World History* (2020). While Parker's book offers a traditional historical survey focusing on military organizations, technology, strategy, and leadership, Lee's work injects culture into the narrative. It includes discussions of non-western societies, including nomadic cultures, China, and Africa. As the authors of its nine chapters show, armies reflect the cultures and societies that produce them. Different societies think about war and wage war differently—and for different reasons. Lee's *Barbarians and Brothers: Anglo-American Warfare, 1500-1865* (2011) is also worth looking at. It examines why some conflicts, such as the American Revolution, were fought more humanely than others, such as the English conquest of Ireland.

Peter Paret, *Makers of Modern Strategy from Machiavelli to the Nuclear Age* (1986). This updating of Edward Mead Earle's *Makers of Modern Strategy*, published during World War II, is assigned to students at every American war college. It offers a chronological and thorough examination of changing strategic thought over the last 500 years. While some of the chapters are a bit dense, all of them repay multiple readings, and they need not be read in order. Those on nuclear war, air power, and mechanized warfare are particularly useful, as are those that examine important strategists, including Clausewitz, Jomini, Mahan, and Douhet. A new edition of this classic, edited by Hal Brands and with many new essays, came out in 2023. The Paret and Earl editions of Makers of Modern Strategy were aimed at policy makers. Anyone with an interest in strategy and general knowledge of military history could read, enjoy, and learn from them. The Brands edition is aimed more at scholars, which may make it difficult reading for some.

MILITARY STRATEGY FOR WRITERS 255

Edward Luttwak, *The Grand Strategy of the Roman Empire* (1976). An influential political scientist and military analyst, Luttwak argues that despite several dozen emperors and regular civil wars, the Roman Empire maintained a consistent and rational approach to foreign policy and grand strategy. The Romans garrisoned the borders of their empire with legions who operated aggressively and sought to counter potential threats before they penetrated the empire's borders. Over time, as weaker legions faced more dangerous enemies, Rome developed a system of defense in depth that relied on frontier defenses like Hadrian's Wall, fortified cities, and mobile armies that could rush to the defense of threatened sectors. While criticized by many ancient historians for painting with a very broad brush, Luttwak's work established a model for other scholars to assess the grand strategies of a host of major powers, past and present.

Gerhard Weinberg, *A World at Arms: A Global History of World War II* (1992). Thirty years after its publication, Weinberg's masterpiece remains the best single-volume history of World War II. The narrative flows smoothly, providing a wealth of detail and incisive critiques of important political and strategic decisions, major military operations, the home front, and more. Unlike too many histories of the war, Weinberg adeptly weaves the Holocaust into the story of the war, demonstrating its centrality to Nazi policy, strategy, and war making. It is a masterful example of how one should write military history.

Mark Clodfelter, *The Limits of Air Power: The American Bombing of North Vietnam* (1989). Clodfelter's book remains the best analysis of the American bombing of Vietnam and why that prolonged bombing campaign failed to produce victory. While focused on the Vietnam War, Clodfelter explores the utility of bombing and what air power can and cannot do in war. It remains important today when the first response of too many American politicians to international crises is to consider bombing something or someone.

Hal Brands, *What Good is Grand Strategy? Power and Purpose in American Statecraft from Harry S. Truman to George W. Bush* **(2014).** In this clearly argued book, Brands looks at four post-World War II American presidents and examines how their administrations formulated and implemented grand strategy. The case studies are well chosen, highlighting both the successes and failures of the carefully crafted grand strategies of Harry Truman, Richard Nixon, Ronald Reagan, and George W. Bush. For novelists, they provide remarkable examples of how even the "best and brightest" can get things wrong and how the relentless pursuit of a flawed strategy leads to disaster.

Max Brooks, John Amble, M.L. Cavanaugh, and Jaym Gates, *Strategy Strikes Back: How Star Wars Explains Modern Military Conflict* **(2018).** While not as focused on strategy as the title implies, the short essays in this book offer an entertaining discussion of a host of military issues within the context of the *Star Wars* canon, both film and television. Among the standouts are Max Brooks' plea for nation building on Endor, demonstrating that you don't need a doctorate to think strategically, and M.L. Cavanaugh's "A Strategist Yoda was Not," which offers an apt critique of the revered character's strategic ineptitude. As Cavanaugh points out, there is no evidence of any strategic education in Jedi training, and it shows.

Acknowledgments

I've taught strategy for the Naval War College and military history at the University of Memphis for more than 20 years. During that time numerous colleagues shaped my understanding of strategy. I've also benefitted from and been enriched by invigorating and challenging classroom discussion by hundreds of students, many of whose questions I've sought to answer in this book.

Dave Farland and Eric Flint, who I first met at the Superstars Writing Seminar in 2020 and now sorely miss, encouraged me, and gave me helpful advice in the early stages of this project. The Superstars Tribe and founders encouraged me, for which I'm grateful.

Kattie Hanna, Konrad Bennett Hughes, and John D. Payne commented on the manuscript and provided helpful suggestions. Eva Papier gave helpful suggestions on the cover design.

As always, Carolyn Ivy Stein, my wife of more than 35 years and writing partner for longer, was invaluable, both in the intellectual development of this book, and in its editing and publishing. I could not have finished it without her.

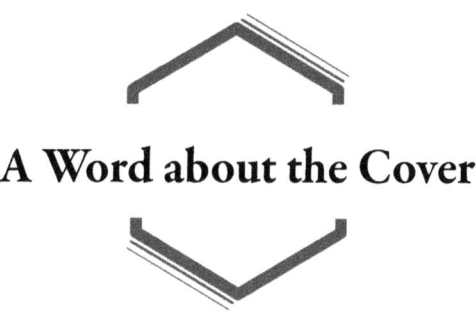

A Word about the Cover

Carolyn Ivy Stein designed the cover using the following art with permission.

Nataliya@stock.adobe.com

askib@stock.adobe.com

No generative AI was used in either the text of this book or to create the cover.

Bibliography

A

Ansoff, H. Igor. *Corporate Strategy* (1965).

Aussaresses, Paul. *The Battle of the Casbah: Terrorism and Counterterrorism in Algeria 1955-1957* (2004).

B

BEAR, GREG. *Forge of God* (1987).

Bergerud, Eric. *The Dynamics of Defeat* (1993).

Brands, Hal. *What Good is Grand Strategy? Power and Purpose in American Statecraft from Harry S. Truman to George W. Bush* (2014).

Brodie, Bernard. *The Absolute Weapon* (1946).

Brodie, Bernard. "More about Limited War," *World Politics* 10, no. 1 (October 1957).

Brodie, Bernard. *Strategy in the Missile Age* (1959).

Brooks, Max, John Amble, M.L. Cavanaugh, and Jaym Gates, *Strategy Strikes Back: How Star Wars Explains Modern Military Conflict* (2018).

Bujold, Lois McMaster. Barrayar (1991), *The Vor Game* (1990), and *Warrior's Apprentice* (1986).

C

CAMPBELL, JACK. *Dauntless* (2006).

Chesney, George Tomkyns. "The Battle of Dorking" (1871).
Clarke, Arthur C. "The Rocket and the Future of Warfare," *Royal Air Force Quarterly* 17, no. 2 (March 1946), 61-69.
Clarke, Arthur C. "Superiority" in Clarke, *Expedition to Earth* (1953).
Clausewitz, Carl von. On War (1976, trans. by Peter Paret).
Clodfelter, Mark. *The Limits of Air Power: The American Bombing of North Vietnam* (1989).
Cohen, Eliot A., et. al., *The Gulf Air Power Survey* (1993).
Corbett, Julian S. *Some Principles of Maritime Strategy* (1988).

D

DICKSON, GORDON R. *Dorsai!* (1960).
———. Tactics of Mistake (1971).

E

EDELSTEIN, DAVID M. *Occupational Hazards: Success and Failure in Military Occupation* (2008).

F

FINCH, MICHAEL P. M. *A Progressive Occupation?: The Gallieni-Lyautey Method and Colonial Pacification in Tonkin and Madagascar, 1885-1900* (2013).
Flint, Eric. *1632* (2000).
Fraser, George MacDonald. *Flashman* (1969).

G

GALLIPOLI (1981)

Galula, David. *Counterinsurgency Warfare: Theory and Practice* (1964).
Galula, David. *Pacification in Algeria* (1963).
Gat, Azar. *War in Human Civilization* (2006).
Gold, H.L. "Gloom and Doom," *Galaxy* (January 1952).

H

HACKETT, JOHN. *The Third World War* (1978).
Haldeman, Joe. *The Forever War* (1975).
Handel, Michael. *Masters of War* (2000, 3rd ed.).
Harrison, Harry. *The Stainless Steel Rat's Revenge* (1970).
Heinlein, Robert A. "The Long Watch" (1949), *The Moon is a Harsh Mistress* (1966), and *Starship Troopers* (1959).

J

JANIS, IRVING. "PSYCHOLOGICAL Aspects of Vulnerability to Atomic Bomb Attacks" (1949).
Jervis, Robert. *The Meaning of the Nuclear Revolution: Statecraft and the Prospect of Armageddon* (1989).
Jomini, Antoine-Henri. *Art of War* (1862, trans. by Mendell and Craighill).

K

KEEGAN, JOHN. *The Face of Battle* (1976).
Kennedy, Paul. *Grand Strategies in War and Peace* (1991).
Kennedy, Paul. *The Rise and Fall of Great Powers* (1987).
Knox, MacGregor and Williamson Murray. *The Dynamics of Military Revolution, 1300-2050* (2001).
Kornbluth, C.M. "The Luckiest Man in Denv" (1952).
Krepinevich, Andrew. *The Army and Vietnam* (1986).

L

LARTEGUY, JEAN. *The Centurions* (1960).

Larrabee, Eric. *Commander in Chief, Franklin Delano Roosevelt, his Lieutenants and Their War* (1987).

Laumer, Keith. *Bolo: Annals of the Dinochrome Brigade* (1976)

Lawrence, T. E. *Seven Pillars of Wisdom,* 1926 (rev ed. NY: Anchor, 1991).

Lee, Wayne E. *Warfare and Culture in World History* (2020).

Libicki, Martin C. *Cyberspace in Peace and War* (2016).

Liddell-Hart, B. H. Strategy (1967).

Luttwak, Edward. *Grand Strategy of the Byzantine Empire* (2011)

Luttwak, Edward. *Grand Strategy of the Roman Empire* (1976)

M

MAO, ZEDONG, *On Protracted Warfare* (1967).

Mao, ZeDong, *Selected Military Writings* (1963).

Marshall, S.L.A. *Sinai Victory* (1958).

Meilinger, Philip. *Air War: Theory and Practice* (2003).

Miksche, Otto. *Is Bombing Decisive? A Study of the Organization and Tactical Employment of Modern Air Fleets* (1943).

Moltke, Helmut von. *On Strategy* (1871).

Morgan, Richard K. *Altered Carbon* (2002).

P

PAINE, S.C.M. *The Japanese Empire: Grand Strategy from the Meiji Restoration to the Pacific War* (2017).

Papers of the Presidents of the United States, Dwight D. Eisenhower, 1957.

Paret, Peter. *Makers of Modern Strategy from Machiavelli to the Nuclear Age* (1986).

Parker, Geoffrey. *The Cambridge History of Warfare* (2020, 2nd ed.).

Pierce, Hayford. "Unlimited Warfare" (1974).

Plutarch. *Lives* (Dryden translation, 1992).

Pressfield, Steven. *The Afghan Campaign* (2006)

S

SCHELLING, THOMAS. *The Strategy of Conflict* (1960).

Strachan, Hew. *The Direction of War* (2013).

Sturgeon, Theodore. "Thunder and Roses" (*Astounding*, 1947).

Sun Tzu, *The Art of War* (Griffith translation, 1963).

Syrett, Harold G. *The Papers of Alexander Hamilton* (1961).

T

TAYLER, HOWARD. *Schlock Mercenary* (2000-2020).

Teller, Edward. "A Concise History of the Crostic Union War" in *The Legacy of Hiroshima* (1962).

Tolkien, J. R. R. *The Hobbit* (1937) and *The Lord of the Rings* (1954-1955).

Trinquier, Rogier. *Modern Warfare: A French View of Counterinsurgency* (1961).

U

U.S. ARMY, *ADP 3-0: Unified Land Operations* (2011).

U.S. Army, *FM 3-0: Unified Field Operations* (2017).

W

WEIGLEY, RUSSELL F. *The American Way of War: A History of United States Military Strategy and Policy* (1973).

Weinberg, Gerhard. *A World at Arms: A Global History of World War II* (1992).

Wohlstetter, Albert. "Delicate Balance of Terror" (1958).

Additional Books by Stephen Kenneth Stein

History

Teaching and Learning History Online: A Guide for College Instructors (Routledge, 2023), with Maureen McLeod.

From Torpedoes to Aviation: Washington Irving Chambers and Technological Innovation in the New Navy, 1877-1913 (University of Alabama Press, 2007).

Sadomasochism and the BDSM Community in the United States: Kinky People Unite (Routledge, 2021)

The Sea in World History: Trade, Travel, and Exploration (ABC-CLIO, 2017).

Voices from the Second World War (Cognella, 2018), with Paul Doerr.

Twenty-Five years of Living in Leather: National Leather Association, 1986 - 2011 (Adynaton Publishing, 2016)

Gaming

TIME'S PRISONERS (Jeweled Sea Press, 2023), with Carolyn Ivy Stein.

Amelia's Friends (Jeweled Seal Press 2022), with Carolyn Ivy Stein

GURPS Vehicles War Galleys (Steve Jackson Games, 2022), with Carolyn Ivy Stein

Fiction

THIEVES BERTH (Jeweled Sea Press, 2023), with Carolyn Ivy Stein

Don't miss out!

Visit the website below and you can sign up to receive emails whenever Stephen Kenneth Stein publishes a new book. There's no charge and no obligation.

https://books2read.com/r/B-A-FVPAB-TOKOC

BOOKS 2 READ

Connecting independent readers to independent writers.

About the Author

Stephen K. Stein is a Professor of History at the University of Memphis where he teaches courses on American, diplomatic, military, and maritime history, as well as the history of technology. He is also an adjunct professor of strategy for the College of Distance Education of the U.S. Naval War College for which he's taught for more than 20 years. The author of six books and numerous shorter works, his previous works include *From Torpedoes to Aviation: Washington Irving Chambers and Technological Innovation in the New Navy, 1877-1913* (2007), *The Sea in World History: Trade, Travel, and Exploration* (2017), which was featured in an episode of "Adam Ruins Everything," *Sadomasochism and the BDSM Community in the United States: Kinky People Unite* (2021), which is the first comprehensive history of that community, and *Teaching and Learning History Online: A Guide for College Instructors* (2023, coauthored with

Maureen MacLeod). His article "The Greely Relief Expedition and the New Navy," *International Journal of Naval History* 5 (December 2006) won the Rear Admiral Ernest M. Eller Prize in Naval History. Read more at https://stvstein.wixsite.com/stevestein.

www.ingramcontent.com/pod-product-compliance
Lightning Source LLC
LaVergne TN
LVHW041611070426
835507LV00008B/189